CW01619409

ARC

FARNHAM

IN OLD PHOTOGRAPHS

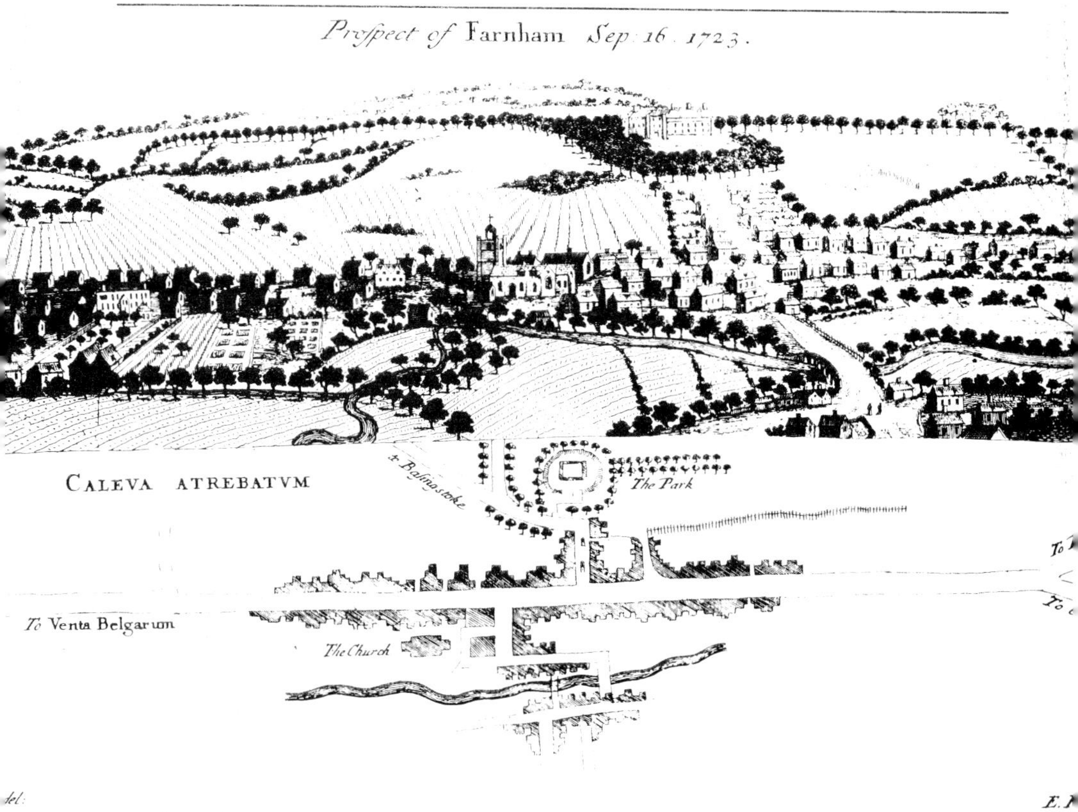

A RARE DIAGRAMMATIC AND PICTORIAL MAP OF FARNHAM which was engraved in 1723.

AROUND FARNHAM IN OLD PHOTOGRAPHS

COLLECTED BY
JEAN PARRATT

ALAN SUTTON

Alan Sutton Publishing Limited
Phoenix Mill · Far Thrupp · Stroud · Gloucestershire

First Published 1990

British Library Cataloguing in Publication Data

Around Farnham in old photographs.
1. Surrey. Farnham, history
I. Parratt, Jean
9.42.219
ISBN 0-86299-8131

DEDICATION: To Edward Griffith, local press photographer for sixty years, a man who always had an eye for a good picture, and to Mollie Saunders, a former teacher-training college principal, who showed me how to widen my horizons.

Front Cover Illustration:

RANGER'S, WEST STREET, soon after it opened in 1894. The right of the picture shows the area which was once a gate room leading to the stable-yard behind. Today it is the sales area for vinyl floor covering. The shop is still trading.

Typeset in 9/10 Korinna
Typesetting and origination by
Alan Sutton Publishing.
Printed in Great Britain by
Dotesios Printers Limited.

CONTENTS

INTRODUCTION

Farnham, the most westerly town in Surrey, is steeped in history. It is an urban community set amid the rural greenery of encircling villages and a place to which visitors return again and again, each time noting something new and interesting.

When evidence of five mesolithic pit dwellings was found here in the 1930s the town was added to the national map of archeological sites as it could then claim to have the oldest village in Britain within its boundaries.

Remains of Bronze Age burial mounds, an Iron Age road, Roman villas, Saxon crofts, medieval houses, Elizabethan shop fronts, Georgian buildings and Victorian artisans' cottages can all be found in the town and surrounding villages alongside the post-Second World War housing of the 'jerry-built' variety and the more thoughtful designs of the seventies and eighties.

Dominating the whole scene is the castle on the hill, the fortress built almost 1,000 years ago which still commands attention and is in use every day as a centre for the briefing of people who are to go abroad.

In the past Farnham's sons worked with their hands – at farming and brewing for the most part. There was also a large charcoal-burning 'industry' from Roman times until well into the twentieth century.

Farnham's daughters worked on the land, too, particularly at hop-picking time, and they were also involved with the wool industry and sack manufacture, thousands of hop pockets (sacks) being needed each year for hops to be packed into before being sent away to market.

Farnham's daughters were a tough group of women. When their menfolk were away fighting, the women defended their town against the Danes in a battle which took place in AD 893.

Farnham has always been a hospitable place and visitors have stayed here en route for London or Southampton from time immemorial. The Bush Hotel, the George and the Lion and Lamb Hotel have all seen the comings and goings of horse-drawn coach parties and, later, families and individuals stopped their cars to look around the town. The George, where the Argos store is today, was just about inside the enclosed area of the town, in medieval times, when The Borough, encircled by the town ditch, was the centre of Farnham. Even the parish church and group of small cottages, the present Church Lanes, were not part of the main town at that time.

Bear Lane, or Bar Lane as it should really be called, formed the barrier where a toll was demanded when entering the town from the east. From the west the toll had to be paid near The Round House (now a traffic island at the top of Downing Street).

In medieval times the road structure of the town was much as it is today: Castle Street leading to the castle, the home of the Bishops of Winchester; West Street stretching to the roads towards Alton, Winchester and Southampton; East Street, the route to London, and Downing Street which took monks and others to Waverley Abbey, built in 1128. South Street alone was not marked on maps until the middle of the nineteenth century and at first this was called by a different name – New Road. All streets in Farnham are numbered consecutively along one side of the street and back along the other as opposed to the more normal odd numbers on one side with even numbers opposite.

Waverley Abbey, the first Cistercian abbey in England, did much to influence the number of visitors who came to Farnham. Kings and Queens of the realm were amongst them and the Farnham Pageant, first enacted in 1910 in order to offset a debt of £800 which was owed on the Church House building, records that in AD 1486 there was a royal baby at the castle. In *The Book of the Words*, the Revd H. Neville Lovett, Rector of Farnham, wrote, 'This episode brings before us a curious incident in Farnham's history. While the Queen of Henry VII, Elizabeth, daughter of Edward IV, the last blossom of the White Rose of York, was preparing for her coronation at Greenwich, her infant child, Prince Arthur, lately baptized at Winchester, was lodged at Farnham Castle with a retinue of lady-mistresses and nurses. The child throve so heartily here, that his thankful father, at the request of the parishioners, founded a chantry at the altar of St Mary, on the north side of the Church.'

There are many people who wonder why the housing estate, at the west end of the town, is called The Chantrys. It is because the land on which the houses were built was once part of chantrys from the parish church, land owned, and donated by, the Church.

Kings and queens often stayed at Farnham Castle in order to be able to hunt in the park. The Old Park stretched to the Hampshire boundary, at what is now known as Dora's Green, and the New Park, together with the Old Park, stretched almost to Windsor Forest, a much larger wooded area in the Middle Ages than it is today. Most sovereigns appear to have loved hunting and this was a good place in which to pursue the sport.

Henry III came to Farnham sixteen times and King John bettered this total by two. Queen Elizabeth I visited Farnham around the time of the Spanish Armada, and George III paid an informal visit to the town in 1774. Queen Victoria sometimes called into town when she visited her troops at Aldershot three miles away. At one time it was suggested that East Street should be renamed Queen Street, and the public house on the corner of Bear Lane was known as the Queen Street Tavern although it had been known as the Fourteen-penny House. If a customer paid 1s. 2d. (14 pennies) he could drink as much as he wished, all evening, on the condition that he did not leave the bar to relieve himself. Queen Victoria gave the Royal Appointment to Charles Borelli, a watchmaker who operated from The Borough. George V also passed through the town. During the 1960s Queen Elizabeth II drove down upper Weybourne Lane, Heath End, and was welcomed by local Brownies. Twenty years later her daughter, the Princess Royal, attended a Save the Children fête in Farnham Castle and Park.

In the seventeenth century many of the Pilgrim Fathers must have passed through the town en route for Southampton to join the *Mayflower*. They would have seen evidence of a great wheat market here. Wheat grown in Hampshire and Sussex had to be sent by road to London, and Farnham made a good place to stop halfway between the fields where the wheat was grown and the city where it was to be used. Large wagons from Alton, Chichester, Petersfield and Winchester rolled into town and were kept safe for the night in one of the many yards leading off the main streets. Take a walk along West Street or The Borough, today, and look into every opening between shops. At the side of each gap there is evidence of gates having hung there, which would have been closed at night to protect the carts and horses within. Most of the gates have long since gone but the brackets for the hinges still remain.

Farnham moved into modern times through the influence of local people like William Cobbett, Radical politician, author, and the founder of the *Political Register,* the journal on which *Hansard* was built.

Whereas in the past people had worked with their hands (including the 150 women employed in the corset factory which now houses the Conservative Club in Ivy Lane, and to which, until very recently, women were not admitted as members in their own right), most of today's townspeople work with their brains.

Banks, building societies, estate agents and finance houses are the 'street traders' of the 1990s. The market stall at the foot of Castle Street still remains but the affluence of the town is determined nowadays more by fluctuations at the Stock Exchange and in interest rates, than by how well the new potatoes have grown. Local people deal with financial and property matters either from the town itself or because they commute to London each day to work.

At the Vine Bar in the Bush Hotel, the town centre's most famous and ancient hotel, members of society from all walks of life are brought together in a way which seems unique. At any one time it is possible to find there, drinking and rubbing shoulders, the multi-millionaire and the out-of-work drunkard, the 'resting' actor and the very-much-in-demand television announcer, the unemployed poet and the hard-working professional author. There are journalists, factory workers, jobbing carpenters and hack musicians, each indulging in his or her chosen drink, alongside solicitors, national trade union officials and artists. The Vine Bar sums up Farnham as a place of antiquity which has not been afraid to taste some of the present, and where anyone and everyone can mix together in harmony, none any better, or worse, than another.

The town is proud of its inventors, such as John Henry Knight of motorcar fame, and its sportsmen like Mike Hawthorn, Britain's first World Motor Racing Champion. International connections are made via the students who attend the West Surrey College of Art and Design from all parts of the globe. The two-minute silence observed in their own countries on Armistice Day each year originated in Farnham. When 'Rock of Ages' is sung in church or a meeting of Toc H is held, it is to Farnham that one looks for the birthplace of the hymn's author and the home of the founder of the latter.

It is a town which lives. Every day there is something new happening and with commercial and community centres like the Redgrave Theatre and the Maltings, as well as the still considerable number of public houses, among the many social outlets in town, the chances are that it will continue to make its mark in the history of this country as it has done for the past 8,000 years.

SECTION ONE

Gone but Not Forgotten

Many of the town's old buildings were razed to the ground prior to 1970 and replaced with 'modern' units which were often out of keeping with the old market town. More recently though, developers such as Alan Taylor, Ken Kent, Michael Campbell and Andrew Sturt have replaced old with well-designed new, giving us the Lion and Lamb Courtyard, Borelli Yard and St Georges, all of which have enhanced the areas they occupy. Nevertheless, the many buildings, such as the cinemas and gas showrooms, which have been demolished will not be forgotten by those people who shopped or spent their leisure time in them.

A CLOSE-UP VIEW OF THE COUNTY CINEMA, formerly The Electric Cinema, which closed in 1956 to make room for the new Cambridge Place. It was reached by going underneath the arch at the front of Cambridge Place, off East Street. The original fascia boards, on which 'Tonight's Film' was written, still exist.

A VIEW DOWN LONGBRIDGE showing John Mills and Sons, builders, before the building was demolished in the early 1960s to make way for the present Farnham Police Station. Farnham Castle can just be seen in the far background and the furnishing department of the Co-op forms the junction space to this picture.

SOUTH STREET IN THE MID-1960S before the shops were knocked down to make way for Sainsbury's supermarket. Many bargains could be obtained in the Oxfam shop, the first charity shop in Farnham. I once bought a large pillowcase full of antique lace in this shop for one shilling. J.H. Wilcox, established in 1883, now trades from a shop in East Street and Babyland was the last specialist baby shop in town. G.E. Day's antique shop is next to Miss Tigwell's toy shop and on the extreme right is the studio of David Melville, photographer.

THE FORMER GAS COMPANY SHOWROOM in East Street, which was knocked down to build The Woolmead complex. The milestone outside the showroom, by the gate on the left, was moved and resited by the traffic-lights at the East Street – Borough junction.

FRANK SPENCER, PHOTOGRAPHER, of 51 Downing Street, took this photograph of Worsam's the bakers around 1880. The bakery was also a confectioners where sweets, chocolate and cakes could be bought as well as bread and, according to the notice in the window, 'Key Yeast' was also available. Each shelf in the right-hand window holds a different type of bread, tin loaves at the top, cottage in the centre and bloomer on the bottom. The base of the window has an assortment of bread shapes. Worsam's remained in Downing Street for over 200 years.

FARNHAM GASWORKS AND RETORT in East Street before the development of the Riverside industrial estate.

THE BOROUGH, around 1920, when traffic was still two-way and cars, bicycles, tricycles and horse-drawn carts could all be seen. On the right the letters ST on a blind show where Sturt's bookshop was situated. Frank Sturt who ran the business was the brother of George Sturt, author of *A Small Boy in the Sixties, Change in the Village* and *The Wheelright's Shop* among a number of books.

THE FORMER CO-OP BUILDING, IN UNION ROAD, just before it was demolished in 1989. The building was used for a variety of purposes including a mortuary at the back, a hairdresser in part of the first floor and a hall for dances and parties. The hall was known as Owen Hall (see p. 46) and stretched most of the length of the building. On the left, the building behind the road sign was once a chapel and the words of the Lord's Prayer could be seen on the painted wall.

THE CINEMA IN EAST STREET (centre), next to the Labour Exchange. The cinema was closed down, overnight, in 1985 and demolished two years later in spite of many attempts to retain this major example of art deco architecture (see p. 17). The Labour Exchange was rebuilt in 1988 by Ken Kent of Kents Developments and Mr Kent retained the building's former name of The Chestnuts, planting two chestnut trees on the forecourt to replace the one which was felled during the building work. The earlier example can just be seen on the left of this picture.

THERE ARE FEW PEOPLE who live in Dollis Drive today who know that the name of their street is a corruption of the surname Dolley, being the man who owned a nursery on the site in Guildford Road. This is believed to be the only picture of the greenhouses which formed the nursery and it was taken when the auction notice for the sale of the land, and the house adjacent to it, was already posted up, as can be seen in the photograph.

A & G BARNES, FURNITURE DEALERS, operated from this spot in East Street until the early 1970s when the building was knocked down to make way for the construction of the Dogflud loop road. The tree which can just be seen on the left was outside the Seven Stars, but was uprooted in the hurricane of 1987.

YARD BROOMS, DOG KENNELS AND GARDEN GNOMES were among the many things sold at M.A. Rose & Son Ltd, now demolished and replaced by three shops made of metal and glass. The building on the extreme left is at the entrance to Cambridge Place, East Street.

CAESAR BROS OF HALE started work on this building in Bear Lane which was to be the town's first cinema on 15 May 1911. It had a seating capacity of 450, electricity was generated on the premises and its sponsors were two men living in Aldershot and Farnborough, who promised it would be open for business by 22 June – 38 days later – and it was. The first piece of film shown was the coronation of King George V which had been filmed in London earlier that day and rushed to Farnham by train. The building was demolished in 1990.

FARNHAM POLICE STATION now stands where these buildings were, and the wall on which the present murals are set is approximately where the double doors of part of John Mills and Sons, builders, can be seen on the right. The poplar trees are in Gostrey Meadow.

SPENCERS, the shop which stood at the top of Downing Street until 1964, was one of the oldest shops in town for ladies wear. It is probably one of the very few shops which had the abbreviated Latin word, etc, as part of its fascia board; to the right of the word Spencer can be seen 'underclothing etc'. When customers made purchases the money was put into a small, metal container and this was screwed into a socket on a wired system above the assistants' heads. A handle was pulled, the container shot up to the cash desk on the wire and was then returned to the assistant with a receipt and change. To the left of the half-demolished building is J. and M. Stone, a company which sold radios and televisions.

FARNHAM HAS HAD THREE CINEMAS. The first, known as The Picture Palace was in Bear Lane. In 1913 The Electric Cinema opened in East Street and later became The County Cinema. It was designed by Harold Falkner and built by Mardon and Ball, local builders. Shoppers in Sainsbury's today are walking on the ground where once sat hundreds of cinemagoers. The entrance to this cinema is still in existence. Stand in front of the archway and look at the board which says Cambridge House. With a little imagination it is possible to see the title of this week's film on the fascia board. 'The County' was demolished in 1956 leaving just the Regal, a few doors along the same street, and built in the 1930s. This was unceremoniously demolished just before Christmas 1987.

EAST STREET in the late 1950s before The Woolmead was built. The Marlborough Head and infamous Watney's Red Barrel can be seen on the left of the picture. Other shops, in addition to Dawson Electrics and J. Smith, butcher, both of which can be seen clearly, include a cobbler, the Regal laundry, R. Miller, mowers and Heath Bros, cycles. Traffic went two-way in East Street when this picture was taken from the bus stop outside the Regal.

THOUSANDS OF SMALL NOSES must have been pressed against the window of Miss Tigwell's toy shop in South Street while, next door, adults looking for something beautiful with which to decorate their homes would browse awhile in G.E. Day's antique shop. On the extreme right is Stratford's, the butcher outside whose shop Charlie Wenham's horse would stop each day, without any instruction from its owner, so that the Wenham family's meat could be taken out and put on the cart (see p. 95). These buildings were demolished to make way for the Sainsbury's supermarket.

ROSE'S, THE CORNCHANDLERS, which had been an important shop, was demolished in 1968. It was a sad day for Farnham and even though a new shop was opened in Cambridge Place, only a stone's throw away, the replacement was no substitute for the original. On the right of this picture can be seen the side of Smyths, a ladies' and children's outfitters, which closed in 1989.

SECTION TWO

At Your Service

Napoleon called England a nation of shopkeepers and even today, with supermarkets and chain stores in the town, Farnham retains many small businesses. In spite of the difficulties created by higher taxes, competition from cheaper multiple stores and the greater choice in larger towns, the small firms still exist. In Downing Street, for example, there is only one multiple store and even in West Street, which is a mile long, there are only seven retailers who operate via major concerns.

GRANDADS AND THEIR GRANDDAUGHTERS have a special relationship and this grandfather, Thomas Browning, is holding his granddaughter, Eileen, outside his bakery in Abbey Street, around 1932. Eileen's sister, Sheila, can be glimpsed in the background. The girls lived in the building on the left and their grandparents on the right with the bakery behind the building and the window on the right acting as a shop front (see p. 64).

A.H. BARLING, grocer and dealer in wines and spirits, had a shop on the site of the right-hand area of the present Midland Bank. It was well established by the turn of the century. Alfred Barling also had a brewery in East Street.

BEFORE THE SHOPS ON THE NORTH SIDE OF EAST STREET were demolished in the early 1960s, to make way for The Woolmead precinct, there used to be plenty of tiny, independently-owned businesses some of which, like Ye Olde Tuckshop, had been there for almost a century. C.A. Rogers was a 'wireless specialist', the first word almost unheard of today.

W & G BUNDAY, PORK BUTCHERS, operated from 25 East Street, a couple of doors away from A.H. Barling's brewery, and close to A & G Barnes (see p. 14). This Christmas display would seem to have been somewhat dangerous, healthwise, but Dr E. Coffey was just down the road at 19 East Street if he was needed. The dog has a rabbit in its mouth. Whether this was given or stolen nobody will ever know.

S. JEFFERY, WATCH AND CLOCKMAKER as well as jeweller, and R. Jeffery, gunsmith, operated from 15 and 16 The Borough from the middle of the nineteenth century. There was a forge behind the premises possibly used in connection with the manufacture of guns. It may also have been of use to Charlotte Smith, ironmonger, next door at No.14. The old couple are believed to be Walter Jeffery and his wife, Mary, possibly with their errand boy.

BEFORE THE NORTH SIDE OF EAST STREET was demolished there were many small shops selling a variety of goods from prams to antique furniture. In the latter category was Arthur Hardingham who can be seen in the doorway. It is said that if someone asked the price of an item and considered it to be too expensive, Mr Hardingham would reply, 'That's the price here. Woolworth's is up the road.'

AT ONE TIME EAST STREET included Shrubb's Photo Stores and Studio. The gated side entrance to the business is unusual. Although there were many gates leading into courtyards in West Street, The Borough and Castle Street the same did not usually apply to East Street.

SOON AFTER THE SECOND WORLD WAR this photograph of Elphicks was taken by Edward Griffith, for many years a local press photographer. To the left of Elphick's is the Farnham Dairy and cafeteria, then Nelson and Goodrick, Hedley Bartlett, the optician, Emily Chilcott's ladies wear shop and Darracotts' bakers and restaurant. Augustus Toplady, the composer of the hymn 'Rock of Ages', was born in the building which formerly occupied the site of Nelson and Goodrick's outfitters.

WEST STREET looking east before the First World War. William Kingham and Sons, grocers, occupy the building on the right and the first two letters of Elphicks can be seen on the sign which sticks out over the road. The town's post office was then situated in the tall building at the end of the left-hand side of the street. The shop of J.E. Spencer, silk mercer and fancy draper (see p. 16), is in the centre of this photograph.

THOMAS HILL,

Electrical Engineer,

19, DOWNING STREET,
FARNHAM, SURREY.

Electrician always in Residence. 'Phone 127 Farnham.

LIGHTING, HEATING, POWER, TELEPHONES,
BELLS and REPAIRS.

"OSRAM," "WOTAN," "EFESCA," and all makes of Lamps.

ESTIMATES FREE.

THOMAS HILL, ELECTRICAL ENGINEER, was responsible for installing electric lighting into most of the principal houses and shops in town. The premises is owned by Lasletts, linen drapers, today. Mr Hill was also responsible for installing telephones, bells and heating which included heavy iron radiators. It is interesting to note that although Osram lamps still exist those from Wotan and Efesca have long since vanished.

EAST MEETS WEST in this picture, as far as street names are concerned. The upper view looks east along East Street while the lower shot shows where West Street joins The Borough and looks east towards the top view. The lamp standard on the right of the lower picture is at the top of Downing Street, with Spencer's immediately behind it. The second building on the left was where the *Surrey and Hants News* was first published in 1859 (see pp. 109 and 120). In the upper picture the Royal Deer is on the right. The shops on the left have been replaced by The Woolmead.

EDWIN CLARKE OF 37 DOWNING STREET, sold fish, poultry and ice. He was both retailer and wholesaler and had premises at the Fish Dock, Grimsby. Its seems unthinkable, today, to have fish and poultry on show on the pavement as in this photograph but it was considered quite normal in the days when horses and carts rather than cars and lorries used Downing Street as a thoroughfare. On the right of Edwin Clarke's shop was the Parish Clerk's office in a building also used as a café.

FARNHAM WAS A QUIET COUNTRY TOWN in the 1930s, where afternoon tea, cucumber sandwiches, scones and strawberry jam were a way of life. There were a number of tearooms including the Castle Café in Castle Street. Today the building in this photograph is a Chinese restaurant and a gentleman's outfitter and although the left-hand window has been enlarged the one on the right has altered little in sixty years. As late as the mid-1970s boys from the Grammar School popped in for a pot of tea and a natter – something it seems hard to imagine today.

A RARE VIEW OF EAST STREET, looking east, taken in the late 1920s. The Regal Cinema had yet to be built, on the site of the garage to the left of the Marlborough Head, and Coombs were the house furnishers nearest the camera on the left of the picture. H. Wharton, The White House, was situated next door to Smyths, which can be glimpsed on the extreme right, and Mr Brown, the window cleaner, had just propped his ladder up where the lady is mounting the pavement with her pram.

ALL THE BUILDINGS on the left of this picture were knocked down to make way for the Sainsbury's car park in South Street. Ernest Langham, who founded the *Farnham Herald* in 1892, operated from the building on the left and Stratford, the butcher (see p. 95), has put up his blind to shield the meat from the sunshine. The Liberal Club, the square building in front of the church, was designed by Sir Edwin Lutyens in 1894.

M

ESTABLISHED 1873.

GEO. J. BEARD,

PICTURE FRAME MANUFACTURER,

Mount Cutter and Gilder,

DECORATOR AND UNDERTAKER,

Artists' Colourman and Art Potteries.

PICTURES REPAIRED, CLEANED AND RESTORED.

FARNHAM ART DEPÔT

(Opposite the Station).

GEORGE J. BEARD ran a varied business from his premises on Station Hill, the thoroughfare which started where the farthest point of the above picture can be seen. One of Mr Beard's successors in the premises, now an off-licence, was a chemist, L.P. Rowe, who retained for his own use the long, mahogany drawers in which Mr Beard had stored his paint brushes. It is to be regretted that these drawers no longer exist.

IT WOULD BE IMPOSSIBLE to stand in this stretch of The Borough today, as these children were doing in the first decade of this century. Today, when vehicles rush by at a rate of thousands an hour, such tranquillity as can be seen here seems almost impossible. Waterloo House is on the site of the building now occupied by the Alliance and Leicester Building Society and is at the entrance to Bear Lane. Between Ransom's, the baker and pastrycook, and A.J. Bentall, milliner and upholsterer, was the site of the bar (now corrupted to 'bear') where a toll had to be paid before one could enter The Borough.

H.C. PATRICK, THE TOWN'S FOREMOST UNDERTAKER, whose name appears on many of the tombstones in the Ypres Salient, marking the graves of soldiers who died there during the First World War, has had premises in several parts of East Street. This building was in the part of the street demolished in the 1960s.

THE WEST END OF EAST STREET just before the buildings were demolished to make way for the Woolmead development. Mrs Rose and Bert Watson who had run Heath's cycle shop opened up their own business, Farnham Cycles, farther along East Street and have remained trading there ever since. To the rear of Heath's was part of the wall of the old police station in Bear Lane, the bars of the cells facing the back of the cycle store. During the Second World War the building in the centre of this view was used as a tearoom for military personnel.

C. SMITHER, with a window full of Lucas lamps and car oil, nestles next door to the Central Garage offering both Shell and BP petrol, Aladdin paraffin and a taxi service. The building with EKCO on it is still in existence and forms part of the boundary to the footpath leading from Downing Street to the central car park. Gateway's supermarket now occupies the site on which the garage stood.

THE BIRTHPLACE OF AUGUSTUS TOPLADY, who wrote 'Rock of Ages'. The building in the photograph was demolished in 1875 and replaced by a Georgian-style building of red brick. This was altered again in 1960 to make the present building adjacent to Elphicks. A stone above the windows of the present shop reads, 'Here was born Augustus Montague Toplady 4 November 1740. This stone was taken from Burrington Coombe'. Legend has it that Toplady had the inspiration for his famous hymn, first published in 1775, when sheltering from a storm at Burrington Coombe in Somerset.

J. SAINSBURY'S

NEW STORE,

18 & 19, THE BOROUGH, FARNHAM.

'Phone : Farnham 0953 - 4.

We had a wonderful opening and beg to offer our thanks to all old friends and new customers.

\- - -

REMEMBER—
The prices are genuine examples of the Sainsbury value.

\- - -

YOU WILL ENJOY BETTER QUALITY AND SAVE MONEY BY SHOPPING AT

SAINSBURY'S

TODAY J. SAINSBURY HAS A LARGE SUPERMARKET in South Street (known as New Road for many years after it was constructed in 1868), but its first branch in Farnham was at 18 and 19 The Borough, now Halfords. Take a look inside this shop today and see the ornate ceiling which was once above the butter counter and take note of the finger holes at the base of each window, from the time when the shop-fronts used to be pushed into the room above so that Sainsbury's wares could be touched from the street. This advertisement was published when the shop opened in The Borough in September 1933.

THIS MAGNIFICENT DISPLAY OF FRUIT AND VEGETABLES was part of Hewitt's window display in the Farnham Industrial Exhibition held at Church House probably in 1949. Hewitt's was situated in West Street, adjacent to Church Passage.

COMFY COACHES operated from an office next to Tily and Brown, now Robert Dyas, in Castle Street, and was also an agency for Farnham Travel. The company moved into premises in The Woolmead during the 1960s. This building, with its unusually large curved top windows, is now an antiquarian bookshop.

THE OLD KNIGHT'S BANK, considered by many to have been one of the worst buildings ever erected in Farnham, was pulled down in the 1930s and its two chimneys erected again by Harold Falkner, one of the town's most prominent architects (see p. 96). Today one can see the chimneys on the Bush Hotel and at the eastern end of The Borough shopping arcade. The letters of Watney Combe and Reid can still be seen today on the wooden bar which is on the left of this picture. The entrance is now that to St Georges.

SWAIN & JONES first opened for trade in 1908. Owned by Frank Swain and John Lewis-Jones the premises which they first acquired was at 38 East Street, the site of a former coachmaker's workshop. The company still flourishes today and has properties on both sides of the street including one which has incorporated the wheelwright and coachmaker's premises of George Sturt (see p. 39). The row of cottages on the right is still in existence although several have now been incorporated into one of Surrey's longest-established Chinese restaurants, the Kar Ling Kwong.

THIS TIN, MADE BY THE SURREY CHEMICAL CARBIDE COMPANY, was filled at a unit in Darvill's Lane, close to the present Farnham bypass. Carbide gas was used for lighting on bicycles and motor cycles. On one side of the tin is this legend, 'Dangerous if not kept dry. Caution. The contents of this package are liable, if brought into contact with moisture, to give off a highly inflammable gas. Keep your carbide airtight.'

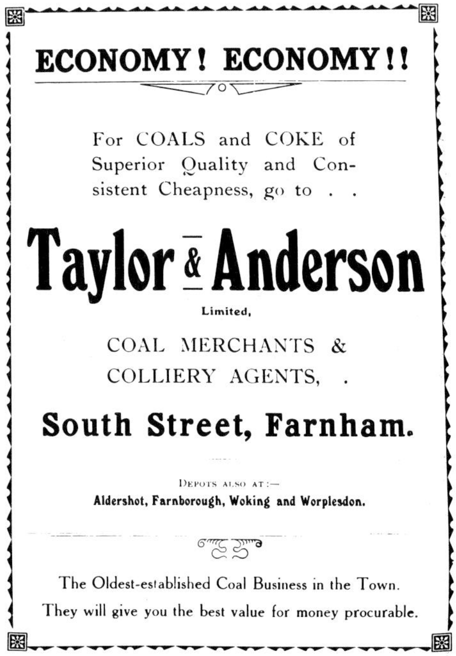

IT PAYS TO ADVERTISE, it is said, and Frisby's certainly stood the test of time only closing in the mid-1980s (see p. 47). Taylor and Anderson lasted almost as long, but Nash's bakery at Hale, established in 1900 in spite of its modern vehicle, ceased production at its plant in Folly Hill many years ago. Interestingly, for men who worked with flour, each of these delivery staff is wearing a flower in his buttonhole.

THE MOST FAMOUS FISHMONGER ever to have traded in Farnham was 'Fishy' Stevens. Lionel Stevens had a shop close to the top of Downing Street and sold both wet and fried fish. A sit-down service was also possible (the door beneath the lamp says 'cafe') and many people spent a cheap evening here having fish, chips, a piece of bread and butter and a cup of tea for 6d. (2½p). This photograph was taken around 1955 and shows the present betting shop as part of The International Meat Company. At the extreme left of the picture is the wall of Worsam's, the bakers, which stood on the same site for 200 years until it closed in the mid-1980s (see p. 11). On the wall at the rear of the building formerly occupied by 'Fishy' there is some grafitti which must have been written about forty years ago.

W.G. FROOM, ARTIST AND PHOTOGRAPHER, of 50 East Street, took this photograph of a baker at the end of the last century. As the photographer was only six doors away from Alfred Rawlins' sub post office, provision merchant and baker, one might assume that it is Mr Rawlins in the picture. In 1902 the postmaster in Farnham sought permission to close Mr Rawlins' sub post office at noon on 9 June because Jeanette Rawlins was marrying Albert Edward Hughes, son of Henry Hughes, outfitter, of 4 West Street that afternoon.

SECTION THREE

Inside Information

Until recent years it was almost impossible to take photographs of the interiors of shops because of insufficient light. Most interior shots could only be taken in photographic studios so few people will have any idea of what the insides of shops and other businesses once looked like – until now.

LONG BEFORE SWAIN & JONES TOOK OVER the north as well as the south side of East Street, Heath Bros, motor cycle dealer, occupied the premises from where this picture was taken looking across to Swain & Jones' forecourt. Part of the Heath Bros building was the former wheelwright's shop recorded in several of the books written by George Sturt, or George Bourne as he was often known. The offices of Heath Bros were the old cottage in which George Sturt's uncle and father used to sit by the fire. Parts of this house, recorded in *A Small Boy in the Sixties,* are now at the Old Kiln Museum, Tilford.

INSIDE SWAIN & JONES' WORKSHOP in 1955. The clock on the far wall, given by KLG Plugs in the 1920s, still hangs in the workshop today although it no longer tells the time. Among the workforce who can be seen in this picture are Ted Strickland, Jimmy Beadle, John Dunlevy, John Nash, Ron Lloyd, George Goacher, Tom Voller, Arthur Marsh, and brothers Maurice and Doug Deadman who later opened their own garage at Heath End. In the centre of the workshop Fred Law, left, discusses business with Donald Lewis-Jones, son of the firm's founder.

WHEN GEORGE HIBBARD WAS MANAGER of W.H. Smith and Son in The Borough he had the tiny office, just one yard square, which can be seen in the photograph. Here he hired, fired and handed out the weekly wage packets to staff such as Mrs Joan Mills, Mrs Hazel Fisher (centre) and Miss Jean Bowdery. When this picture was taken in 1953 the latter's wage was 39s.11d. (just under £2) for a 44½-hour week. Behind the rows of Everyman books which can be seen, was the Lending Library, the rival to that in Boots the Chemist (see p. 47).

THERE IS STILL A BLACKSMITH'S FORGE in Upper Church Lane, as there has been for a century. This shot, taken in the 1930s it is believed, could have been taken a century earlier had it not been for an electric light bulb hanging from the ceiling just above the raised sledge-hammer. The window looks out on to the street.

ELPHICKS INTERIOR in 1926, photographed by *Town and Country News*. There were plenty of chairs for the customers to rest on and plenty of assistants to give meticulous attention to their needs. Goods could be delivered, if required, by a boy on a trade cycle who would cycle to Frensham and back with something as simple as a pair of stockings from the St Margaret hoisery range if he was required to do so.

WHEN THE MARINDIN HALL was first built at Millbridge, the billiard tables were in the room with the stage. Later an extension was built to make it possible for other events to be held in this room and billiards and snooker were played in the new area.

THERE ARE A NUMBER OF WELL-KNOWN FACES in this photograph, taken inside the post office in West Street after it had been rebuilt. The opening on 5 January 1973 was attended by the planning officer for Farnham, John Wainwright, centre front, and on his left is James Hockey, former principal of Farnham School of Art (later to become the West Surrey College of Art and Design). In the background, silhouetted against the doors, is Dave Warner who still delivers letters in Farnham.

AN INTERIOR VIEW of part of the lounge inside Waverley Abbey House, for many years the home of the Anderson family and a building used as an army hospital in the First World War (see p. 52).

IT WOULD BE HARD TO IMAGINE A SCHOOL LIBRARY looking like this today but when Farnham Girls' Grammar School was housed in the former Boys' Grammar School in West Street, the library on the upper floor was as can be seen in this photograph.

INSIDE THE BAKERY OF R. STURT at Millbridge, Frensham, when the dough for every loaf was kneaded by hand and baked in the huge oven at the back of the picture.

WHEN THE CLAYTONS RAN WEST END RADIO, at 21 West Street, nowadays a charity shop close to The Wheatsheaf, they used to work above an area which had been a bakery. On one occasion an elephant, part of a circus, was walking up Downing Street, put its trunk through an upper window of Worsam's and stole a loaf. A runner was then sent along West Street, to the baker at No. 21, telling him to shut his windows to prevent another loaf being stolen. Until it was gutted to make way for the charity shop, the interior of West End Radio was panelled in oak and offered customers Lloyd Loom chairs in which to relax while watching television sets they might wish to buy.

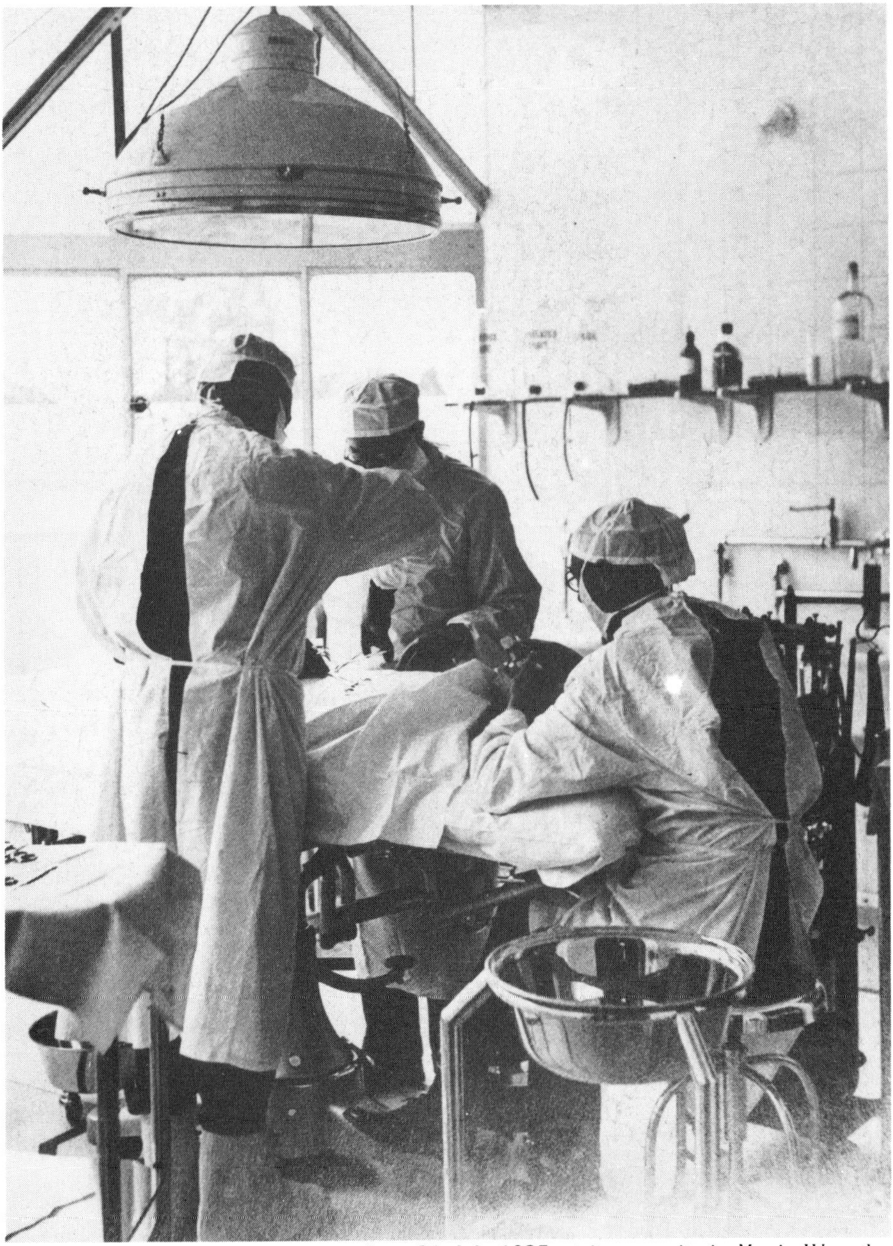

WHEN TRIMMER'S HOSPITAL was opened on 31 July 1935, at its new site in Menin Way, the doctors who used its facilities were delighted with the light and airy operating theatre. The total cost of building the new hospital had been £16,500. The building is now known as the Phyllis Tuckwell Hospice and relies entirely on charity for its maintenance.

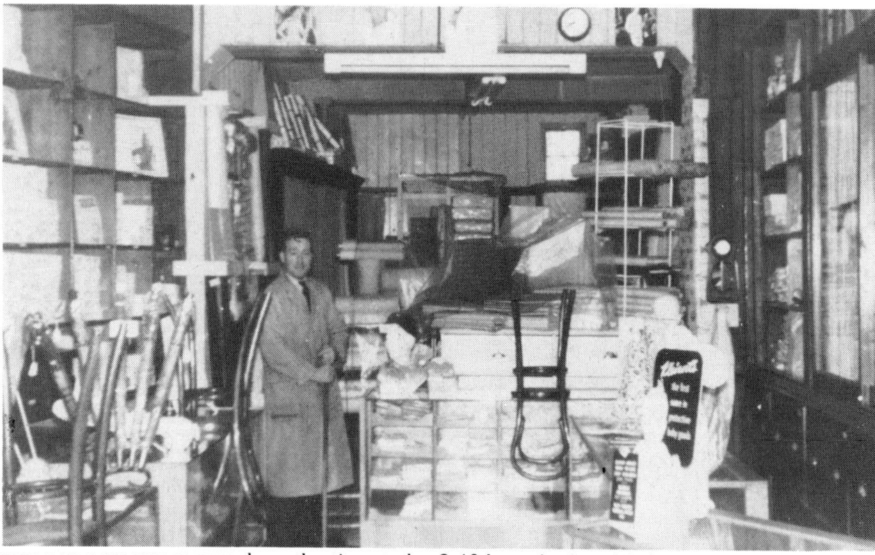

THE HANDS ON THE CLOCK show the time to be 8.40 but whether this is morning or evening is not known. Evening is most likely. Stan Phipps is cleaning Nelson and Goodrick in West Street, sometime in the mid-1950s. Although strip lighting tubes have been installed the ground area of the shop still gives the appearance of the 1930s.

THE INTERIOR OF OWEN HALL IN UNION ROAD, where many parties and dances were held, in the mid-1930s. This was the occasion of Harold Cole's 21st birthday (he is in the centre holding the key). Also in the picture are Lily Sparks, who later ran her parents' sweet shop in The Borough; Peter and Lottie Cole; Les Muddell; Muriel Payne; Daisy Young; Jack Worner; Charlie Holdship; Stan Budd; Lil Fosbury; Ethel Arundell; Marie Wakeford; Jack Sargeant and Sid Young. The band was the Twilight Rhythm. Harold Cole later became a firm favourite with the royal family and attended many functions at the express invitation of its members.

BOOTS LENDING LIBRARY was on the first floor of the chemist's shop in The Borough. Library books were ranged on oak shelves, there were curved-back chairs to sit on and the staff made sure that the customers' wishes were met. In this photograph, taken in the early 1960s, the assistants are Jane Doe, Barbara Chuter, Margaret Bowdery and Eilene Henderson. A single deposit of 2s. 6d. (12½p) was all that was required to PAYR (pay as you read). The library is decorated for Christmas, in this picture, and a note above the pelmet stated that the decorations were for sale.

FRISBY'S SHOE SHOP IN THE BOROUGH lasted for over ninety years. This photograph, taken in the 1960s, shows the stocking counter as well as the shoe boxes. Prices for stockings ranged from 3s. 1d. (15½p) up to 6s. 11d. (34½p). The staff fitted the customers' shoes while the latter sat on chrome and coloured plastic seats and rested their legs on footstools.

THE FARNHAM STREET SCENE changed completely in the early 1930s. The old Town Hall was demolished before the present buildings (now used by the Nationwide Building Society) were built. This picture shows the few remaining walls of the part of the building known as the Corn Exchange, before it was committed to brick rubble and dust.

THE CARS IN THIS PICTURE look incongruous set beside the table with carved legs and comfortable chairs. However, this was the scene as one walked into Swain and Jones' car showroom in East Street in 1927. The table was the original one used in the boardroom and continued to be used until the early 1980s.

THE INTERIOR OF THE PRESENT BIGGS, WEST STREET, when trunks, cases and similar equipment were sold there. In 1925 it was owned by Emily Chilcott, milliner. Later Franklin and Chilcott, outfitters and milliners, operated from 8 West Street, immediately opposite. When Emily Chilcott opened the latter shop in 1936, she had non-reflecting glass in the windows which attracted considerable attention.

WHEN *THE HAPPY PRINCE* WAS PERFORMED in Farnham Parish Church by members of the Farnham Girls' Choir in the mid-1960s the church was packed to capacity. The story had been specially adapted for the choir by Malcolm Williamson and the performance was for part of the Farnham Festival. The prince was played by Margaret Daniels, who is wearing a tricorn hat. To her left is Susan Seymour as the bluebird. Other members of the choir are in the background, in costume for the operetta rather than in their formal choir dresses.

A FAVOURITE SHOP for adults and children alike was that of Wm. Cox in The Borough. This was a family business, opened in 1908 by the parents of Miss Lily Sparks, left, and eventually closed in 1972. All the chocolates sold were handmade and 'fork-dipped' by William Cox, son of the owner, in Winchester. Wm. Cox, senior, was Miss Sparks' uncle. Toffee was always cut with tongs in this shop and, like the loose sweets, was sold in white bags with brown lettering.

THE LION AND LAMB was once a coaching inn. Today the area formerly occupied by travellers is a picture showroom and jewellers, but sixty years ago the upper floor was used by staff of William Kingham and Sons, grocers, as a rest room where a table-tennis table was supplied for staff use. The photograph shows a view through the window, along the balcony which still exists.

SURREY AND HANTS NEWS REPORTERS have made their marks in a variety of ways over the past forty years. One was drowned while attempting to row the Atlantic, another is a regular contributor to radio, television and stage productions and, of the current team of four editorial staff, three have a total of ten published books to their credit and three more in the pipeline. However, it is unlikely that there will ever be another reporter who will sit in the ruins of an historic building, Firgrove House, and play what remained of a grand piano, as Peter Chapman did here.

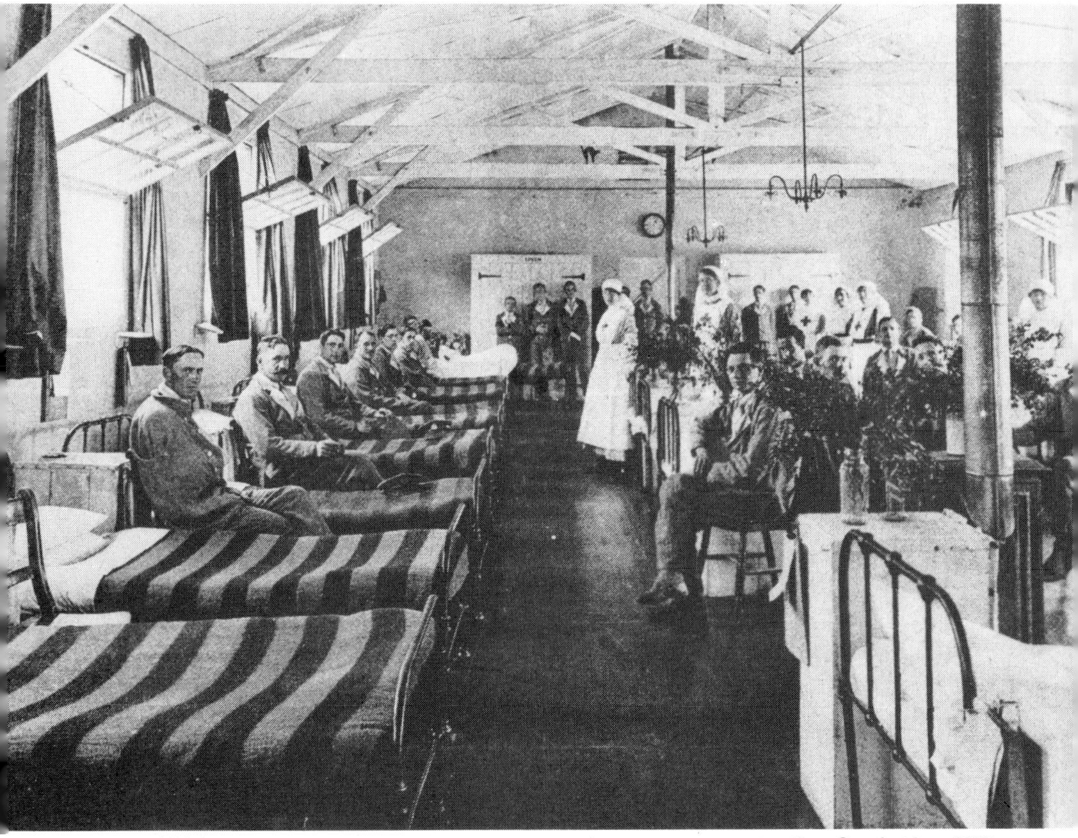

IN 1914 WAVERLEY ABBEY HOUSE was accepted as an annexe to the Cambridge Military Hospital in Aldershot. Robins and Sons of Farnham converted the ground floor of the house in the summer and on 24 September seventeen wounded officers were moved into what was called the Waverley Abbey Hospital. In October 1914 the *Daily Mirror* featured this hospital with photographs of Mrs Rupert Anderson, whose home it was until taken over by the War Office, and her daughters, Amy, Nancy and Betty, all of whom were nurses at Waverley, and Millie who was in France. This picture is of the wounded in Rob Roy ward and was possibly one of the scenes which the *Daily Mirror's* journalist reported upon.

A CELEBRATORY LUNCH inside the Marindin Hall, Millbridge, in 1931 with the Lady Constance and Mr Richard Combe superimposed on the photograph. The Combe family, part of the Watney, Combe and Reid brewing empire, owned Pierrepont, Frensham, and the diners were staff on the Pierrepont estate. It is interesting to note that in spite of the neat outfits worn by the waitresses it was considered all right to have bottles of beer (it must have been from the family firm) on the tables.

THE INTERIOR OF STURT'S BOOKSHOP in The Borough (see p. 12). Sturt was also a publisher of postcards and it could therefore be expected that the rack on the left of the picture is full of his productions.

IN WRECCLESHAM POTTERY time has almost stood still since the days when it was opened by Absolom Harris in 1873. It is still in the hands of the same family and pots are still made from clay turned by hand on a wheel, a twig taken from the hedge outside being used as a height measure. In 1990, however, the company exhibited at the Ideal Home Exhibition, proving that even the most traditional methods of manufacture can still survive in a technological age. This photograph was taken soon after the pottery opened a century ago.

SECTION FOUR

On the Move

Since the Middle Stone Age man has been on the move in and around Farnham. The first meeting of the Automobile Association is said to have taken place at Barfield, near Farnham, and several men in the town made good livings from wheels, among them Sturt and Goacher, wheelrights, Heath and Wiltshire, motor cycle and cycle dealers, and Swain and Jones, who have sold cars in East Street since 1907.

MOTOR BIKES WERE ALL THE RAGE in the late 1920s and 1930s. Len Heath, the motorcyclist who lived at Frensham, was competing in a six-day international trial in Salzburg when the Second World War was declared. He returned to England and continued running the motor cycle firm he had started a decade earlier with his brother Joe, operating from their father's shed. Here the 'ton-up' boys of the early 1930s, who had bought their machines from them, are just leaving the Spotted Cow at The Bourne. Frank 'Punch' Parratt, their unofficial leader, is on the extreme right (see p. 89).

HEATH AND WILTSHIRE ran a garage from a site in Union Road, almost opposite to Church House, from early in the twentieth century. In the early 1960s it was demolished and Expedier House was built on the land. Then, in the late 1980s, this too was demolished, and Wey Court, the present building was erected. The trees of Gostrey Meadow can be seen in the background.

THE CHURCH ARMY, which had its headquarters in the Edgware Road in London, sent out its evangelists to preach in country villages. This Church Army caravan was photographed at Frensham about 100 years ago.

CHARLIE WENHAM, Farnham's best-loved rag-and-bone merchant, is seen here cutting some grass for his horse, Topsy, around 1960. The cart is standing on the verge by the Farnham bypass on land which belonged to Charlie by dint of a gentleman's agreement. It is below the built-up area of The Fairfield and faces towards Farnham town centre. It might become the site of a petrol station if the 1990 campaign against BP's plan is not successful.

IN 1947 AN AMERICAN ARMY LORRY skidded on a slippery surface and smashed into the front of the International Meat Company's shop at the top of Downing Street. The International grocery shop in West Street can just be seen at the top of the picture, and the building then known as the Alliance public house is adjacent to the shattered butcher's shop. The Alliance was once run by Jessie Matthews, star of stage, screen and *Mrs Dale's Diary* on radio. At the time this accident took place Downing Street had a two-way traffic flow.

MR GEORGE PARFITT with the car he built in 1897 for John Henry Knight. The vehicle is now in the Montagu Museum at Beaulieu. It was one of the first petrol-driven cars in this country and was built in West Street in a workshop almost opposite The Jolly Sailor public house. A plaque on the wall of the building records the construction of this vehicle.

MIKE HAWTHORN at the wheel of a sports car. Mike later won the World Motor Racing Driving Championship but died in a road accident in 1959 when he was at the height of his career.

GYPSIES WERE A FAMILIAR SIGHT in Farnham at hop picking time and this family has stopped its caravan on the outskirts of town, probably on the Farnham to Bentley road. In the early 1920s the landlady at The Bull Inn, Bentley, was said to have become tired of the travellers who stole bottles of beer from behind the bar when she had gone out to the kitchen to fill up glasses from the barrel, so to pay them back and to stop any further pilfering, she filled bottles up with urine and it is these which the gypsies are said to have stolen. It may have seemed a nasty trick to play but it stopped the thieving.

DAVID WICKINS, once owner of British Car Auctions, is seen here checking a car about to be offered for sale in the early 1960s.

JOHN HENRY KNIGHT, inventor, photographer and author, designed many strange devices including an automatic brick-wall-building machine and the wood-spring tyre, a wheel made from small pieces of wood set in a flexible frame, as well as a motor car. This picture, though, is of an oil engine, possibly made by a Guildford firm, which Mr Knight chose to photograph at his Barfield home. Perhaps he is not certain that the machine will work because the blacksmith is in evidence to the right of the picture, possibly waiting to effect a repair on the 'device'.

DOWNING STREET in flood during the early years of this century. The man on the left of the picture is holding up his trousers so that even if his boots get wet his trousers will not. Scenes like this were commonplace in Farnham until the river bed was widened in the 1960s. On the side wall of the Hop Bag public house is an advertisement for *The Weekly Dispatch* which must have been a national rather than local paper. The picture is believed to have been taken prior to 1891.

IN MARCH 1990 THE FIRST TURF WAS DUG to start the Blackwater Valley Route through part of Farnham. This road is a further development in the town of the Farnham bypass, started fifty years earlier. The tractors in the picture above have ploughed so many furrows it is hard to comprehend that the land on which they are standing would soon be the A31 dual carriageway. Edward Griffith took this photograph in 1938 from the western side of town at the new road's future junction with Red Lion Lane. Farnham Parish Church can be seen in the background.

ALL LINED UP AND READY FOR WORK is this team of men from Victoria Transport. The firm operated from what is now part of the central car park. The tower of the United Reformed Church, in South Street, can be seen in the distance.

PLOUGHING THE FIELDS by hand (and horse) on the outskirts of Farnham a century ago. This photograph was taken by John Henry Knight.

ALTHOUGH FARNHAM IS ONLY ABOUT FIVE MILES from Farnborough, where aircraft displays have been held for decades, the Graf Zeppelin was seldom seen over the town. However, one afternoon in the 1930s a Zeppelin 'stopped play'. These people had been playing bowls at Gorsehanger, Greenhill Road, when one of the strange, cigar-shaped objects passed overhead.

SMYTH'S, DRAPERS AND OUTFITTERS, traded in East Street for over a century closing in 1989. For at least half of that time the shop was run by a band of unmarried sisters who always wore black. This van, the company's pride and joy, once won a prize for its driver in a Farnham carnival for being the 'best in show'. The award was a pipe and tobacco although the driver was Miss Rose Smyth. In the days between the two World Wars it was unusual for a woman to drive a van and win a prize for it.

EDWARD GRIFFITH, to whom this book is dedicated, faithfully recorded the town on glass plate and film, for sixty years. Here he is standing by the wall which ran along the side of the former Regal cinema at the side of his Lea Francis car. Before it was taken to the scrapheap in 1936, Edward removed the clock from the dashboard, and the dickey seat. These continued to be used, the seat in his photographic studio in Downing Street, which he later sold to Martin Rice, and the clock, which he wedged on the parcel shelf of each new car he had, was still working in 1981.

COMMUTERS FROM FARNHAM STATION TODAY would have difficulty in believing that between 1925 and 1927 a train called 'the Micheline', with pneumatic tyres, ran for a trial period on a nearby track. This photograph was taken by an amateur photographer, Alec Shepheard, on the 'up' platform in Farnham Station.

WHEN THOMAS BROWNING operated his steam bakery from Abbey Street he was justifiably proud of his immaculate van. The bakery backed on to the river and the house in which the Browning family lived is adjacent to the archway in the terrace of houses on the north side of the street. Before South Street was built the only exit from Farnham, southwards, was via Abbey Street and the Cistercian monks, on their way back and forth from their abbey in Moor Park, would walk this stretch of thoroughfare, hence its name. Thomas' daughter, Ivy, can be seen in the doorway (see p. 19).

FREDERICK WRIGHTON seems to be as pleased with his twenty-year old Lagonda in 1957 as he would have been had he had it new in 1937 when it was built. The picture was taken in Mavins Road by Edward Griffith, outside whose home it was parked.

A FAMILY GROUP AT BARFIELD, ready for a cycle ride. John Henry Knight is in the centre. This picture is from a glass plate negative in Farnham Musuem.

ONE OF THE STEAM WAGONS belonging to the Pharo family of Badshot Lea and used in their haulage work. The company is still in operation today.

ST JOHN AMBULANCE BRIGADE had a specially built horse-drawn ambulance constructed for them in 1894 by George Sturt of East Street. However, by the early months of 1913 the brigade was able to have its first motor ambulance at a cost of £120. This picture was taken in Castle Street outside the Watney, Combe and Reid brewery depot.

SPECIAL OCCASIONS warrant special postmarks, and the marks on this group of three envelopes commemorate the opening of the Sixth Form College in Morley Road on 12 September 1973, the Tenth Commonwealth Forestry Conference at Alice Holt on 7 September 1974 and, most unusual of all, a stamp made up by hand on a child's printing kit, to record the 'First Ever Balloon Post From Farnham'. This took place on 27 July 1968 when Malcolm Brighton took the specially stamped envelopes up in a balloon from The Bourne to Hurtmore. Mr Brighton died in an attempt to cross the Atlantic by balloon.

LITTLE IS KNOWN about this photograph or the occasion being celebrated. It is interesting to note, though, the 'stop' line on the road outside what is now the Royal Deer and the wooden signpost at the junction of Bear Lane and The Borough. Alfred Wyles shop is on the corner and the gas showroom (see p. 11) is in evidence on the right.

ONE OF THE PHOTOGRAPHS taken by John Henry Knight a century ago. It is believed to have been shot on the Farnham to Guildford Road, close to Junction Bridge. The wall in the background was demolished in the spring of 1990 to make way for a new stretch of dual carriageway.

READY FOR THE ROAD, at least that seems to be the prospect for this row of cars in the Swain & Jones garage on the north side of East Street in the late 1920s. A notice on the wall behind the second car from the left states 'Another Lea Francis success'.

SECTION FIVE

Seen Through an Artist's Eye

Many amateur and professional painters and engravers have attempted to capture on canvas or paper the way in which they saw various places in the town. These range from the complicated and stilted engravings of Moor Park to the watercolour of the tiny cottage in Rowledge, which looks idyllic but which had wild cats living in the roof space as late as 1951. Before the days of photography it was only through paintings and engravings that people and places could be recorded for posterity. Farnham was a town which attracted many artists whose work, if unsung generally, lives on today.

'Lion & Lamb,' West Street, 1900.

FARNHAM still has many courtyards leading from the main streets, but a century ago there were many more than today. One such courtyard was that which led from West Street into the stabling area of The Lion and Lamb Hotel in West Street. Marshall Barnes, the artist who drew many of the landmarks of Farnham, produced this sketch of the hotel for the centenary booklet of William Kingham and Sons in 1952.

A VIEW OF EAST STREET from The Borough, drawn in 1919. The distinctive concrete shield above the Royal Deer can be clearly seen although the door beneath this ornate work has been blocked up. At about this time the world famous boxer, 'Boy' McCormick, who lived in the town, used to spar in the rooms above this pub.

FARNHAM about 150 years ago, as drawn by H. Prosser. The view is from the south side of the river and looks across the meadows where sheep appear to be grazing. At least three oast-houses can be seen on the right. The drawing was made before the church tower was heightened in the middle of the last century.

MOOR PARK, SURREY, *circa* 1800

THIS ENGRAVING OF MOOR PARK HOUSE was made by F. Evans in around 1800. It was here that Jonathan Swift, author of many works including *Gulliver's Travels*, lived and wrote while he was secretary to Sir William Temple. There has been a house on this site since 1307.

MOTHER LUDLAM'S CAVE as depicted by an engraver with the surname of Hawkins and 'published according to Act of Parliament by Alexander Hogg, 16, Paternoster Row'.

THE INTERIOR OF FARNHAM PARISH CHURCH as depicted by F.G.D. LaMotte, sculptor, in 1800.

THE INTERIOR OF QUINETTES FRUIT DRINK COMPANY'S OFFICE, off Castle Street, in the early 1930s. The firm was proud of its excellent reputation for fruit crushes and it decorated this office in shades of orange, lemon and green to represent the three most popular flavours of the company's products. The logo was a roundel in which were three owls' heads – Quizzit, Quoffit and Quenchit. The firm, owned by Mr Palin-Evans and his mother, was bought out by Kia-Ora. The building later became part of the Castle Theatre (see p. 121).

SWAN COTTAGE, in the High Street, Rowledge, as painted by Eric Mort, an artist who lived in the village. Although wild cats lived in the roof and the toilet was in a shed, it was home to a number of families before it was demolished in the 1970s, although one of the two yew trees which once stood at the entrance to the garden still remains.

WHEN GLADYS AYLING PAINTED THIS SCENE about fifty-five years ago, she could not have imagined that the peace and tranquillity would be lost forever when the building was demolished to make way for The Woolmead. This painting shows the side view of her father's cycle shop, looking up from East Street towards the bowling green area. One day a flock of sheep squashed into the tiny shop floor area and pinned Lilian Ayling née Ranger, Gladys' mother, behind the counter. On other occasions cows and bullocks would walk up the path shown in the picture, frightening Doris Ayling, her sister, so much she hid in the bicycle tyres. The forge at the back of the building was used by William Ayling as a place to make some of the bikes he sold. Lilian and William had two other children Binny and Bob who later, together with other members of their family, ran Ranger's shops in West Street which had been owned by their grandfather.

BETWEEN 1850 AND 1900 JAMES SMITH, carrier, corn, hay and straw dealer operated from the shop depicted in this painting. Fifty years later Gladys Hardingham ran a secondhand bookshop from the same building. The alley to the right of the shop runs up into Timber Close, one of the sites in Farnham where it is believed the roof trusses for Westminster Hall in London may have been constructed.

AN ENGRAVING OF WAVERLEY ABBEY RUINS, made in 1785. The two men depicted on the left with their scythes have evidently been cutting hay in the fields around the abbey. The ruins can still be seen today and are of historic interest as Waverley Abbey was the first Cistercian Abbey in this country.

MOIRA KELSEY, an accomplished artist as well as having once won a beauty queen title, drew this sketch of the Bush Hotel's courtyard when she worked there with her husband, Peter, who was the manager. The Vine Bar, to the right, is one of the most cosmopolitan of bars to be found anywhere, and also offers some of the least expensive real ales to be found in town. When the fountain is playing and jazz musicians give Saturday lunchtime concerts this sixteenth-century inn is one of the best places to be in Farnham. Moira and Peter Kelsey now own The George at Odiham.

SECTION SIX

Hospitality on Tap

Farnham is reputed to have once had more pubs per head of population than any other town in the country. Hop gardens surrounded the entire town and at the end of the nineteenth century Farnham hops were the most expensive in the world. With so many men involved in the cultivation of one of the four main ingredients of beer, it is only natural that they should be interested in the final product, and a number would ask to have a few coppers from their wages retained by their employer, so that he could provide them with beer at the end of the week. It was in this way that a number of Farnham pubs had their origins in private houses, the Bat and Ball at Boundstone being an example.

THE RAILWAY HOTEL, renamed The Blue Boy, has been one of the first places seen by visitors arriving in the town by train since 1849. The building is said to be haunted by a ghost – a tall figure wearing a black cloak and hood which tend to merge into one. At one time there was an undertaker's opposite and the occupants of the flats, into which the undertaker's was converted, have also seen the same tall, dark stranger.

A SCENE INSIDE FARNHAM MALTINGS some time before 1946 when malting ceased. The men are using large wooden shovels to turn over the grain. The man on the left is holding a thermometer which would have been used to test the temperature of the grain which was heated. The Maltings is now an arts centre. Farnham brewers, who made use of the malt from these premises, were generous benefactors to the town. Sampson and Trimmer both founded almshouses and Trimmer also founded a hospital. The smaller brewers became united in 1890 and were known as Farnham United Breweries. In 1926 Courage and Company took over these pubs.

WHEN ALMOST THE WHOLE OF THE LAND surrounding Farnham was covered with hop gardens there was a great need for oast-houses in which to dry the hop cones. Most have now been demolished but these buildings beside the Wey, about half a mile east of Farnham, still exist as a private house, though the conical roofs have been removed.

A GROUP OF BARMEN waiting to pull pints for thirsty customers. The poster over the door on the left advertises Farnham United Breweries Pale Ale and Stout. The photograph is believed to have been taken in the Running Stream at Weybourne (see p. 143).

THE FOX INN, at the foot of the hill which separates Farnham from The Bourne, once one of the pubs under the Farnham United Breweries livery. The building has altered very little over several hundred years, and still serves a good pint of real ale today.

THE FOREST INN was, until the mid-1980s, a small, comfortable roadside public house. Then it was bought from Courage and Company and extended to its present massive proportions. At first the name was changed to The New Forest Inn and then, when it was bought by Bernard and Anthea Monk, it became The Merrie Monks Motel. When this picture was taken, at the beginning of the century, customers arrived either on foot or bicycle. Tradesmen making deliveries used a horse and cart. The ground behind this building was used for playing cricket and is known as The Oval. At one time the pub had an entire cricket team with the surname of Parratt.

THE PUB SIGN on the wall at the left of this picture indicates The Feathers Inn in Lower Church Lane. Although it is about eighty years since a pint was pulled in this pub the iron bracket on which the sign hung can still be seen. This is one of the very few thoroughfares in the country where the gutter and drains are in the middle of the road rather than at the sides.

THE BLUE BELL, DOCKENFIELD, now a free house but once under the livery of Farnham United Breweries.

THE JOLLY FARMER, Bridge Square, renamed the William Cobbett in recognition of one of Farnham's most famous sons. William Cobbett, politician, author, and political agitator was born here in 1763, the son of poor peasants. He loved the town in which he was born and was always concerned for those who worked on the land. Writing was the means he used to stir people to political awareness on both sides of the Atlantic. He is buried just outside the north door of Farnham Parish Church (see p. 96).

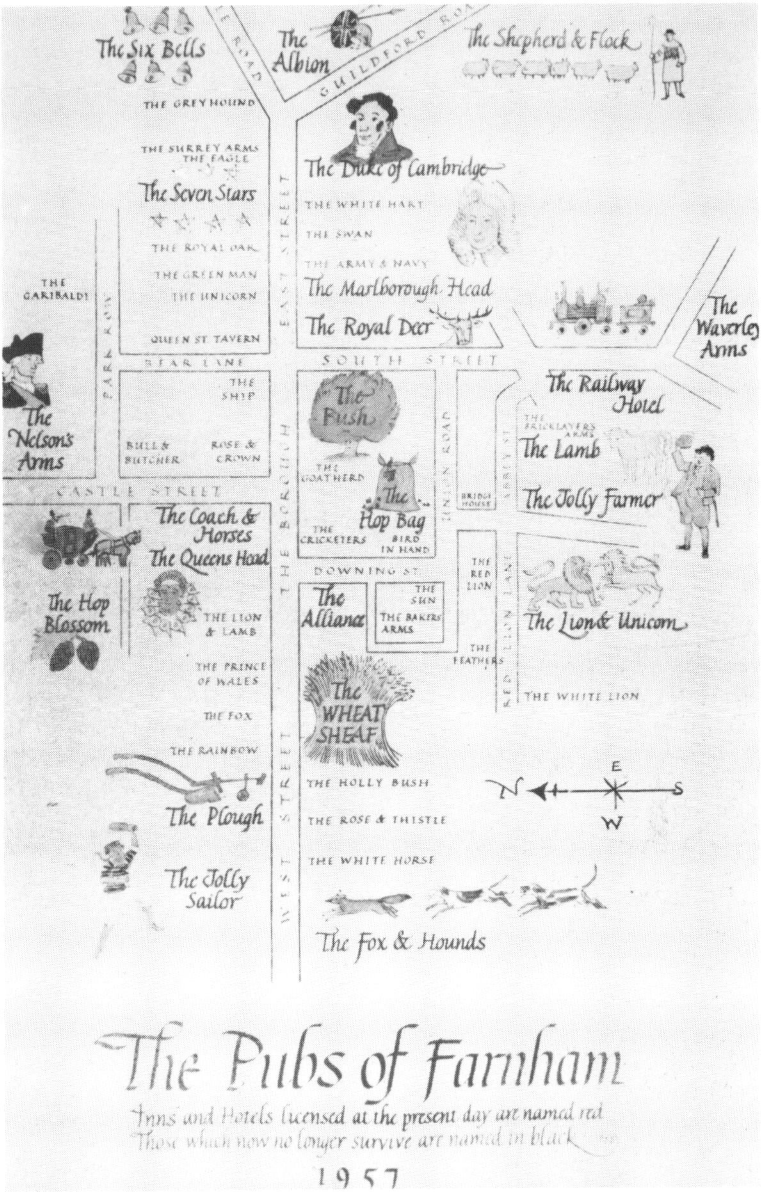

ALTHOUGH IT IS SAID that Farnham once had more pubs per head of population than any other town in the country, by 1957 many of them, even those in the main streets, had disappeared. In this pictorial map those pubs in heavy type still dispense drinks, the exceptions being the Hop Bag (which changed its name to the Downing Street Club and was then demolished in 1990), the Fox and Hounds and the Lion and Unicorn. The Jolly Farmer is now called the William Cobbett (see facing page) and the Railway Hotel has become The Blue Boy.

THE HOP BAG was demolished in 1989. A pub has stood on the site for around 250 years. In 1755 it was known as The Adam and Eve but by 1794 the name had changed to the King of Prussia. This name did not last long and it became known as The Hop Bag or The Pocket of Hops. Fire almost destroyed the building in 1868, and a man was murdered outside in May 1987 when the building was known as The Downing Street Club. It bore a sign similar to a London street sign, but with the SW1 part crossed through. The building on the right side is a chapel which was knocked down to make way for the entrance to the central car park.

THE SANDROCK on Sandrock Hill, Boundstone, is now a free house although for many years, while it was run by two sisters who scrubbed every inch of the floor and interior woodwork every day, it was under Farnham United Breweries and later Courage. Today it has a strong inclination towards charitable works and a group of men who meet there, known as The Sandmen, help local people and raise funds for the needy.

SURREY.

FARNHAM, GODALMING, NORMANDY,

TILFORD & WRECCLESHAM.

PARTICULARS AND CONDITIONS OF SALE OF

ELEVEN FULLY LICENSED

PUBLIC HOUSES,

SITUATE IN THE TOWNS OF FARNHAM & GODALMING,

AND

THE VILLAGES OF NORMANDY, TILFORD & WRECCLESHAM,

The whole of such Public Houses being let on a repairing Lease to Messrs. R. T. & J. BARRETT, for a term expiring at Midsummer, 1889;

ALSO

THREE COTTAGES, SITUATE IN CASTLE STREET,

FARNHAM, ADJOINING THE NELSON'S ARMS PUBLIC HOUSE,

And producing an aggregate rental of £23. 8. 0 per annum,

Which will be offered for Sale by Auction, by

MR. J. ALFRED EGGAR

(Under instructions from JOHN HENRY KNIGHT, Esq.)

AT THE BUSH HOTEL, FARNHAM,

On FRIDAY, APRIL 6th, 1888,

AT THREE O'CLOCK PRECISELY.

J. ALFRED EGGAR, whose premises stood in Castle Street, in front of the Watney, Combe and Reid depot, and who is reputed to have initiated the two-minute silence nowadays observed worldwide on Armistice Day, had the task of selling eleven local public houses in 1888. Some of them, including The Fox, West Street and Green Man, East Street, neither of which is any longer in existence, included a sum which had to be paid to the Lord of the Manor of Farnham even after the property had been purchased. Bills of sale at this time used a wide range of typefaces as can be seen on this notice.

THE MARLBOROUGH HEAD is the name of a pub which has stood on the same site in East Street for at least 250 years. It was rebuilt in 1929 in a mock-Tudor style, as were a number of other pubs in the town including the Seven Stars, the Plough and the Jolly Farmer at Runfold. In the middle of the last century the licence was held by the Revd Dann Harrison. To cater for the troops who used to visit the town from Aldershot, there was a soldiers' room above the wash-house of the pub in the 1860s. It is likely that this building will be demolished in late 1990. The building on the left is the former Regal Cinema (see p. 13).

SECTION SEVEN

People

Famous authors, soldiers, architects and inventors have all made Farnham their home and in many cases have been nationally acclaimed for their work. However, it is the ordinary man and woman who carries on business without applause who is the backbone of any community so, although the 'mighty' are included here, the 'salt of the earth', such as Charlie Wenham, the rag-and-bone merchant, and Annie Martin, greengrocer, are among them, representing the town's hitherto unsung workforce.

FIELD MARSHAL VISCOUNT MONTGOMERY OF ALAMEIN was one of the best-known figures of the Second World War. Although he lived just outside Farnham he always came into town to draw his old age pension. His car had a number plate which struck chords in the minds of former service personnel even though the letters were not exactly those of the establishment in which they found comfort in their days under military discipline. A chauffeur would stop NAA1F outside the post office and 'Monty' would alight, collect his state pension, and then be driven back again to his home at Isington.

WHEN OLD JOSEPH HENRY BROWN started his window-cleaning business from his home in Bullers Road, Weybourne, he could not possibly have imagined that his grandson would still be cleaning the town's windows almost into the twenty-first century (see p. 90).

THIS VIEW SHOWS LESLIE HAWTHORN, OWNER, with two of his staff inside one of the offices at the Tourist Trophy Garage, East Street, in 1947. Leslie's son, Michael, later became the 1958 World Motor Racing Champion, but when he became a daredevil on four wheels he was only following in his father's footsteps. Leslie was a motor cycle racing champion.

FRANK 'PUNCH' PARRATT, one of Farnham's best-loved characters, lived all his life at The Bourne. He drank in The Bat and Ball public house for seventy years and a plaque commemorating his connection with the pub is on the wall in the place where he sat and which is still known as Punch's Corner. He was loved by all who knew him and after his death it was found that he had left money, and guest lists, for all his friends to have a party at his expense. Such was the affection in which he was held that he has had three books dedicated to him, *A Guide to the Parratts of Farnham, Bygone Farnham* and *Name Your Poison!* in which the dedication reads, 'To my late cousin Frank 'Punch' Parratt, who drank well, but wisely, for 84 years'.

DURING THE SECOND WORLD WAR women took on many jobs which they had not, hitherto, been considered able to undertake. Irene Brown helped her father, Arthur, to clean windows in Farnham. This picture was taken in South Street.

CHARLES BORELLI, clock and watchmaker to Queen Victoria, was said to have looked out from his shop, which faced the bottom of Castle Street, and felt inspired by the flat ironstone cobbles at the junction with The Borough. Many people tried to replace these paviours but Charles Borelli, possibly aided and abetted by his architect friend, Harold Falkner, held to his objection against their removal. Thus, today, pedestrians cross the same cobbles their forbears did more than half a century ago. In the photograph Mr Borelli is constructing a model of the former Market House which stood at the bottom of Castle Street. This model is now in Farnham Museum.

WHEN GLADYS HARDINGHAM SOLD BOOKS from this shop in West Street over forty years ago she often sat out in the sun and chatted to passers-by. The shop was later demolished to make way for a new office block. Mrs Hardingham and her husband, Fred, came to Farnham from London where his father had run an antique shop in Petty France. Mrs Hardingham has never lost her interest in books and bric-a-brac and at ninety-two years of age can still be seen at jumble sales and fêtes, looking for bargains.

A GOOD BOY SCOUT is always prepared to do anything and in this picture, taken in 1933, Lord Baden-Powell, founder of the Scout movement, ties a show number to the sleeve of his daughter, Heather, before she takes part in 'A Legion of Frontiersmen' gymkhana which was held in Farnham.

ANNIE MARTIN, Farnham's best-known greengrocer, and champion beetroot boiler (even at eighty-four years of age), in the 1960s. Annie came to Farnham during the Second World War and started her stall at the foot of Castle Street. Now the fourth generation of Martins run the business but 'Granny' is still the revered figurehead. In this picture Outspan oranges cost 4d. each, mushrooms 9d. per quarter and Granny Smiths apples 2s. per pound.

THE FLOOD FAMILY played its part in the history of Farnham between 1949 and 1989. In this picture, taken on their wedding day, Ann and Gerald Flood are being congratulated in the Castle Theatre by members of the theatre staff including, third from left, Peter Byrne who, like the bridegroom, later made his name on television. Gerald Flood became a national star when he took the part of Inspector Mahmoud in *The Rat Catchers*. Gerald died in 1989 a few months before the couple were due to celebrate their fortieth wedding anniversary. Many stars of the showbiz world attended his funeral at Rowledge Church where he is buried.

FARNHAM POST OFFICE FOOTBALL CLUB 1948/9, when they were winners of the Home Counties Region Postal Cup, the Surrey Midweek Cup and the Guildford and District Wednesday League. Back row, left to right: C.S. Hayter (trainer), W.S. Wilkins (head postmaster), D.H. Weedon (secretary), D. Tanner (reserve) and T.J. Hutchings (reserve). Middle row: A. Hewins (reserve), B.T. Kirk, A. Cobbett, N.D. Garrett, L.L. Harrison, A.P. Godwin, R.S. Buckell (team manager). Front row: R.G. Harris, L. Vince, R.R. Kirk, -?-, F. Rivers and A.G. Mills.

BERT HOLDAWAY, in a magnificent costume made of feathers, believed to have been made for a carnival in Farnham. Young Bert worked in the motor industry, making leather seats for cars.

CHARLIE WENHAM, the rag-and-bone merchant who lived at Wrecclesham, was one of Farnham's best-loved characters, until his death in the 1980s. Every day he would tour the streets collecting old iron and rags then, around lunchtime, he would make his way along Hale Road towards Aldershot. At the Six Bells he would stop and sort out his 'stock' and then let his horse, Topsy, pull the cart on into Aldershot where he sold his wares to the scrap dealer. On the return journey he would stop at The Running Stream, in Weybourne, and remain there until closing time. Then his faithful steed would take him home, usually half-asleep, a journey of over two miles. The horse knew the red and green colours of the traffic-lights, it is said, and always obeyed them at the South Street – Borough junction before stopping at Stratford the butcher, in South Street, for Charlie's meat order to be put on to the cart (see p. 18).

HAROLD FALKNER, Farnham's greatest and most eccentric architect, reading a newspaper and drinking a cup of tea.

IT IS HARD TO BELIEVE, from this painting of William Cobbett, that he was born into a very humble family. He was a prolific writer and in 1802 started the *Political Register,* the forerunner of *Hansard.* In the *Oxford Junior Encyclopaedia* he is described thus, 'As a crusader he was a total failure. He became one of the best-hated men in England. His attacks were often so violent and even misdirected that he failed to get the recognition for the wisdom and truth of his teaching.' There is a Cobbett Society today and many of his works, including *Cottage Economy,* have become classics and are still in print.

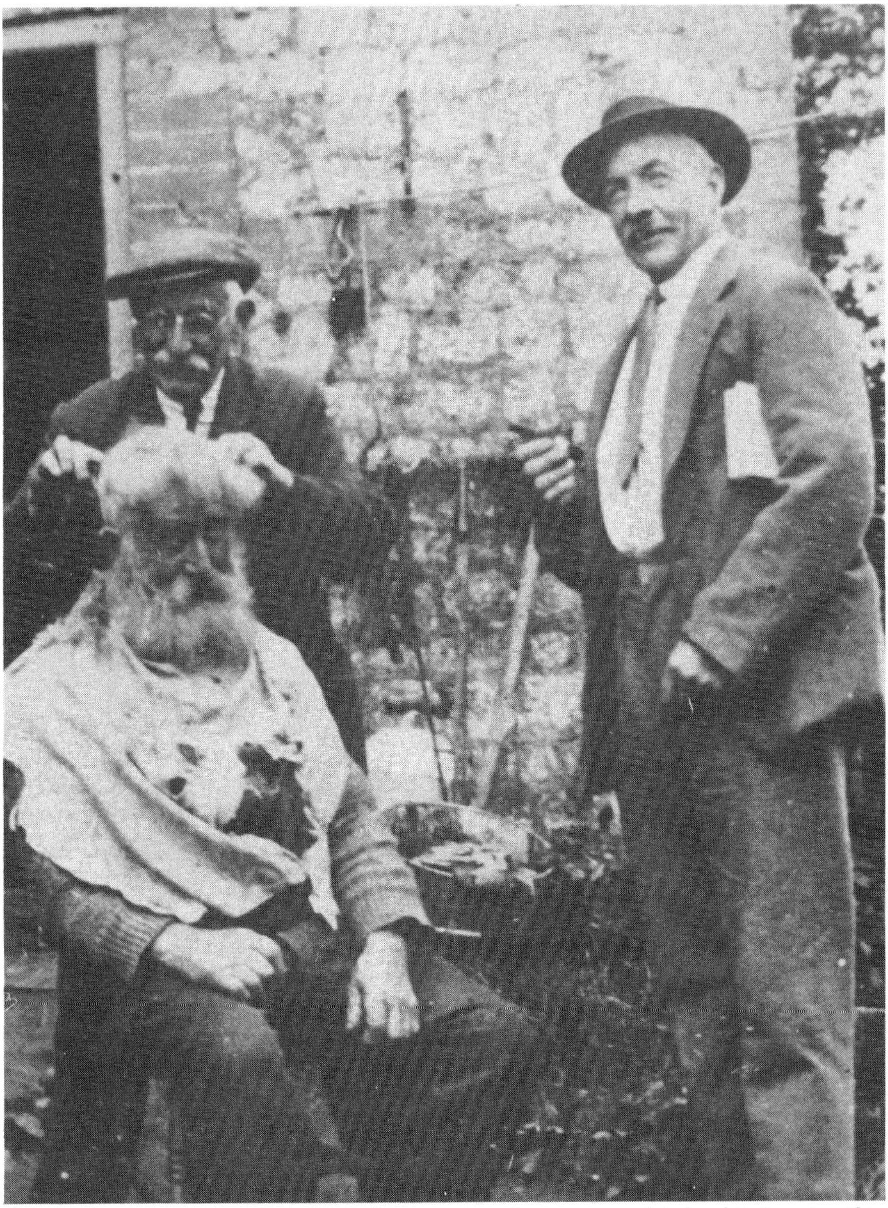

IN THE DAYS OF HIGH CLASS HAIR SALONS for men as well as women, it is hard to imagine this scene, in The Bourne, when Harry Nixon, one of the village's best-known characters, had his hair cut out in the open. The barber, in his cloth cap, appears to know what he is doing and he obviously had satisfied customers because the gentleman on the right seems to be waiting his turn in the queue.

VI MASON, the much-loved village shopkeeper in Weybourne, who died in March 1990, was patronized by Dame Vera Lynn, the Forces' Sweetheart, when Vera was a child and visited Weybourne each year. Jessie Matthews, actress, singer and at one time landlady of The Alliance in West Street, Farnham, also shopped at Vi's little shop at Weybourne crossroads.

MR RAYMOND FOSTER with the pair of boots made for a paratrooper to wear when he walked across America. The picture is taken inside R.H. Foster's in Downing Street where the cobbler used to sit close to the window to mend his boots and shoes. After the paratrooper's return the boots were on view in Foster's window.

SUPERINTENDENT SIMMONDS, of Farnham Police, sits in the centre of his station's sports team in Farnham Park, just before the First World War.

ALTHOUGH THIS PHOTOGRAPH WAS TAKEN IN HAM, near Richmond, it shows a lady born in Farnham in 1786. Sarah Parratt, who married a Mr Morfew, was featured in *Tit-Bits* magazine in 1890 under the heading 'The Oldest Widow in England'. She was interviewed in this cottage on Ham Common when she was 104.

DURING THE VERY SEVERE WINTER OF 1962/3 Margery Marshall delivered prescriptions on skis, to housebound sick people. She was employed by G.E. Thomas, the Downing Street chemist, and the picture was taken in Upper Church Lane.

THE PHOTOGRAPHER, EDWARD GRIFFITH, in front of some of his prints around 1945. The photograph on the right is of Castle Street and the young Mr Griffith is looking at an album of other photographs for possible inclusion in an exhibition.

WHEN JOHN HEWETT WAS A WITNESS at Farnham Police Station, in 1898, he objected very strongly to having his photograph taken so, in spite of having three burly policemen hold him down, he still managed to partially hide his identity by keeping his eyes closed. As a fairly long time exposure was necessary at this time the photographer had even more difficulties than a photographer, confronted with a similar objector, would have had today.

GEORGE STURT, author of *The Wheelwright's Shop, A Small Boy in the Sixties, The Bettesworth Books* and many others, poses in the garden of his Vine Cottage home at The Bourne, on 20 September 1903. His cat, Mac, is on his shoulder. He was born in The Bourne, Farnham in 1863 and took his pen name of George Bourne from his native village. His book *Change in the Village*, first published in 1912, has become a classic and is an analysis of how and why change came about in the rural community he loved so much.

MISS IRENE TIGWELL'S TOY SHOP in South Street, closed to make way for the Sainsbury supermarket, was tiny and dark, but crammed from floor to ceiling with toys of every description. As late as the 1970s it was still possible to buy wooden 'Dutch' dolls and lead soldiers here, decades after they had ceased to exist in any other toy shop in the area.

MIKE HAWTHORN, at the height of his career, standing in front of his family's garage, Tourist Trophy (now called Romans), in East Street. When he won the World Motor Racing Drivers' Championship in 1958 he was given a civic dinner in appreciation at the Bush Hotel by the Farnham Urban District Council. The menu was grapefruit cocktail, fried fillet of sole, roast duck with vegetables and fruit salad with ice-cream. The entertainment was by Mary Joynes (see p. 136).

WHEN TRIMMER'S HOSPITAL FIRST OPENED in 1935, the matron, Miss Brammer, was a Yorkshirewoman who was considered by her colleagues to be 'an absolutely super' lady. In this picture, taken on the steps of the hospital in Menin Way, the doctors are, left to right: Dr Humphrey Ward, Dr Pemberley, Dr Town-Jones, Dr Roberts, Dr Bardsley and Dr Caldecott. Dr Town-Jones was at the hospital from the time it opened until it closed to become the Phyllis Tuckwell Hospice (see p. 45).

THERE WAS A MILITARY HOSPITAL AT SHORTHEATH, known as The Highlands Auxiliary Hospital, during the First World War, and this photograph of four patients was taken in either 1915 or 1916.

THIS PICTURE OF ERNEST ARTHUR PARRATT was taken in 1877 when he was six years old. He was a charcoal burner like many other members of the Parratt family who lived in the Rowledge and Boundstone area. When he grew up he married Millie Nash whose parents worked on the Pierrepont estate at Millbridge (see p. 53). The couple had a number of children of whom only two, Archibald and Florence survived. Their entire family can be seen on p. 155.

A RARE PHOTOGRAPH of one of the characters in George Sturt's book, *A Small Boy In The Sixties.* It shows 'Old Tom' who was employed by Mr Cottee, a bootmaker, to deliver water from the conduit near the Castle Steps to the people in the town. The charge was 6d. ($2\frac{1}{2}$p) per barrel. 'Old Tom' is wearing a flat hat and one of the local, wide-collared smocks. Sturt wrote, 'He (Old Tom) baled it out with a ladle on a pole . . . to fill a water barrel he had wheeled up from the town on a low, four-wheeled hand-cart. Having filled his barrel he locked the conduit door and trundled back down to Castle Street to deliver his water. . . . What I do get thinking of Old Tom is a notable feeling of having lived in the eighteenth century.'

BETTY DOLLEY, right, and a school friend in East Street, in the early 1930s. The girls attended Farnham Girls' Grammar School and it is interesting to see teenagers wearing short white socks and panama hats. The hats suggest summer but the girl on the left is also wearing leather gloves. Betty Dolley was the only daughter of George Dolley, nurseryman of Guildford Road, and his wife (see p. 14). She married Ronald Ridout, a former pupil at Farnham Grammar School, and the author of many textbooks in English now used all over the world. She died on 21 July 1990.

IN ADDITION TO the large contingent of Home Guard personnel from Farnham post office the men at Farnham railway station also did their bit for their country. This picture was taken one December during the Second World War, but which is not certain. Pictured in the centre front is Henry Jackson, now well-known for his Old Kiln Museum at Tilford and for the annual Rustic Sunday which he organizes there.

MR RICHARD COMBE of Pierrepont, Frensham, and the Watney, Combe and Reid brewery. He was regarded as a kindly man who treated his staff well. He evidently carried considerable weight in the community, too, because he was the other main signatory to the Bishop of Winchester, on a letter of protest to the railway company responsible for Farnham station in 1892. The platform was considered inadequate and the letter was also signed by magistrates, merchants and traders in the town.

TED CANE, the man who, every year, put more flowers into the gardens of Farnham than anyone else. He grew seedlings in his garden in West Street then sold them from his pitch next to W.H. Smith in The Borough.

MR OTWAY McCANNELL, principal of the Farnham School of Art from 1927–46.

DAVID JOHNSTONE, a reporter on the *Surrey and Hants News,* Surrey's oldest newspaper, was drowned while taking part in a rowing race across the Atlantic. David and his friend, John Hoare from Leicester, drowned although their purpose-built boat, *Puffin*, was later found empty and upside-down in mid-Atlantic in October 1966. Two members of the Parachute Regiment, Chay Blyth and John Ridgway (see p. 138) who lived in Farnham at that time, made a successful crossing during the same summer.

JOHN GOODRIDGE, left, founder of the gentlemen's outfitters in Downing Street, which has been a byword in the town for at least seventy years. Wearing a smock which most definitely did not come from Goodridge's is James Hockey, right, head of Farnham School of Art from 1946 until his retirement.

FRANK CARTER, born in 1886, moved to Frensham in 1908. He was under-cowman to Mr Richard Beale at Pit Farm. This picture was taken around 1910 in Hamlash Lane when he was working for Mr Morton Latham at Hollowdene. His horse was called Taffy. Frank Carter was wounded in the First World War and became caretaker of the Marindin Hall before spending twenty-three years as a council lengthsman. He kept this photograph of himself in his pocket throughout the time he was at the Somme and it became very damaged. In the spring of 1990 his daughter, now a grandmother, was given a mint print of the same picture which another villager had treasured for eighty years.

MISS EVELYN 'JO' SIMMONDS, Farnham's first female photographer, who ran the Delaunay Studio, West Street, for her employer, Eugene Fuller, after he was blinded in the First World War. She was engaged to be married, but her fiancé was killed in a motor cycle accident three weeks before their proposed wedding day so she remained a spinster until her death in 1989. 'Jo' was a daughter of Superintendent Simmonds, a much-loved superintendent in the town from the late nineteenth century until his retirement (see p. 99).

SECTION EIGHT

Schooldays

Education in Farnham, both state and private, has always been of a high standard, from the time in the sixteenth century when a school was begun in part of St Andrew's parish church, through to the Sixth Form College in Morley Road today. There have been many schools, including Barfield, Elmsleigh and Miss Murrell's, which have turned out people who later became very successful. There were many others, in town and village, to which pupils crept like snails, unwillingly, every day during term time.

SCHOOLDAYS WERE HAPPY DAYS AT BARFIELD, the building which was once the home of John Henry Knight. In this picture are, back row, left to right: ? Clissold, ? Murray, ? Benson, Mike Hawthorn (see p. 103). Middle row: John Summers-Coy, -?- , David Ford, ? Patten-Bridge, -?-. Front row: Guy Halliwell (son of one of Farnham's well-respected doctors) and Ross Duncan.

EXACTLY ONE HUNDRED YEARS separate these pictures of little girls at East Street School. In the upper picture the young ladies sit demurely in white aprons although wearing heavy boots on their feet. Every child has long hair. In the lower picture only half have long hair, shorter locks being easier to deal with for youngsters who had swimming as part of their school timetable. This group were performing at a special event for the Queen's Silver Jubilee in 1977. Left to right in the back row are: Tina Ell, Patricia Morgan, June Shepherd, Joanne Osborne and Corinne Gore. In front of them are: Andrea Morton, Gala Dawson, Clare Huggins, Jill Osborne and Victoria Fry.

THE INFANTS' CLASS at St Peter's School, Wrecclesham, in 1932. The teachers were Miss Lee, seated at the piano, and Miss Baker, standing. The toy box was only opened on Friday afternoons but, as a special treat, it was opened on the day the photographer took this picture. The children are mostly unidentified but Ethel Gilliam is fifth from the left, with Douglas Snooke on her left. Harry Wright, fourth from the right grew up and joined the merchant navy in the Second World War. He later became the composing manager for Farnham Castle Newspapers. Douglas Snooke ran a garage in Rowledge until his retirement in 1989.

INSIDE THE BELL TOWER of Farnham Parish Church during the Second World War. The small boys were from Farnham Grammar School and were tutored in ringing skills by the master in the picture, a Mr Knight. Included in the picture are Tony Maxwell-Aylwin, Maurice Sturt, Jim Bodkin, Bill Bodkin and John Crowhurst plus ? Lampard, ? Locke, and Clifford and Keith Dolley (see p. 122).

HALE JUNIOR SCHOOL in 1969. The teacher is Miss Denny and among the pupils in this class are: Adrian Watts, Roger Tonkin, Penny Carmichael, Mark Parratt, Amanda Perry (who was a child star, advertising Kellogg's cornflakes around this time), Martha Oakes and Christopher Burton.

MISS VICKY KING taught at Hale Junior School, above, but worked even harder in her retirement than in her career. She led the local Writers' Circle, was on the board of management committees of many organizations including the Redgrave Theatre, Farnham Society, Farnham Maltings and the Museum Society, and wrote a booklet about her childhood memories. When this picture was taken she was attending the launch of the 1990 Ian St James Award for writers.

THE CLASS OF 1972 AT THE PARK, formerly East Street School, on a hillock in the school grounds. Reading from right to left, from the back to the front, are: Louise Wise, Susan Orgill, Karen Grassie, Victoria Stewart, Catherine Savile, Sandra Eastwood, Jane Allaway, David Wolverson, Paul Butler, Helen Piercy, Andrew Moran, Paddy Varnham, David Wilkins, Tracy Warren, David Royle, Catherine Price, Jason ? , Julie Reader, Hugh Baker, Damien O'Brien, Roger Day, Simon Kilcross, Gary Willis, John McAndrew, Shaun Lunn, Kevin Brooks, Nicola Fisher and Sarah Stevens. The Park School was closed in the mid-1980s and is now a Social Services Centre. At the time this picture was taken Denis Kelly was the headmaster of the school and the children were given a musical and broad-minded form of education under this much-loved and respected man.

THE CHILDREN OF ST ANDREW'S SCHOOL, under the directorship of Mr E. Paye, gave creditable performances every Christmas while he was the senior teacher at the school. Among those performing in this picture are: Linda Bentley, Mark Parratt, Asad Butt and Linda Ellis.

FARNHAM GRAMMAR SCHOOL, although an all-male establishment, managed to find one 'girl' to appear in their production of *Latin For Love* which was produced in the early 1950s. In the back row, extreme right, is Terry Blackwell, who became a teacher and then a lecturer in art education, and on the extreme right is David Grigor.

EDDIE GODSIL, was a teacher, deputy head and acting head at Farnham Grammar School. Mr Godsil, like Miss King (see p. 114), seemed to be even more active in retirement than he was as a schoolteacher, although his Irish brogue never seemed to lessen in its intensity. Eddie, like Vicky, belonged to many organizations including the Redgrave Theatre, Farnham Visitors Council and the Town Guides. In spite of having had hundreds of boys through his classes he always found time to ask about the success, or otherwise, of his former pupils if he met them in the street. From the time he joined the school on 1 November 1939 until he retired in the late 1970s, he had only one half-day's absence.

THE PURPOSE-BUILT FARNHAM GIRLS' GRAMMAR SCHOOL was opened in July 1939, by the Duchess of Gloucester who can be seen in this photograph accompanied by Mrs Philipson-Stowe. The Girl Guides formed a guard of honour and many other notables were in attendance on the day. Friends of the school provided a grand piano, an oak armchair and a refectory table which had a trestle top. It is recorded in *The Story of a School, 1901- 1973,* that many years after the opening ceremony a distinguished guest decided to give his talk to the school while sitting on the end of this table. The story goes: 'To save his face, and possibly his bones, the headmistress, Miss Dorothea Inman, had to sit on the opposite end of the table to save him from being catapulted into the choir.'

MISS BETTY HAIR joined the staff of Farnham Girls' Grammar School in 1948, nine years after the photograph above was taken. She remained there until she retired in 1973. Although she was scarcely five feet tall she was held in awe both by pupils and fellow teachers, mainly because she set such high standards for herself and her pupils and no piece of work ever escaped the closest scrutiny. However, she was fair and just and her wide circle of friends, many of them former pupils bore testimony to this. A higher proportion of her pupils than might reasonably be expected, went on to careers in journalism, librarianship and English teaching – evidence of her high standards. She died in 1988.

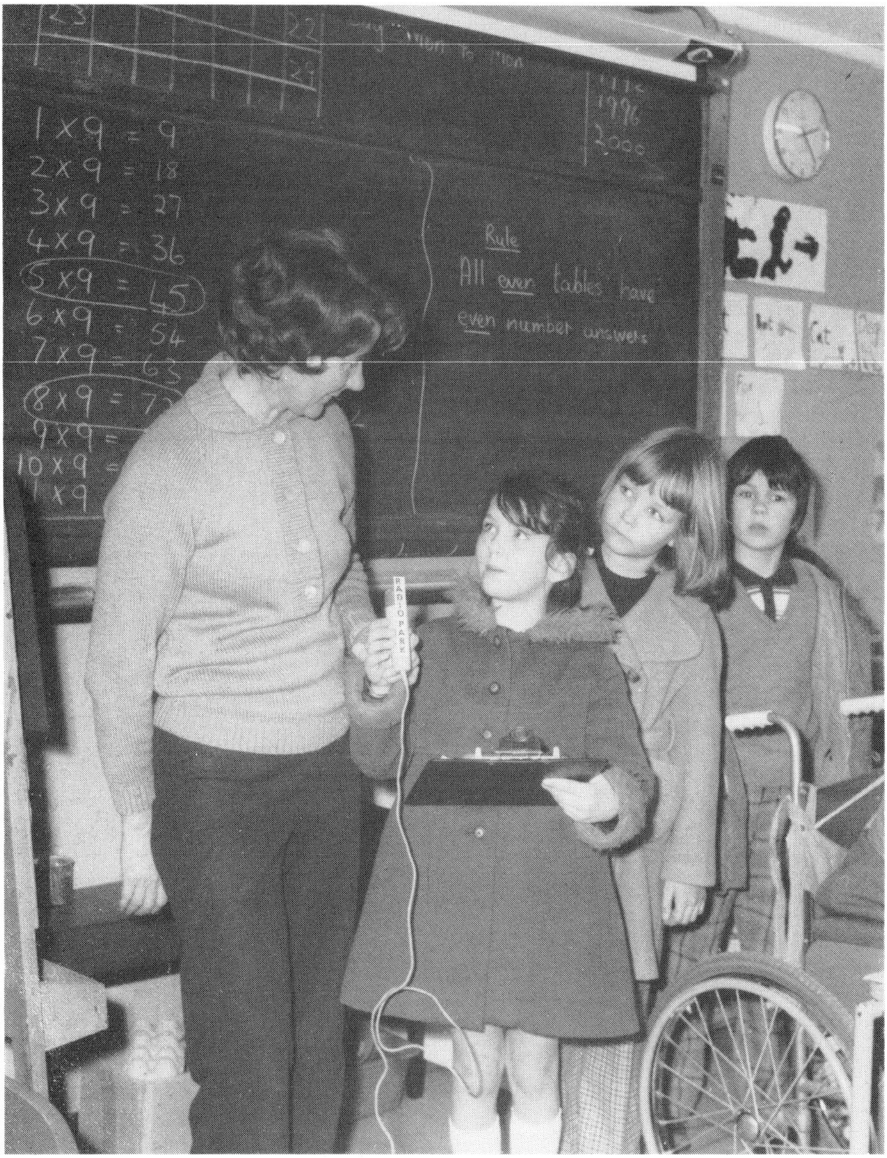

JEAN THORPE, the Farnham teacher who did more than anyone else for physically disabled but mentally alert children in the area, was interviewed for a school radio station in 1975. The young interviewing team, from the former Park School in Hale Road, Maria Clark, Joanne Fraser and Jamie Rose, took their mobile recording unit to the William Cobbett School at Weybourne and spoke both to Miss Thorpe and some of her pupils, one of whose wheelchairs can be seen in the picture. Radio Park, as the station was called, gave many youngsters the opportunity to interview and learn skills needed for radio work although not one child was over nine years old.

SECTION NINE

A Farnham Miscellany

The pictures in this section are a miscellany – those which cannot be omitted, but which do not fall naturally into any special category. From the record of a church service for the Relief of Mafeking through to the opening of the Regal Cinema with one of the most famous films of all time – Snow White and the Seven Dwarfs *– this section captures the photographs that nearly got away.*

FARNHAM HAS ALWAYS 'GONE TO TOWN' FOR ROYAL OCCASIONS and the coronations of King George VI and Queen Elizabeth brought out the best in the townsfolk. Castle Street had two large, plywood towers built at its foot and all the way up there were poles with banners and hundreds of flags on the buildings. At Ransom's, the sign informed the public that coffee was 'Roasted Daily By Experts' and exhorted shoppers to 'Try Our Noted Sausages'. The sign for The Castle Café (see p. 27) can just be seen behind Ransoms' shop. The bus is an Aldershot and District Traction Company vehicle *en route* for London.

THE FRONT OF THE *SURREY AND HANTS NEWS* OFFICE at 104a West Street is one of only two such fronts in the country. The second one is now in the Museum of London but both fronts originally came from a pastrycook's in Cornhill, London, called Birch, Birch and Co. The right-hand archway of the door has, under layers of paint, gilt letters which can be discerned in the right light and give information about what could be sold in the shop. It was brought to Farnham by Harold Falkner (see p. 96) to be used for the shop front of Surrey's oldest newspaper.

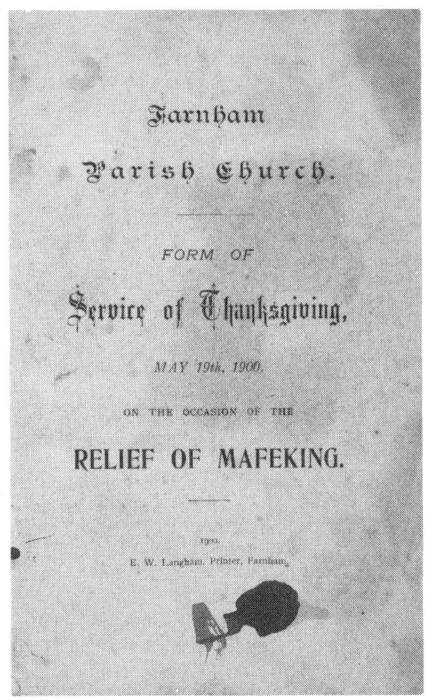

Farnham

Parish Church.

FORM OF

Service of Thanksgiving,

MAY 19th, 1900,

ON THE OCCASION OF THE

RELIEF OF MAFEKING.

1900.

E. W. Langham, Printer, Farnham.

FARNHAM has always celebrated special occasions and the Relief of Mafeking was no exception. A special booklet was produced for the service held in the parish church of St Andrew on 19 May 1900.

SOME SMALL COTTAGES were knocked down at the bottom of Downing Street in the early 1930s and replaced by shops. This picture was taken between demolition and the construction of the premises now known as The Toy Shop by Edward Griffith. The hole in the centre, at pavement level, was where coal used to be emptied into the cellar of the cottage on the site. The herringbone brickwork on the present building was apparently constructed from bricks used for work being carried out at Farnham Castle at about the same time.

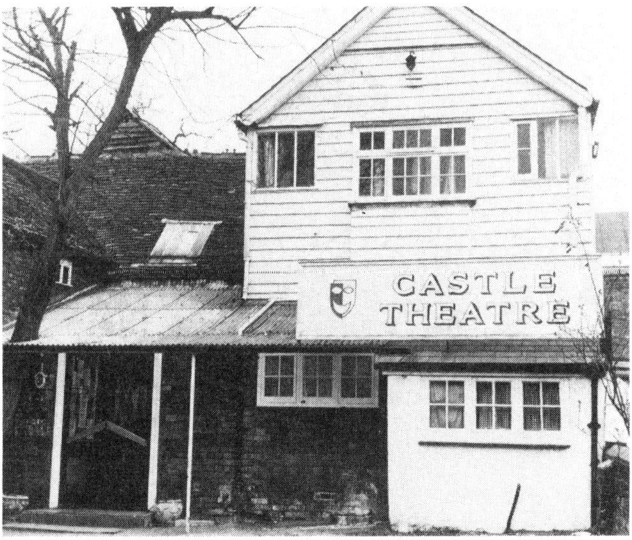

THE CASTLE THEATRE, now an Italian restaurant, was in a Castle Street courtyard. The building had been used for many purposes including sleeping quarters for servants at the castle, a skating rink and a de-lousing station for soldiers returning from the battlefields of the First World War. It remained Farnham's only theatre until the present Redgrave Theatre was built.

TWO YOUNG MEN in the lamplight of the Coach and Horses public house in Castle Street. Douglas Mount held the licence at this pub and the Royal Antediluvian Order of Buffaloes No. 8570, Borough Lodge, used to meet there every Monday. The photographer, Edward Griffith, asked two men to pose for a picture which he wanted to take under the light. 'Nobody will ever see it or know who you are' he told them. Later this picture was used on a map of Farnham and thirty-five years after it was taken it now appears in a book. So much for the anonymity which Keith Dolley, left, and Richard Clark thought had been guaranteed them.

FIRGROVE HOUSE was demolished to make way for Trafalgar Court, at the bottom of Firgrove Hill. The house was built in 1688 and refronted in the nineteenth century. Inside the house was a magnificent carved staircase, brought to Farnham around 1820 when it was taken from Merton House which was being demolished. Firgrove House was said to have been connected with Horatio Nelson and his lover, Emma Hamilton, and it is possible that Lady Hamilton brought the staircase to Farnham. What is certain is that her black slave, Fatima, given to her by Lord Nelson, lived in the workhouse in Bear Lane, Farnham, after Lady Hamilton gave up Merton House.

A ROW OF COTTAGES IN FACTORY YARD, West Street, now called Arundell Place. These were demolished in the early 1970s, and an attractive office unit is now in their place.

IT IS BELIEVED that this photograph, of an unknown gentleman, was taken in 1860. The elderly man probably found the climb up to the castle rather a strain, so sat on the steps leading to it and was captured on film. The steps are known as The Blind Bishop's Steps because there are seven steps with seven strides between them all the way up to the castle and this pattern enabled blind Bishop Fox, who lived at the castle, to go up and down into town without help.

THIS SHOT LOOKS THROUGH THE WROUGHT-IRON GATE towards The Grange, for many years the home of the Percival family. The Grange is situated at the top of Castle Street, close to the entrance to Farnham Castle.

A VIEW DOWN EAST STREET, towards the traffic lights, in the early 1960s, before these buildings were pulled down to make way for The Woolmead. To the left of the Bristol and West Building Society is Gordon's carpet shop; the Mikado, tobacconists; Aldershot and District Traction Company office and, on the extreme left the Regal Service laundry.

ONLY THE TRAFFIC ISLANDS and the wall on the extreme left of this picture remain today. John Mills and Sons, builders merchants, established in 1850, was being demolished to make way for the present police station at Longbridge when this picture was taken in the 1960s. The twin cowls on the roof of the Maltings can just be seen to the right of the route signs.

A GROUP OF LOCAL MEN posed at Farnham station for this photograph before they left to 'do their bit' for their country in the First World War. How many returned is not known.

A CENTURY AGO the owner of Moor Park tried to prevent people walking in or taking carts across his land. There was an uprising among the local people who, on Sunday 17 January 1897, at the Bourne Place entrance to the park, broke down the chains which had been fixed to the gates. It was a snowy day but between 400 and 500 townsmen stood their ground against a handful of lodgekeepers and six ex-City of London policemen. The sheer weight of numbers of the locals gave the town a victory which has never since been challenged. These men, sitting on Farnham Urban District wheelbarrows, were among those responsible for keeping the park open.

SNOW FEATURES IN BOTH PICTURES on this page, although in this one it is only to describe the purity of the young lady who took up residence with seven small men in Walt Disney's *Snow White and the Seven Dwarfs.* The charity performance at the opening of the Regal, in the mid-1930s, is probably the only occasion when a bishop, in this case His Grace the Lord Bishop of Guildford, opened a cinema. (See p. 13.)

AN AERIAL VIEW OF FARNHAM taken in the mid-1970s. Farnham parish church can be seen in the centre, marked 5. The cinema (3) was demolished in 1987. A development of shops and flats overlooking Gostrey Meadow can be seen on the left (4) and to the back is part of the West Surrey College of Art and Design (1) and the Upper Hart car park (2).

WHEN FARNHAM UNITED BREWERIES' FOOTBALL TEAM, 'The Bungs', ruled supreme, the eleven men who made up the team which won these trophies found themselves beside nine supporters and the team's president, Mr William Loe, third from the right in the back row, all of whom wanted to muscle in for this shot.

THERE WOULD HAVE BEEN very little alcohol-generated football violence among those supporting 'The Bungs' if their followers had stopped at this hotel for the night before a big match. This is the Temperance Hotel on Station Hill, situated immediately opposite the Station Hotel where beer and wine were freely available, in contrast to the temperance hostelry where none was on sale.

IN SPITE OF ITS PROXIMITY TO FARNBOROUGH it is hard to imagine Farnham having an aircraft manufactory, but a number of planes, including this one, were built at Wrecclesham and some, such as the Whitlet Training Aeroplane (above), were tested in the old Lion Brewery in West Street.

SECTION TEN

Only Yesterday

To the young people who find themselves featured in a book about Farnham in old photographs I offer no apology. Even yesterday is history. The first free playscheme sponsored by Waverley Borough Council, in 1975, should be recorded. So too should the radical changes to road traffic-flow directions which were formerly two-way. Street parties for the Coronation of Queen Elizabeth II and the contribution of the Farnham Girls' Choir in developing relationships between the town and other countries should be on record although they took place only yesterday. Therefore, if you find yourself in this section and are only twenty-five years old, remember that everyone is making history all the time.

A VIEW ALONG EAST STREET before the buildings in the centre were demolished to make way for the Dogflud loop road. The shop with a downpipe (centre) was for many years the East Street post office and was for a while a drop-in centre for teenagers, run by Canon Donald Gray, and known as 'Nowhere' because the youngsters had said they had nowhere to go.

FARNHAM POST OFFICE in West Street, on the left of this picture, was vacated on 18 January 1969 and local people had to get their pensions and allowances from a temporary building in Bear Lane. On 16 May, four months later, the building was demolished and work started soon after on the new building which is in use today. This was opened on 5 January 1973 (see p. 42).

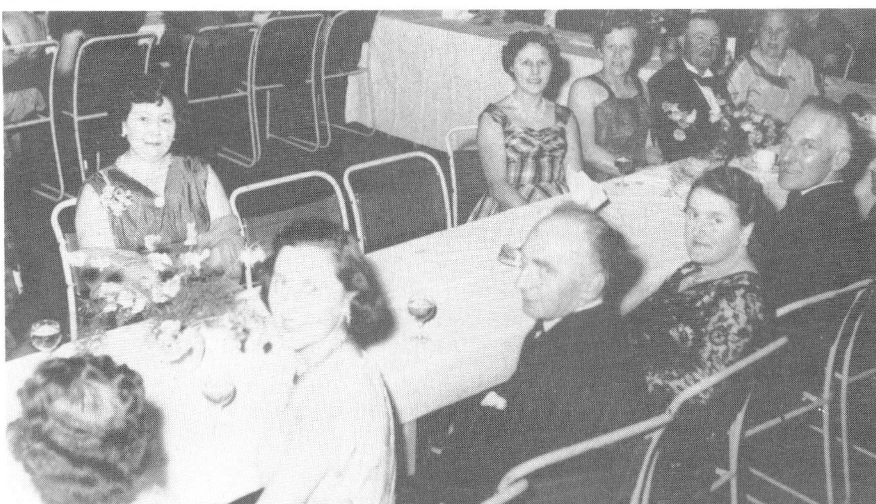

OLD TIME DANCING AT THE 'MORGUE' (The Memorial Hall built to commemorate the men who died for their country in the First World War) was one of the weekly social events for many people in Farnham in the 1950s. This picture was taken at a dinner (although there seems to be only wine left on the table) and includes Nancy Goodall, George, Gladys and Jean Bowdery, and Marie Siggery.

ELPHICKS OF FARNHAM often lent dresses to be worn at children's fashion shows in the 1960s, as publicity for the firm. This picture was taken around 1966 in Hale Institute when Hale Young Wives' children modelled the garments. Among the 'young ladies' in this picture are Cherry and Melanie Watts, Laura Pearce, Juliette Hiller, Jane Kingdon, Karen Withall, Wendy and Debbie Parratt and Janine Seignot, the tiny girl on the right, who grew up to be a traffic warden in the town, albeit one who was not typical of the conventional 'ogre' in this occupation.

A GROUP OF YOUNG MEN FROM THE FARNHAM YOUTH CLUB pot-holing in the 1950s. Some of them, including John Thomas, front row, extreme left, formed a charitable group known as The Hedgehogs and the group has continued in this area for almost forty years. One of the best-known leaders of the youth club was Peter Watts.

TWENTY-FIRST BIRTHDAYS were very sedate events in the mid-1950s. This photograph was taken at one such party in Echo Barn Lane and includes Doris Leitch, Nora Ransome, Sylvia Turner, Pat Brooks, Jean Bowdery, Stella Davies and Fred Dugan.

WHEN WILLIAM KINGHAM AND SON, grocers, who had a retail shop in West Street, with a bacon curing department behind and a warehouse in The Hart, celebrated their centenary in 1953 two small girls, Bernadine and Margaret Bowdery, on the right of this picture, dressed up as 'Let's Go To Kingham's 100 Years Ago'. Their father George Bowdery was a sales representative for the firm. Others in the picture include Alan Dadley, Rosemary Painter and Ann McNair.

WHEN QUEEN ELIZABETH II WAS CROWNED in 1953 there were many street parties arranged in Farnham. The Queen of the North/East/South/West Avenues party, at Heath End, was Anne Valiant. Her sister, Sonia, was one of her attendants. Behind the queen is Mrs Spencer, whose husband collected insurance money from the people on the estate. The two ladies to the right are believed to be Mrs Joyce and Mrs McGuire.

MARY JOYNES AND THE FARNHAM GIRLS' CHOIR AND FARNHAM SINGERS sang their way through thirty-nine years in this country, on the continent and in America. In Farnham they frequently gave concerts in St Joan's Hall, Waverley Lane, where this picture was taken in the 1960s. Mrs Joynes, the founder and conductor, is in the long dress.

MEMBERS OF THE FARNHAM GIRLS' CHOIR sang at many weddings. This picture was taken outside the Methodist Church in South Street, when John Hibberd took Phyllis Barnes to be his lawful, wedded wife. Choir members included Margaret Bowdery, Christine Norfolk, Hazel Thomas, Linda Hicks and Mary Sly.

WAVERLEY BOROUGH COUNCIL ran a playscheme for children in Farnham in 1975. It was held at the Memorial Hall Ground and the total attendance over twenty days was 2,785. This group includes the scheme's leader, Jean Parratt, right, with her assistant, Erika Johnson. Among the children are David, Gary and Peter Wolverson, Nicholas, Benjamin and Oliver Kannemeyer, Janice, Stephen, Richard and Mandy Frizell, Karen Tucker, Wayne Horsefall, Juliette Van Noorden, Christopher Collins, Barry Lawrence and Dawn, Stephen and John Anderson.

ONE OF FARNHAM'S MORE ADVENTUROUS RESIDENTS, photographed by Edward Griffith. John Ridgway, who rowed the Atlantic in 1966, is smiling at his baby daughter, Rebecca, while his wife, Marie-Christine, looks on. John rowed with Chay Blyth, a fellow paratrooper, in a 20-ft dory. Their attempt was successful, but that of David Johnstone and John Hoare ended in tragedy (see p. 109).

SECTION ELEVEN

Badshot Lea and Weybourne

About a mile out of Farnham are two villages separated by half a mile of what was once a muddy track but which is, today, a metalled road. Badshot Lea is probably a closer-knit community than Weybourne, although the reason for this is not clear except that Badshot Lea has its own church whereas Weybourne is part of the Parish of St John at Hale. Both villages have their own schools, both have their own pubs and both have post offices. Both are on main roads and both have halls where residents can gather for Women's Institute meetings, jumble sales, or to vote in elections. Each maintains its own identity however similar they appear on the surface.

ALL ABOARD THE *SAUCY KIPPER* before she set sail from Badshot Lea Docks in 1904. This boat was built for one of the Farnham carnivals at a site close to the Blackwater River, which divides Farnham from Aldershot at the county boundary. Although there is usually only a trickle of water through what is little more than a ditch, the area became known as Badshot Lea Docks because of the 'ship building' which took place there. It has become as famous a place in local folklore as the nearby Tongham Treacle Mines, a field in which cans of treacle, left over army rations from the First World War, were buried and later pierced open by a farmer when ploughing.

ST GEORGE'S YOUTH CLUB of Badshot Lea on an outing. On the extreme right is Nicolette Fisher and her father, Ron. Nicolette swam for Britain in the paraplegic games in 1990. Two years earlier her sister, Cheryl, roller-skated from Lands End to John O'Groats, to raise money for her sister who was hoping to be picked for the Paraplegic Olympics in Seoul.

A GROUP OF HAPPY PENSIONERS at Badshot Lea.

THE ELM TREE at Weybourne crossroads from which the nearby public house took its name. This photograph is from a glass plate negative made by John Henry Knight about a century ago.

PHARO'S STEAM ENGINES at Badshot Lea. The vehicle on the right has carbide drip lamps for night travel (see p. 35).

WHERE CHILDREN NOW PLAY in the William Cobbett School playground at Weybourne, cows once chewed the cud. It is believed this picture was taken by John Henry Knight, who lived in the village. Weybourne Cottage can be seen through the leafless trees and as the cows have been given additional hay one can assume that this picture was taken on a fine day in winter.

TWO PUBS within a quarter mile of each other, each with a single, common purpose to please its customers. The Elm Tree at Weybourne crossroads is above, and the Running Stream, below. The stream referred to is the one which runs down from Rowhills Copse at Heath End.

THE FARM BUILDINGS on the right of this picture were adjacent to a small bakery which served delicious bread. During the late 1960s and early 1970s it employed a delivery girl who rivalled Sheridan's Mrs Malaprop for using the wrong words. Her favourite malapropism, used to describe those she thought were double-crossing her, was 'hipplecritts'. The cyclists are *en route* for Badshot Lea from Runfold and are passing Bridge Farm.

THE PRINCE OF WALES public house in Upper Weybourne Lane was kept by Tom Lawrence. His son, Ron, ran a smallholding, keeping chickens and geese as well as cultivating the ground around the pub. Ron, who is seen here standing in front of the former pub door among the flowers in his garden, continued to live in the building until his death in 1989 although he never had it altered inside. The wooden seat around the wall of the public bar, the glass windows around the bottle-and-jug department and the small, ladies bar, where the floor was worn so badly that even the counter had to be cut crookedly to stand straight, remained exactly as they had been for thirty years after the pub closed.

SECTION TWELVE

Hale and Heath End

Hale, at its lower reaches, has the distinction of being recognized as the oldest village in England. When men, women and children lived there around 6,000 BC wolves were an ever-present danger; today thousands of cars pass through the villages every day, making Hale especially, one of the most dangerous places in the area. Stone Age man chipped his flint tools on the common land behind Hale Schools and in the Victorian period soldiers sharpened their bayonets and cleaned their boots here. Heath End, the village which separates Weybourne from Hale, but which is really an integrated part of the latter village, is rather a no-man's land. It has no meeting place, no church of its own and no club or institute, although it does boast three public houses, an Indian restaurant and a pizza parlour!

TWO OF THE MOST FAMOUS WEALTHY FAMILIES in Hale were the Caesars and the Swansboroughs, the latter pictured above in the garden of their home.

THE TWO LITTLE GIRLS in this picture stand on the Farnborough Road where cars and lorries, by the thousand, rush up and down each day. The Halfway House is the white building in the centre and Wigmore's bakery is on the left. Wigmore's later moved up the hill to the bakery they built close to the Alma Way junction. Many hundreds of local people still cherish the memory of going to the bakery, which was situated behind a private house, and buying minute loaves made from Hovis flour, then taking them home and having the tiny slices buttered for tea.

WHEN HALE WAR MEMORIAL was unveiled in 1921 the village turned out in full force. The local Boy Scouts and Girl Guides were closest to the memorial and every woman wore a hat. The Ball and Wicket public house is on the left and the porches of the Hale Hospital Cottages (now private houses) can be seen just down the hill from the pub. A path, no longer in existence, goes across the green, on the right, to the Methodist Church.

IT WAS A RARE OCCURRENCE for a politician to visit a local village so when an MP spoke in 1911, George Hale, photographer, took the opportunity to record the event on film. It is believed the picture was taken on Hale Recreation Ground on a weekday judging by the lack of men in the photograph – they were probably all at work. Their womenfolk made the most of the opportunity afforded by the visit to put on their best 'bib and tucker' and leave the household chores for a while.

THE STRAIGHT LINE which stretches across this picture is the Farnborough Road. The large building is the former Hale Laundry and the narrow lines in the foreground are lines of washing. The present Willow Way and White Cottage Close are where the washing hangs. The large field to the rear is now built up with Oak Tree View and Whitmore Green and the row of prefabricated buildings to the rear, left, is part of the old Heath End School. The water for this laundry came from springs at Heath End, in a stretch between the top of North Avenue and Alma Way.

UNTIL THE NEWCOME FAMILY SOLD HALE PLACE, the local WI group and church organizations, used to hold events in the gardens of the house every year. It had, at one time, been the home of the Sellwood family and was visited on many occasions by Alfred Lord Tennyson when he was courting Emily Sellwood. This photograph shows some of the Hale WI members in fancy dress with, second from left, Mrs Gladys Bowdery.

THE LADY AT THE DOOR of 3 Wellington Lane, Heath End, a wooden cottage demolished in 1973, is Mrs Kempson who once ran the Rose and Crown public house at 79 Farnborough Road, Heath End. Mrs Kempson died in 1945 aged ninety-eight. The Rose and Crown later became a café run by a Mrs Winters and her son, Fred. Her other son, Arthur, was a thatcher and travelled around the locality. The café operated until after the Second World War when it was turned into a fruit and vegetable shop. It used to carry the Cyclists Touring Club sign to show cyclists they were welcome to eat there.

Particulars and Conditions of Sale

of

THE IMPORTANT FREEHOLD PROPERTY

known as

THE ARMY COLLEGE
HEATH END
FARNHAM, SURREY

For Sale by Auction

at The Bush Hotel, Farnham, on

Wednesday, 30th June, 1948

at 3 p.m. precisely.

(unless previously sold by private treaty)

Solicitors :

MESSRS. MURRAY, HUTCHINS AND CO.,
11, Birchin Lane, London, E.C.3.,
(Mansion House 9631/2).

Auctioneers :

MESSRS. EGGAR AND CO.,
74, Castle Street, Farnham, Surrey
(Farnham 6221/2).

THE ARMY COLLEGE AT HEATH END was built in 1880 by Mr Courtney Welch as a private military training college. It was used in this capacity until 1939 when it was taken over by the RAF. In 1948 it was put up for auction. Lot one, which included the college, a small cottage and grounds bordered by Warren Road, was eventually converted into private flats before it was demolished in the mid-1970s and the flats, now known as Hillcrest, were built. The second lot consisted of the college playing fields and spinney which were bought by Farnham Urban District Council for recreation purposes and the land is now the home of Heath End Wanderers Football Club.

UPPER HALE ROAD, at its junction with Wood Road, before the First World War. The shop doubles as a grocers and post office and a postman is standing by his bicycle just before going on his round. Children stand in the roadway and the horse and cart in the background show a leisurely life-style in complete contrast with the rush and roar of traffic which now passes this spot every hour of the day and night.

THE LAND BEYOND THE HEDGE WAS ONCE A COPSE in Wellington Lane, Heath End, part of the grounds of Heath End House, now 114 Farnborough Road. Prior to the construction of bungalows in The Fairway, houses in Wellington Lane and one or two houses in Upper Weybourne Lane, all this area was covered in trees although in some places the land was very marshy. The lamp-standard is at about the spot which is now the entrance to The Fairway.

THIS WEDDING GROUP, pictured outside the bride's home in Hale in 1925, is delightful inasmuch as the whole family, even tiny babies, have been included in the formal photograph. The bridegroom is James Hughes and his bride is Doris Lamb. The bride's parents are second and third from the left in the back row and her sisters Evelyne and Christine are the bridesmaids on the left. In the front row is Mrs Salter, one of the bride's sisters, on the left and another of her sisters, Mrs White, on the right. The *Just William* character with the striped tie is one of her nephews, W. White. The bride's home was a prefabricated-type building known as The Huts. These wooden units were demolished when the Alma Lane and Bricksbury Hill houses were built.

SECTION THIRTEEN

Round and About Rowledge

Rowledge, or Roughditch at it used to be called, and Wrecclesham were separated by a wide ditch a century ago. Fights used to take place over the ditch and the residents of Rowledge were considered to be the roughest types imaginable. Wrecclesham residents were not much better, according to the folklore of the time. The village was almost a mile from Farnham and well-wooded, making it an ideal place for vagabonds and thieves to hide if they were being hunted by the police. Just as with Wrecclesham and Rowledge, where one place has developed into a commuter-belt dormitory village and the other has remained essentially a working and residential community, so with The Bourne and Frensham – the latter is where one goes for the weekend, the former where one lives during the week.

IN THE SQUARE AT ROWLEDGE two horses and a carriage belonging to Mr Porter are waiting outside the post office, possibly for the passenger to carry out his or her business inside the premises which advertised itself, above the door, as being a money order office and savings bank. The post office business was obviously not enough to make a living on, though, because lamps, mantles, spades and tin baths were also stocked in the shop which was next door to the village grocer.

WHEN THESE PICTURES WERE TAKEN posing for a photograph was still a novelty. The top group includes the Wrecclesham postmen, centre, and other villagers, and in the lower scene the potters at Wrecclesham Pottery take a breather. Note how even the youngest worker, second from the right, is wearing a cap (see p. 54).

FAMILY LIFE has been an important part of village communities. This picture, taken in the garden of a house in High Street, Rowledge, in 1949, shows left to right: Ken Parratt, his mother, Elsie, and his father, Arch. Next to Arch is his mother, Millie, and father, Ernest (see p. 105), and Flo, Millie and Ernest's daughter. On Flo's left is her son, Austin and husband, Steve, with Ted Parratt, Arch and Elsie's second son, on the extreme right. In the front are Arch and Elsie's 'little ones', Julia, Ena, Victor (Julia's twin brother) and Rosetta. The garden in which this picture was taken has Ernest's cider press recorded in *Name Your Poison!*, a book written by Ted Parratt and published by Robert Hale in 1990.

THE TINY GIRL at the front of this Parratt wedding was a very disappointed child. She had been a bridesmaid, wearing a salmon-pink dress, and wanted to sit near the bride for the picture. She was moved but that did not make it her duty to smile, so the present Marjorie Worsfold did not.

THE PHEASANT, Wrecclesham, was almost opposite The Bear and Ragged Staff. The couple are Mr and Mrs Attfield and the child standing on the wall is D. Piper.

THE GIRLS' FRIENDLY SOCIETY in Rowledge probably sitting in the vicarage gardens. All are wearing their best hats.

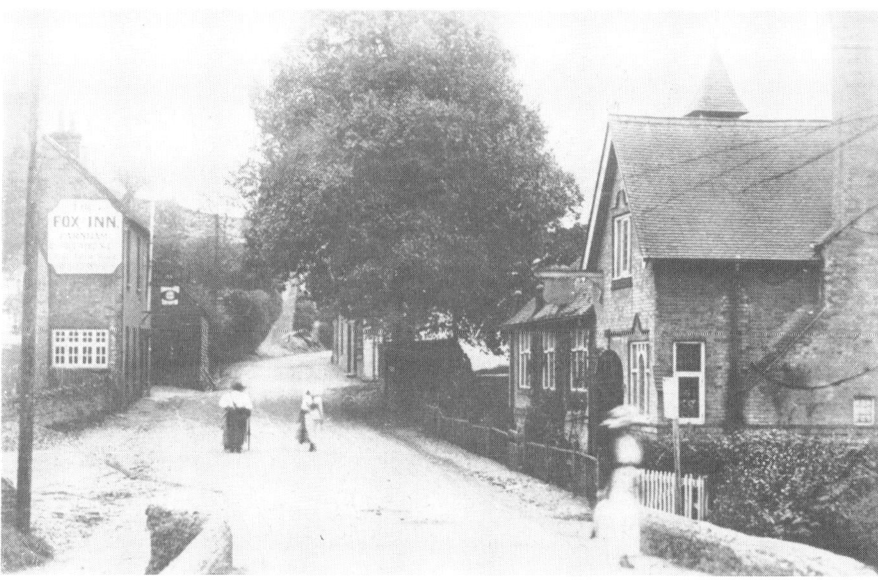

WHEN ONE CONSIDERS how many cars rush down the hill at this point on the Farnham to Frensham Road at The Bourne, it seems almost impossible that when The Fox was under the Farnham United Breweries livery the women in the picture, who had undoubtedly walked back from a shopping expedition in Farnham, should be able to walk safely in the centre of the thoroughfare.

MENTION THE NAME OF PARADISE WOOD to middle-aged men in Farnham who had been pupils at the Grammar School in the 1940s and 1950s and glazed looks will often appear on their faces. This beauty spot at The Bourne was given to the town by Miss M. Shaw Le Fevre in July 1918 and was part of the ground covered by Farnham Grammar School boys when they went on cross-country runs. Perhaps the name inspired them, because Paradise Wood was also the scene of many a kiss and cuddle between the boys and girls from the town's respective grammar schools.

GEORGE DADSON, one of the Dadson family of Millbridge, Frensham, dressed up for a spin on his bicycle. The picture was probably taken by George Sturt of Millbridge, a relative of the George Sturt who was an author in Farnham.

THE BAKERY AND GROCERY SHOP belonging to Mr R. Sturt was at Millbridge crossroads, Frensham. The bakers worked long and hard (see p. 44), as did the delivery boy (photographed by George Sturt) as he pushed his hand-cart round the village.

TWO SMALL CHILDREN stare at the photographer as he snaps the two routes indicated by the signpost around 1914. The road on the left leads to Rowledge, a mile-and-a-half away, the other to Farnham and Aldershot. On the pole above the children's head a poster announces public meetings to be held at Frensham and The Bourne.

ACKNOWLEDGEMENTS

This book has been made possible by the co-operation of a number of friends and relatives who have willingly put their treasured photographs at my disposal. Unfortunately many pictures loaned to me have had to be left out due to lack of space but they are all recorded for a subsequent volume. I should like to thank the following people for giving me permission to use their pictures and for help in the preparation of this volume:

Edward Griffith • Martin Rice and Downing Street Sudios • Gladys Hardingham Dennis Stone of Farnham Castle Newspapers • Harold Cole • Lily Sparks Peggy Chapman • Anne Jones of Farnham Museum • Margaret Mullery Bernadine Collins • Keith Dolley • Jean Cole • Florrie Coles • Ron Fry Doug Tanner • Hetty Friend • Mr and Mrs R.H. Foster • Jack Hardingham Harry Wright • the William Cobbett Society • Chris Bonner •Doris Addy Allan Elphick • the Goodridge family • Arnold Perera • Peter Lewis-Jones John Boas • Frank German • Mary Joynes • Peter Watts • Jonathan Durham Arthur Brown • Judith Halliwell • Sheila Phillips • Moira Kelsey Chris Shepheard • Guy Bellamy • Raymond Kirk • Nora Blissett • Sainsbury's Marjorie Worsfold • Mark Parratt • Surrey Archaeological Society • Surrey Constabulary • Annie Martin • Ted Parratt my husband.

I should also like to thank the unknown photographers of the past who provided some of the material for this book of the 1990s with their cumbersome cameras of more than a century ago. If anyone has been left out of these credits then I apologize and will acknowledge them in the future.

THIS PICTURE MUST BE CAPTIONED 'GOODBYE'. It shows families waving goodbye to husbands, brothers, fiancés and lovers as they left the town to fight in France in the First World War. The men had been brought into Farnham by car from outlying villages and then marched to the station, led by a man blowing a flute, before catching the train to London and eventually the battlefront.

Massimiliano Varrese e Francesco Serino

L'Estate è già finita

SONDA

Prima edizione: novembre 2011

ISBN 978 88 7106 636 3

EDIZIONI SONDA
....
corso Indipendenza 63
15033 Casale Monferrato (Al)
Tel. 0142 461516 – Fax 0142 461523
E-mail: sonda@sonda.it
Web: www.sonda.it

Avevo fatto una promessa, che non ho *mai* mantenuto...
Al mio «Guerriero della Luce» Massimo Pietroni, mio zio.

È un'emozione così grande poter dar vita alle parole! Ogni volta che ho avuto bisogno di sollevare il cuore e lo spirito, e cercare risposte, ho sempre trovato rifugio in un libro...
Per questo voglio ringraziare i nostri editori, per averci dato questo privilegio, per la passione e l'amore che ci hanno messo.

La mia Famiglia, che mi ha lasciato libero di essere e decidere.
I miei amici, quelli *veri*! Pochi... Ma loro sanno chi sono!

La Luce...

Te...

Massimiliano

Dedico questo libro a mio figlio Nicola,
nato il giorno in cui abbiamo consegnato il manoscritto,
e alla mia Silvia, che ha *realizzato* questo magico destino.

Ringrazio mia madre,
perché altrimenti il cerchio non potrebbe chiudersi...

Francesco

Uno

Sono qui, seduto su una scomoda sedia di legno, la gente rumoreggia intorno, l'aria è più leggera rispetto a due giorni fa. Ho in testa un berretto verde militare che mi nasconde il ciuffo e lo tiene in ordine. Erano anni che non lo facevo più crescere, quindici, forse anche di più. Mi sentivo affascinante con la mano che ogni tanto passava tra i capelli e li riordinava a memoria, senza specchio, e il bello era che funzionava davvero, quasi fossero telecomandati. Oggi ho trent'anni e forse non ho più la stessa abilità, ma vorrei riprovarci, vorrei tornare un po' indietro nel tempo e sentirmi di nuovo come allora, con l'unica differenza che adesso il mio ciuffo ha una bella e vistosa *frezza* bianca. Non mi sono tinto per fare il figo, l'ho ereditata da mio padre. Lui sì che è «bianco», praticamente da quando è nato. L'ho sempre preso in giro per questo, gli dicevo che è «nato vecchio».

Non so perché, ma in certi momenti di malinconia mi viene spesso da paragonarmi a lui, è stato un modello da emulare per la forza che ha dimostrato ogni volta nel ricominciare da zero, per la capacità di reinventarsi sempre. Non è stato fortunato nella vita. Ma, in fondo, cos'è la fortuna? Dove sta? Esiste davvero o dipende solo da noi e da cosa scegliamo e da come agiamo?

Credo di aver capito che nella vita bisogna imparare a dire di no! Che non vuol dire negare qualcosa a qualcuno, ma più semplicemente dire di sì alla propria volontà, al proprio desiderio. È solo così che ho imparato a liberarmi da alcuni miei sensi di colpa. Quali?

Non ve lo posso dire, ancora.

Oggi qui al mare si sta bene, l'acqua è incavolata nera, i bambini in spiaggia corrono e schiamazzano. La gente è tornata a fare bambini, vedo.

Anch'io ho voglia di essere padre, voglia di poter condividere le mie esperienze, voglia di poter prendere in braccio il mio cucciolo e sentire la gioia che si impossessa di ogni mio poro. Cavolo, stamattina ho parlato con Checco, e tra meno di un mese diventerà papà!

Appena ho sentito la sua voce, è stato come finire sotto una di quelle grosse onde: contentezza e nostalgia, nostalgia e contentezza, e in un attimo mi sono passate davanti agli occhi le immagini di noi a diciotto anni. Sarà per il ciuffo che nascondo sotto il berretto, o forse più semplicemente perché vorrei tornare a quei giorni, a quell'estate del 1994, quando noi due vivevamo come dentro un sogno, quando contava solo correre sui nostri scooter tra i campi di girasole e farci domande, le più assurde, le più belle, le più strane. Tutto era spontaneo, naturale, senza pensieri a tenerci legati. Eravamo pieni di sogni, della nostra amicizia che nessuno poteva intaccare. Nessuno mai.

Checco oggi sta per diventare padre, cura una collana per un piccolo editore e legge molto, soprattutto libri sugli angeli e strane teorie di vita, e manuali spirituali sull'educazione dei bambini.

Io per lui sono il Massa di sempre! E sono anche un artista, per di più affermato, le mie opere si vendono bene, non mi lamento degli affari.

Ma io, per me? Chi sono davvero? Dove sto andando? Cosa voglio dalla mia vita? Vorrei addirittura cambiare nome! Così sarebbe più facile ricominciare...

Mi sento a un bivio e non so decidere. Mi sento come quel giorno, davanti a quel campo di girasoli, noi due fermi, l'uno di fianco all'altro e una sola domanda in testa: - Checco, ma la vita è così com'è, nel senso che è già scritta, o siamo noi che la disegniamo? Che decidiamo il nostro destino?

Vorrei che tu, Checco, fossi qui adesso e mi rispondessi, questa volta senza teorie strane e originali. Vorrei un po' di concretezza, perché tu oggi sei capace di dimostrarla. Volevi fare lo scrittore, e lo fai. Volevi una donna al tuo fianco, e ce l'hai. Volevi un figlio, e sta per arrivare. Tu sei sempre stato più concreto di me, più reale.

Io cosa voglio, invece? Me ne sto qui seduto da un po'... Su questa scomoda sedia di legno, gialla come quel campo di girasoli, a chiedermi come sarebbe salire di nuovo in sella a uno scooter, correre via e ridere col vento in faccia, quando oggi so che dovrei smettere di sognare e iniziare a pedalare con le mie gambe.

Ho perso il conto di che giorno è oggi, forse è il sette o forse è il dieci di settembre. So di sicuro che è giovedì, e stasera la luna sarà piena.

Mi ricordo quella mattina come se fosse adesso...

Quando suonò la campanella corsi in strada, chiamai Checco e partimmo.

Era il quattordici giugno 1994, ed era finito l'ultimo giorno di scuola. L'estate stava scoppiando, in Toscana.

Checco viaggiava ondeggiando sul suo Piaggio Zip verde pistacchio, io lo seguivo sicuro, in sella al mio scassato Benelli s50 rosso Ferrari - il primo scooter con bimarcia automatica, quello con le ruote piccole piccole. Forse non ve lo ricordate, ma di certo almeno una volta nella vita l'avrete visto passare guidato da un simpatico vecchietto che non si sposta mai.

L'aria si faceva gustare come un gelato alla fragola e cioccolato, i nostri due motorini vagavano per le strade e io osservavo la città, osservavo il paesaggio che sfilava al mio fianco, l'asfalto correre veloce sotto gli pneumatici consumati del mio mitico *Benellindson*, il soprannome che gli avevo affibbiato per via della strampalata posizione calata all'indietro che assumevo imitando i motociclisti dei chopper americani. Continuavamo a superarci a vicenda. Checco ogni tanto mi guardava dagli specchietti e si girava indicandomi la strada da seguire. Era buffo vederlo così, con quel casco giallo fosforescente.

Abbandonammo il centro abitato di Grosseto, e dopo aver superato l'ultimo semaforo ci immettemmo lungo la piccola provinciale puntando dritti verso la costa. La pianura si stendeva piatta, colorata di giallo e di verde, punteggiata di cavalli al pascolo, liberi, proprio come noi. Una meraviglia, la Maremma. I poderi in pietra, le case coloniche, l'odore degli alti pini marittimi, il sapore del vento e dei pinoli.

Checco, che mi aveva superato di nuovo, frenò all'improvviso fermandosi sul ciglio della strada. Per poco non gli andai a sbattere contro, e lo evitai davvero per un pelo. Scese dallo Zip e si posizionò: gambe leggermente divaricate e ginocchia morbide, molleggianti. Poi si girò dalla mia parte facendo delle smorfie con la bocca. Due libellule variopinte dalle ali trasparenti si librarono in aria scomparendo lontane da qualche parte. Le spighe di grano davanti a noi si muovevano lente su quello che sembrava una specie di mare morbido e dorato.

- Scusami, caro Massa -, disse Checco con la voce attutita dal casco mentre si abbassava la cerniera dei jeans, - ma ho troppa necessità di liberare la vescica -. Poi esclamò con soddisfazione: - Ah...

Sì, era buffo, proprio buffo.

Anch'io feci pipì, ma un po' mi vergognavo a mostrarmi così, al vento. A Checco invidiavo la straordinaria leggerezza con cui affrontava le cose, perché le faceva davvero senza malizia, come natura comanda.

Salimmo su per le colline degli Etruschi, verso Vetulonia, e ci fermammo in un piccolo slargo prima di una curva a guardare il mare. Era blu come un colore a olio. Lo osservai pensando per quanto tempo ancora avrei potuto vivere quei momenti, sentirmi così, all'unisono con tutto e con un amico per la pelle accanto. Tirai fuori dallo zainetto foglio e penna e feci uno schizzo del profilo dell'orizzonte. Al contrario di Checco, io non ero molto loquace, e preferivo starmene così, in silenzio, a fissare con le immagini ciò che le parole non riescono a spiegare. E ogni volta, sentivo il cuore gonfiarsi di gioia.

La vita quotidiana, la scuola, il bar erano distanti almeno dieci chilometri...

Quando ero piccolo e abitavo ad Albinia, un paese vicino al Monte Argentario, ci pensavo poco, al futuro. Credevo solo che sarei diventato un portiere, come papà Antonio. Ne ero sicuro. Al massimo, mi corressi un giorno, se non fossi riuscito a parare come lui, sarei potuto diventare come «Giorgione» Chinaglia. Allora, papà faceva il rappresentante di noccioline americane. Con mamma, Luisa, si erano trasferiti lì da Roma in cerca di tranquillità, e l'avevano trovata, almeno all'inizio. D'estate poi, io e mia sorella Monica andavamo al mare tutti i giorni con la mitica Graziella, che guarda caso era verde pistacchio! Ricordo gli aquiloni che volavano nell'azzurro bottone del cielo sopra le stradine vicino alla spiaggia. Quanto tempo ho passato a giocare su quella sabbia biancastra! Amavo cercare le cose nascoste sottoterra. Non era un lavoro difficile: bastava iniziare a scavare da qualche parte, qualsiasi punto andava bene. Come tutti i lavori che si rispettino, anche quello, però, aveva un suo lato noioso: quasi sempre non trovavo un fico secco, sepolto lì sotto. A me, comunque, di questo importava poco, ogni giorno poteva riservare sorprese. Una volta, avrò avuto sì e no otto o nove anni, spinto dall'emozione che mi aveva suscitato la vecchia fotografia di un vaso etrusco sul sussidiario di scuola, decisi di andare a scavare nel campo dietro alla chiesa. La mia idea era che in passato, chissà quanto tempo prima, là dietro si fosse trovata un'intera città etrusca, piena di strade e di botteghe, di bambini e di signori con i sandali polverosi ai piedi. Quel giorno, immaginai di cercare una casa, con la cucina e le camere da letto, con le ciotole sul tavolo e una finestra senza infissi. Ricordo che rimasi lì tutto il pomeriggio, finché l'imbrunire del cielo non mi permise più di vedere. Ma a un certo punto, come un fungo spuntato all'improvviso, trovai qualcosa. Era un chiodo, un semplice chiodo, un lungo e grosso chiodo arrugginito sotto venti centimetri di terra, che nessuno, se non il sottoscritto, avrebbe potuto mai trovare. Quando lo sfilai via mi accorsi che era storto, con la capocchia più larga di quanto mi aspettassi, anche se forse la scarsa luce giallastra del lampione vicino mi confondeva un po' le idee. Il chiodo, nella mia mente di bambino, era certamente di fabbricazione etrusca, forse era servito per fissare tavole di legno che poi si erano spezzate. Chi lo sa. Quel chiodo, comunque, diventò il mio portafortuna.

La tranquillità, dicevo, ad Albinia l'avevamo trovata, ma gli inverni erano lunghi, e tutto pareva sprofondare ogni volta in un letargo innaturale. Mamma lì non era felice, aveva smesso anche di dipingere. Quante volte, da piccolo, mi ero perso guardando le sue mani muoversi sui fogli come in una danza leggera e improvvisata... Ricordo il giorno in cui, per farmi un ritratto, mi obbligò a rimanere nella stessa posizione per ore. E quante risate, perché ogni volta che sollevava lo sguardo dal foglio, mi facevo trovare con una smorfia diversa.

Il solo stipendio di papà a un certo punto non bastò più, e fu così che lui decise di cambiare ancora, trovando nel capoluogo toscano l'occasione che tanto cercava: aprire un'attività in proprio. Un suo collega rappresentante gli aveva parlato di un bar in vendita in via Sicilia, nel quartiere Pace. Dopo tre decenni l'anziana signora Maria aveva deciso di andare in pensione. Papà contrattò per diverse settimane, riuscendo infine a concludere quello che definì un «vero affare».

Quando io e Checco scendemmo giù dalle colline ero ancora immerso nei ricordi. Il mio amico salutava gli olivi che scorrevano ai lati come spettatori immobili immersi nelle fragranze della natura. Superammo un incrocio, ma il Benelli all'improvviso cominciò a non sentirsi bene. Faceva come dei colpetti di tosse secca, che a volte sembravano di tosse grassa, e comunque erano un segnale inequivocabile: il *Benellindson* stava invecchiando e a volte gli partiva qualche rotella. Quando si metteva a fare così, tosse e asma cronica, bisognava aiutarlo in qualche modo. Percorsi altri cento o duecento metri, il motore non ne poté più e decise di soffocare i suoi brontolii. Inesorabilmente fiaccato dal solito problema alla centralina, come una candela che consuma lo stoppino diminuì la potenza fino a fermarsi presso un campo di girasoli immenso, giallo e grande come un mare. Senza batter ciglio, scesi e misi il Benelli sul cavalletto basso. Checco, che aveva assistito alla scena dallo specchietto, dopo una rocambolesca inversione a U mi arrivò di fianco. Si tolse il casco liberando tutti i suoi riccioli biondi. Sembrava un cespo di insalata gialla.

- Solito problema alla centralina -, disse con aria riflessiva pulendosi gli occhiali con la maglietta. Scese dallo Zip e si guardò intorno.

Dal minuscolo portaoggetti del *Benellindson* estrassi delle forbicine con l'impugnatura nera, del nastro adesivo e una fascetta di fili elettrici. Mi misi al lavoro, e taglia-lega-incolla-sciogli-passa-sfila-tira-e-stringi bene, in un batter d'occhio avevo finito. Cavolo, meglio di un meccanico di Formula 1 al pit stop.

Gasato, sgusciai da dietro al *Benellindson* e iniziai a correre su e giù per la strada urlando: - Sì, sì, sono il campione di me stesso! Sono il campione di me stesso!

Dopo essermi sfogato, tornai verso Checco. - Ecco fatto.

- Sei impazzito per caso? -, chiese sorpreso dalla mia reazione.

- Perché, è vietato sbrigarsi?

- A parte il fatto che sei sempre così maledettamente lento, e poi cosa sono tutte quelle scenette?

- Be', qualcosa da te devo pur averla presa, no?

Lui disse: - Okay -, ma non sembrava troppo convinto.

D'istinto e all'unisono, come due ballerini coreografati, ci girammo a osservare quel mare giallo di girasoli, con lo sguardo pieno e lontano, complici e inconsapevoli, improvvisatori di uno spettacolo appena cominciato.

Poi, d'improvviso, chiesi: - Checco? Ma secondo te, la vita è così com'è, è già fatta... Mi spiego meglio. Voglio dire, la vita, in generale, dal tuo punto di vista, è qualcosa di unico nel senso che è così e basta, perché è già stata scritta da qualcuno, o ce la scriviamo da soli e non lo sappiamo?

Gli brillarono gli occhi. - Bella domanda, mio vecchio Massa -, rispose felice. Sogghignando, rimase fisso a guardarmi.

Lo ricambiai, poi, ancora eccitato, continuai: - Eh, Checco. Allora?

- Allora? -. Mi osservava soddisfatto, ma sembrava non voler rispondere.

- E allora? La mia domanda? Eh? La mia domanda? -, lo incalzai.

- Eh... Mi chiedi se la vita ce la scriviamo noi e non lo sappiamo, giusto? -, chiese a sua volta.

Annuii.

Lui sorrise, e alzando l'indice domandò: - E se invece lo sapessimo?

Per me le parole di Checco, pur nel suo strampalato modo di fare, erano la conferma che al di là dei libri di scuola, al di là della televisione, e probabilmente di tanto altro, si nascondeva un significato più intimo e segreto che solo un amico può riuscire a capire. Da quando ci eravamo conosciuti, quel giorno del 1989, niente era stato più come prima.

Papà aveva appena comprato il bar Da Maria, e lo aveva trasformato nel bar Paradise. Quella zona mi piaceva perché c'era tutto: il meccanico, il parrucchiere, il campetto da calcio, la scuola - non mi piaceva ma era pur sempre la mia scuola, il tecnico commerciale - e poi c'era lui, Checco. La prima volta che lo vidi era una giornata di fine agosto, mentre stava giocando da solo. Ho sempre davanti agli occhi l'immagine di lui col pallone in mano, che era andato a riprendere nel cortile accanto dopo aver sbagliato un rigore a porta vuota. Non è mai stato un buon calciatore, amava di più il tennis. A un certo punto, da dietro i suoi occhiali da vista tondi, mi guarda e fa una delle sue smorfie. Io scoppio a ridere e allora mi avvicino, come rassicurato da quel suo strano modo di comunicare. - Possiamo giocare insieme -, gli dico, - io sono un portiere.

Checco sembra interessato e mi risponde solo: - Okay -. Gli stringo la mano, come fanno gli adulti.

- Vuoi essere mio amico?

E lui ancora: - Okay.

Fu davvero una passeggiata. Ricordo che a quelle parole un raggio di sole si fece largo tra le nuvole per venire a posarsi proprio lì, in via Sicilia.

A settembre ci ritrovammo nella stessa classe, ma solo qualche giorno dopo scoprii che aveva due anni meno di me. Aveva fatto la famosa «primina», perché a quattro anni sapeva già scrivere e a cinque aveva già letto una versione ridotta de *Il richiamo della foresta* di Jack London. Io, be', col trasferimento avevo perso l'anno scolastico ed ero costretto a ripeterlo. Per dovere di cronaca, dovrei anche confessare che, insomma, non è che fossi proprio una cima, sui ban-chi. Le materie che mi piacevano di più erano le scienze, che per me erano sinonimo di Natura, e ovviamente il disegno, passione che mi piaceva pensare venisse indirettamente da mamma... Dico indirettamente perché è nata così, in modo spontaneo: lei non mi ha mai fatto pressioni. Quando ero piccolo, credevo che quello fosse il suo lavoro, perché a volte a casa veniva qualcuno che non conoscevo, contrattava un po' con mamma, poi le dava dei soldi e si portava via uno dei suoi quadri, di solito tra quelli che mi piacevano di più.

Lei dipingeva sempre in silenzio, nello sgabuzzino con una piccola finestra in fondo al corridoio, proprio accanto alla mia camera, ma amava farsi guardare, ed è per questo che quando mischiava i colori, o tracciava le linee prospettiche, credevo seguisse una sorta di rituale, al quale ogni volta venivo inconsapevolmente iniziato. Le piaceva disegnare ambienti semivuoti, al massimo con una sedia a dondolo e alcuni giochi di legno. Ma c'era sempre un enorme finestrone che affacciava su paesaggi rurali, calmi, vastissimi. Io mi immaginavo di correre su quei campi, entrare in quella stanza per giocare e infine addormentarmi, sfinito, cullato dal dolce movimento del dondolo. Bastava osservarla un attimo per capire che per lei dipingere significava creare un mondo diverso, più bello, più *vero*. Non me l'ha mai confessato, ma io ho sempre pensato che le cose stessero proprio così.

Lo stesso vale per me. E Checco lo sapeva.

Se sono stato fortunato, a conoscerlo, non è compito mio dirlo, o forse sì, ma credo anche che certe *storie* vadano cercate, cercate nel profondo dei nostri desideri. Anche Checco è d'accordo. Lo è sempre stato...

Poi, però, arrivò qualcosa a turbare questo delicato equilibrio.

Due

Balzai in sella al *Benellindson*, attraversai il sottopasso della ferrovia e imboccai il lungo viale della Pace. Dopo i soliti sei minuti e cinquanta secondi ero al Paradise. Grosseto non era certo Roma; se partivi in ritardo era facile che arrivassi pure in anticipo.

Papà se ne stava come sempre appoggiato con le sue grandi mani dietro al bancone. Il calendario accanto alla macchinetta del caffè mi ricordò che era il diciotto giugno, il primo sabato delle vacanze.

Per rinnovare gli ambienti senza spendere troppo, quando aveva rilevato l'attività papà aveva deciso di cambiare la disposizione del banco, che ora era parallelo alla grande porta a vetri d'entrata. Il finto marmo di buona fattura col quale aveva sostituito il vecchio ripiano di legno era illuminato da alcuni faretti montati su un mensolone sospeso su cui stavano allineati gli amari e i superalcolici. In sala, le scaffalature semplici per l'esposizione dei prodotti lo rendevano un classico esempio di bar all'italiana. Con gli occhiali sulla punta del naso, che ogni tanto arricciava per tirarli un po' più su, papà si mise in bocca una grossa manciata di noccioline americane che ormai da anni, per abitudine, erano diventate il suo spuntino preferito. Nel laboratorio, al quale si accedeva da una piccola porta a soffietto proprio dietro alla cassa, la scorta era sempre abbondante.

Durante l'anno scolastico, a occupare i tavolinetti della sala c'era sempre qualche gruppetto di ragazzi che approfittavano dell'ora di religione per venire a ripassare matematica o stenografia. In quel momento c'era solo il signor Osvaldo, che abitava al primo piano proprio sopra al bar, a rendere un po' meno triste l'atmosfera.

- Checco mi ha detto di dirti che stasera ti devi mettere la camicia bianca -, esordì papà.

- La camicia bianca? E perché?

-Aò! -, esclamò col suo accento romanesco. - Ma io che ne so, chiedilo a lui, no? Quée ragazzo è proprio strano...

Checco, che abitava in fondo alla via, a cinquanta metri dal Paradise, ne aveva sicuramente pensata una delle sue. Ma lui era così, imprevedibile, anche se spesso combinava qualche guaio.

L'appuntamento era in centro, al Coenobium, il pub più in voga della città. Checco mi aveva detto che quella parola in latino significa monastero, convento o qualcosa del genere. Da quando avevano messo i telefoni, però, il pienone era assicurato e quel nome suonava proprio fuori luogo. Ogni tavolo, infatti, era dotato di un telefono collegato agli altri da un sistema a circuito chiuso. Tutti potevano chiamare tutti, bastava digitare il numero del tavolo prescelto. Era forte.

Prima di uscire, papà mi ricordò che dovevo portare a mamma la busta della spesa che stazionava sopra al panchetto accanto al registratore di cassa. Presi un succo di frutta alla pera, lo bevvi in un sorso e lanciai la bottiglietta vuota nel cestino. Canestro.

Montai sul *Benellindson* diretto a casa.

Abitavamo in affitto nel complesso popolare del Villaggio Azzurro, a due passi dalla ferrovia. Una volta adibito a caserma, era semplice e per quanto il nome cercasse di nasconderlo, in realtà era piuttosto anonimo, per non dire brutto. I fondi al pianoterra erano quasi tutti magazzini, e a parte qualche camioncino non ci passava praticamente nessuno, lì sotto. Casa nostra era all'ultimo piano, e per fortuna da qualche anno avevano installato l'ascensore: si fermò al quarto piano e le porte si aprirono. - La busta della spesa te la metto sul tavolo in cucina -, dissi a mamma una volta entrato.

- Grazie, Chicco -, rispose lei, chiusa in bagno. Mi chiamava sempre così. Quasi sempre.

Superai il mobiletto dell'ingresso prima del corridoio, dove in una piccola libreria erano disposti l'enciclopedia, qualche libro d'arte di mamma, una biografia su «Giorgione» Chinaglia che avevo regalato a papà e pochi altri volumi. Sulla parete opposta, un quadretto con una Madonna dagli occhi azzurri. Da quando ci eravamo trasferiti dalle pareti erano scomparse tutte le tele di mamma. Avevo provato a farle cambiare idea, all'inizio, ma ogni volta diceva che non le piacevano più e che anzi un giorno si sarebbe dovuta decidere a prenderle dalla soffitta e regalarle. Superai il bagno, la camera di Monica e quella dei miei. Mamma aveva l'abitudine di tenere sempre le porte chiuse. Entrai nella mia stanza e lanciai le chiavi del Benelli sul letto. Sopra la testiera, guardai il poster di Michael, i suoi pantaloni alla caviglia, il suo guanto bianco. Imitai il suo urletto, mi dava carica. Mi osservai allo specchio, cavolo, il ciuffo si era ammosciato. Dopo una doccia e una ricca dose di gel sarebbe tornato a posto. Dalla finestra si vedevano i palazzi di fronte e, più in fondo, il cielo che portava al mare. La luce entrava diretta, e mi gustavo gli ultimi raggi del pomeriggio che allungavano le ombre degli oggetti. Sulle pareti, i poster dei *Gremlins*, di *Nightmare* e una sciarpa della Lazio, ricordo della prima partita con papà, a Roma. Le Nike bianche, per le quali avevo speso metà del mio patrimonio personale e che odiavo sporcare, ai piedi del letto. Senza fretta, tirai fuori dall'armadio la camicia bianca, la studiai a lungo tenendo la gruccia a distanza, prima con la mano destra, poi con la sinistra. Aveva il colletto alla coreana. La posai sul letto e la stirai bene con il palmo, la lisciai come fosse una distesa di capelli e la guardai di nuovo: non ricordavo mi piacesse tanto.

Mi feci la doccia cantando *Billie Jean*, mi vestii, mezza boccetta di profumo Excess di Paco Rabanne spruzzata addosso e l'ultima aggiustatina al ciuffo. Volevo essere il più figo di tutti, quella sera. Mi guardai di nuovo allo specchio: la camicia bianca era la soluzione ideale, i miei due chiletti di troppo non si notavano affatto. Perfetto. Tornai in bagno per l'ultimo rito: lavarmi i denti, già perfetti, fin quasi a lucidarli con certosina meticolosità. Poco prima delle otto chiamò Checco. Mamma, con una specie di sottoveste azzurro cielo, venne a dirmelo. Somigliava alla Madonna del quadretto. - C'è Checco al telefono -. Poi scomparve in cucina.

- Pronto.

- Camicia?

- Sì.

- Allora tra cinque minuti scendi -, e riattaccò.

In cucina, mamma era intenta a scartare della roba. Si voltò di scatto, come colta in flagrante. - Sei già pronto?

- Mila dov'è? -, chiesi, come per scacciare un certo imbarazzo.

- È fuori. È tutto il pomeriggio che sta sdraiata sul davanzale, forse sente il caldo pure lei, povera gattina! -, concluse mamma con un sorriso un po' stanco.

- Be', speriamo che non voli giù un'altra volta... -, commentai, ripensando a una storia di qualche anno prima quando, ancora cucciola, la gatta bianca di mamma era caduta sul balcone di sotto.

- Checco sale? Vorrei chiedergli una cosa.

- No, ci troviamo giù.

- Ah, va be', sarà per un'altra volta.

La salutai e uscii.

Nello specchio dell'ascensore controllai di nuovo il ciuffo.

Fuori si stava proprio bene, la serata era stupenda.

Superato l'incrocio dello stadio, il Benelli cominciò a perdere potenza. E ti pareva. Checco s'accorse subito del problema e con una manovra delle sue tornò indietro.

- Stasera mica ce l'ho, i fili. E mo'? -, chiesi.

Checco mi guardò la camicia. - Dai, monta su, passiamo dalle stradine così i *caramba* non ci beccano.

Il sole stava calando alle nostre spalle, mentre le prime stelle facevano la loro timida comparsa dietro alle colline scure dalle curve morbide. Parcheggiammo e ci incamminammo verso il centro storico passando da Porta Corsica, la più grande della città. I mattoni rossicci delle alte mura medicee scintillavano al tramonto. Attraversammo piazza Dante passando sotto il lungo porticato e sbucammo nella stretta ma vivace via San Martino.

Nella piazzetta della Palma, di fronte al Coenobium, c'era come al solito un sacco di gente.

Ci sistemammo all'unico tavolo ancora libero. Il ciuffo era perfetto, ma non so dire quanto lo fossi io, in quell'ambiente. Insomma, ero contento, certo, la scuola era finita e potevo finalmente pensare più a me stesso, ma contemporaneamente sentivo come un richiamo verso l'aperto, quella straordinaria sensazione di libertà che si prova tra i muri di pietra della vecchia fornace, o sull'argine del fiume, a guardare la città.

Ordinammo e iniziammo a chiacchierare. Checco non la smetteva di nominare il suo idolo del tennis, Jimmy Courier, che proprio quel giorno aveva vinto il Roland Garros. Continuava a elogiarlo per la potenza dei suoi servizi. Secondo una sua teoria, l'americano era in grado di ruotare il polso il 38% in più. Provai a chiedergli cosa significasse saper ruotare il polso il 38% in più rispetto a noi comuni mortali, ma a un certo punto non riuscii più a seguire quei suoi complicati ragionamenti tennistici.

- Checco, basta, con questo tennis hai rotto, non ne posso più! -, sbottai.

- E tu sei il solito ignorante -, mi rimproverò da dietro quei suoi occhialetti tondi. - Ancora non hai capito che il tennis è come una scuola di vita. Anzi, *è* una scuola di vita, dove filosofia e fisica si sposano perfettamente. Quando Jimmy gioca non c'è nessuno che gli dice cosa fare, *è da solo* su quel rettangolo, lui, la sua mente e la sua arte al servizio delle leggi universali del cosmo: dinamica, gravitazione, elettromagnetismo. Non ti sembra straordinario?

Scrollai il capo. Non riuscivo a seguirlo.

Checco cercò di convincermi, ma io continuavo a non capire.

- Ma come non capisci, Massa? Questa è la *vita*! -, si infervorò. - Sei proprio straordinariamente ignorante; non nel senso di analfabeta, che comunque per te sarebbe già un complimento, ma nel senso che ignori -. Abbassò le spalle sconsolato, e si mise a costruire una mega cannuccia per bersi l'aranciata.

Fu allora che successe una cosa che mi si è come stampata nella memoria. La musica era piuttosto alta. Agli altri tavoli stavano tutti giocando a comporre sulla piccola tastiera dei telefoni numeri a caso. Era un passatempo divertente che anche a me, per via della chiamata *misteriosa*, a volte piaceva. Il pub era grande e quando era affollato non sapevi mai chi poteva risponderti. C'era poi un fitto via vai di bigliettini, tipo quelli che ci passavamo in classe. Era la seconda fase della scoperta. Una volta accertati l'interlocutore o l'interlocutrice al di là del filo, decidevi se continuare la comunicazione scrivendo su un foglietto un messaggio da far viaggiare tra i tavoli. Certo, c'era sempre la possibilità che passando di mano in mano alle tue parole ne venissero aggiunte altre - spesso con risultati bizzarri -, ma in fondo il divertimento era proprio quello. I bigliettini rappresentavano l'apoteosi dello stare insieme, singoli individui che si mischiavano tra loro. Era bello. Bellissimo.

Fu allora che, dicevo, una ragazza varcò la soglia del Coenobium. Di solito non mi soffermavo, come gli altri, a guardare chi entrasse, ma quella volta, non so perché, lo feci. Una vampata di fuoco mi salì dal collo fin sopra alle guance e rimasi a bocca aperta per parecchi secondi, credo.

Era una tipa rosso-bionda dalle curve sinuose, con due occhi sfavillanti e una bocca lucida come miele al sole. Avrà avuto la mia età, o anche un anno di meno. Era così bella che mi sembrava impossibile non averla mai notata prima. Voglio dire, non è che andassi in cerca di ragazze ogni giorno, ma una così, cavolo, non potevo non averla notata prima. I capelli, poi, a seconda dell'inclinazione del capo assumevano le sfumature dorate di certe pesche, e lasciavano intravedere i lobi delle orecchie decorati da un paio di piccoli orecchini, che però sembravano enormi tanto erano deliziosi. La tipa tirò fuori dalla borsetta un lucidalabbra e se lo passò sulla bocca. Dietro di lei entrarono altre tre ragazze, ma in mezzo a loro sembrava l'unica donna. Una era vestita praticamente come lei. Saranno amiche del cuore, pensai. Mi girai d'istinto verso Checco, ma era così concentrato sulla sua cannuccia che non mi considerò affatto. Si sistemarono al banco, in attesa che si liberasse un tavolo. Guardando quella ragazza, mentre parlava, mi accorsi che le labbra erano sottili, ma stupende. Le osservai il naso, piccolo, e poi il collo, lungo e abbronzato.

Nel frattempo al nostro tavolo erano arrivati panini e patatine fritte. Iniziammo a mangiare. Checco aveva finalmente terminato di costruire la sua mega cannuccia, e volle subito provarla. Sistemò il bicchiere all'angolo opposto del tavolo, ce la infilò dentro, addentò una patatina e si mise a succhiare. L'aranciata, dopo un percorso tortuoso, arrivò a destinazione.

- È una bella soddisfazione -, commentò col boccone ancora in bocca -. A proposito, vecchio Massa, ma lo sapevi che i venti che spirano dentro a un uragano possono arrivare fino a tremila chilometri all'ora? Pazzesco, vero?

Ogni volta Checco aveva la sua da dire ma, non so perché, le sue stranezze avevano sempre senso...

Mi girai verso il banco, ma lei non c'era più. Chissà a quale tavolo si era sistemata, mi chiesi.

Avevamo spazzolato tutto, e ora stavamo lì a discorrere del più e del meno. Parlammo anche del mare, e dei mondiali di calcio che erano iniziati il giorno prima. A un tratto squillò il telefono del nostro tavolo. Checco rispose prontamente con voce profonda: - Questura di Grosseto -. Dopodiché fece una faccia strana. - Chi? -, per poi rivolgersi a me: - Vogliono te.

- Vogliono me? -. Presi il ricevitore e lo accostai all'orecchio.

- Ho visto, sai, come mi guardavi.

- Cosa?

- Ho detto che ho visto, come mi guardavi...

Era lei. Come vincere al Totocalcio, oppure prendere 10 in matematica. Quella sera, successe che la ragazza più affascinante che avessi mai visto mi stava chiamando al telefono del Coenobium.

Un secondo dopo sentii come una voragine dentro, percorsa da onde che andavano e venivano. E quando lei mi chiese se avevo capito, un fremito, una specie di tremolio alla bocca dello stomaco mi fecero capire che si trattava di emozione pura.

Checco mi guardava con aria interrogativa.

- Sì, ho capito. Grazie -, e riattaccai.

Non so di preciso perché lo feci, probabilmente ero solo troppo imbarazzato. E io che mi ero sempre considerato uno tosto. Che figura avevo fatto? Cercai di non pensarci, ma la testa mi frullava.

Dopo cinque minuti sul tavolo planò un aeroplanino di carta. Mi guardai in giro per capire chi lo avesse lanciato, ma era già troppo tardi. Lo agguantai e lo aprii. Era bianco. Peccato, pensai. Checco mi bussò sulla mano con la cornetta del telefono, l'aria un po' assente. - Tieni, è ancora *lei*.

Ero talmente concentrato sull'aeroplanino, che non avevo sentito squillare di nuovo l'apparecchio.

- Che ne dici di venire al nostro tavolo?

Al loro tavolo? Volevo scomparire. Ma che figura avrei fatto se avessi rifiutato?

- Okay -, risposi col cuore in gola.

- Allora... vado un attimo in bagno e poi ti aspetto. Cercaci... -, e riattaccò.

Santo cielo, non avevo mai provato così tanta vergogna in vita mia. Bastarono quelle poche parole a sciogliermi come un cubettino di ghiaccio al primo sole.

Checco se ne stava in silenzio, in attesa.

Io non sapevo bene cosa dire, mi sudavano le mani. Dopo un profondo respiro, mi feci coraggio e mi alzai. Tra la folla, non era semplice individuare il tavolo incriminato. Li passai in rassegna con lo sguardo: ce n'erano quattro di sole ragazze, ma non *lei* e nemmeno le sue amiche. Feci un nuovo giro. Niente. Per tenere sotto controllo l'ansia andai in bagno. Mi sciacquai il viso, controllai i denti e il ciuffo e tornai in sala. La musica pompava dagli altoparlanti. Il mio cuore pompava all'impazzata. Niente, non riuscivo a vederle. Mi vergognavo come un ladro. Poi, ebbi la brillante idea di uscire a prendere una boccata d'aria. Ed eccola lì. Quasi mi stesse aspettando.

- Ci sei arrivato, finalmente.

- Eh, già.

- Bella la camicia, particolare.

Ero in confusione totale.

Ebbi come un déjà vu. In qualche modo, rividi in lei la bellezza di mia madre, la forma del suo viso, il taglio degli occhi. Forse era per quello che mi aveva colpito, e mi faceva sentire la sua presenza come qualcosa di *familiare*.

- Ehi, ma questo ciuffo è spettacolare... -, continuò passandomi la mano tra i capelli. Non lo avevo mai permesso a nessuno, prima. Nemmeno a mamma.

Una vampata mi percorse fino ai piedi. Le sue dita... Oh, che dita!

La guardai meglio, anche se solo per un istante. Sotto la camicetta indossava una canottierina di cotone rosa a costine e le labbra lucide erano eccitanti. Erano labbra sensuali e sconosciute. Mi sorrise. La osservai: parve di cogliere per la prima volta un sorriso, e pian piano mi sentii risucchiato dalla voglia di toccarlo, di assaporarlo. La guardai negli occhi, avevo una voglia matta di continuare.

Cominciammo a parlare. - Ma le tue amiche?

- Sono in bagno, quelle ci vivono, lì. Specialmente Caty.

Annuii. Ero così emozionato che non avevo capito una sola parola. Scoprii che frequentavamo la stessa scuola.

- Che strano -, dissi subito, - non ti ho mai vista fuori, e nemmeno dentro, per i corridoi.

- Io sì. Però sapevo che tu non mi avevi mai vista.

- Cioè? Che significa, scusa?

- Perché sono io che non mi sono mai fatta vedere...

Sorrisi, ma la sua risposta mi mandò in confusione. Allora era stata così brava da non farsi mai notare da me? Cavolo...

Parlava e si muoveva con tanta sicurezza che ero come ipnotizzato.

A un certo punto se ne uscì con: - Certo che è strano! Stiamo qui a parlare e non ci siamo nemmeno presentati!

- Già, è vero, scusami! -, dissi porgendole la mano. - Io sono Massa.

- Massa?

- Sì, Massa. È l'evoluzione del mio nome.

- Ah, sì? E quale sarebbe?

- Eh -, sospirai aggiustandomi il ciuffo, - è una storia lunga, poi te la racconterò...

- Va bene, Massa, ci sto...

- E tu? Come ti chiami? -. Finalmente, pensai, le hai fatto una domanda.

- Mi chiamo Magghy. Cioè... Mi chiamo Margherita, ma insomma, io mi sento molto più Magghy. Anche i miei mi chiamano così. Forse... siamo un po' matti!

Ci sedemmo su un muretto della piazzetta e proseguimmo a chiacchierare. Le guardai le scarpe, dal tacco alto: mi sembravano scarpe da attrice, tanto erano eleganti. Rimanemmo lì almeno un paio d'ore, anche se a me, a dire il vero, sembrarono molto, molto meno. Magghy non solo era uno schianto, era pure simpatica. Ogni volta riusciva a trovare un argomento nuovo, parlava della scuola e sparlava dei professori, raccontava dei suoi progetti immaginandosi il futuro. Mi piaceva. Mi piaceva tanto.

Per la prima volta nella mia vita, mi accorsi di quanto potesse essere piacevole stare in compagnia di una ragazza. Come diceva il mio amico Vezio, era davvero una questione di alchimia.

Quella sera d'inizio estate non l'avrei mai più dimenticata. Un grillo cominciò a frinire poco più in là, come un discreto compagno notturno. Poi Magghy mi disse che a volte sognava davvero che un principe azzurro venisse a prenderla e la portasse via con sé.

Pensai che il destino non poteva scegliere un momento migliore per farci incontrare. A settembre sarebbe cominciato l'ultimo anno di scuola, l'anno della maturità, l'anno che per molti di noi avrebbe significato l'inizio del lavoro. Ora, invece, l'estate l'avevamo in mano, ed era l'ultima estate di libertà, gli ultimi tre mesi di una vita che nessuno avrebbe mai voluto perdersi.

Magghy mi guardò, poi si avvicinò, socchiudendo gli occhi e dischiudendo la bocca proprio davanti alla mia. Trattenni il respiro. Oh mio Dio, ci stavamo per baciare.

Non avevo mai provato niente del genere.

Il suo respiro, il suo odore, la morbidezza delle sue labbra, la sua lingua tiepida. No, non poteva esistere un'emozione altrettanto forte. Cavolo, il cuore mi pompava come un forsennato, non riuscivo a controllare il respiro.

Quando rientrammo, il locale era ormai semivuoto. Checco se ne stava defilato su uno sgabello, e sembrava addormentato. Con il mento poggiato sul bancone giocherellava col bicchiere vuoto tenendo gli occhi a mezz'asta, quando non li chiudeva del tutto abbassando lentamente la testa per il sonno. In quel preciso momento mi ricordai del Benelli parcheggiato vicino allo stadio. Questa proprio non ci voleva. Mi feci coraggio e dissi a Magghy che il mio amico mi stava aspettando, poveretto, che prima di arrivare al Coenobium mi si era fermato il motorino e che lui mi aveva portato dietro sul suo

Zip passando dalle stradine. Magghy ci rise su, e mi rispose di non preoccuparmi. Su un tovagliolo di carta mi scrisse il suo numero di telefono, e io feci lo stesso. Le lasciai anche quello del bar, così, per sicurezza. Prima di metterlo in tasca guardai il suo biglietto: c'era un cuoricino al posto del puntino della i di Margherita. Ci salutammo con un bacio sulla guancia dandoci appuntamento al giorno dopo.

Per la strada, Checco era silenzioso. Quando gli chiesi il motivo mi indicò l'orologio: le due e dieci. Strabuzzai gli occhi. Era la prima volta in vita mia che facevo così tardi. Per Checco, poi, che si alzava presto per abitudine, tirare fino a quell'ora doveva essere stato piuttosto faticoso. Non so perché, ma avevo la sensazione di averlo quasi umiliato. Mi scusai dandogli una pacca sulla spalla.

Quella notte, solo in camera mia, pensai a Magghy.

Il sonno mi era passato. Presi il mio blocco da disegno, feci la punta alla matita e buttai giù uno schizzo col suo nome. Lo leggevo e rileggevo. Non smettevo di ornare gli angoli delle lettere, gli spazi bianchi. Fregiavo ogni singolo punto del foglio con motivi floreali, con linee sinuose e leggere. Le avrei fatto un ritratto. E lei lo avrebbe appeso proprio accanto al suo letto...

Nella mente ripassavo ogni singolo attimo della serata. Il telefono, l'aeroplanino, i suoi capelli, i suoi occhi, la sua bocca. Cercavo con tutte le energie che ancora mi rimanevano di far risuonare nelle mie orecchie il timbro della sua voce, di assaporare il gusto della sua saliva. Era quella giusta, ne ero convinto.

Si era fatta l'alba. Di là, papà si era alzato e parlava a bassa voce con mamma. Di solito apriva il bar alle sei e trenta, ma ora che la scuola era finita non usciva mai prima delle sette e Monica, che si svegliava sempre con lui, adesso poteva dormire almeno fino alle otto.

La casa era immersa nel silenzio, perciò riuscii a cogliere qua e là stralci del discorso dei miei. Era mamma a fare le domande: «E questo mese?». E poi: «Per quanto tempo?»; e ancora: «Quindi? È peggiorata?». I toni bassi della voce di papà non arrivavano chiari fino in camera, ma capii che le risposte riguardavano proprio il bar, anzi, l'incasso del bar. Per ben tre volte sentii nominare il termine più citato dal prof di ragioneria: «IVA».

Ci fu un attimo di silenzio, quindi mamma riprese: - Lo dobbiamo dire anche a lui? -. Non ci fu risposta, o almeno non riuscii a sentirla.

Ma chi era, il *lui*? Io, forse? E perché? Che c'entravo, io, con il bar?

Poi, oppresso da un senso di disagio, finalmente mi addormentai.

Tre

Il primo pensiero, appena sveglio, fu di nuovo lei: Magghy. Era automatico, naturale, non dovevo far altro che respirare e prendeva forma da solo.

Poi mi venne in mente Checco. Dovevo ringraziarlo per la pazienza dimostrata. Anzi, avrei dovuto scusarmi.

Erano le dieci. Feci colazione.

Dall'odore di cipolla, capii che mamma stava preparando la prima panzanella dell'anno. Mi salutò sbrigativamente. Aveva imparato a cucinarla ad Albinia, e da allora era diventato il suo, e di conseguenza il nostro, piatto estivo preferito.

Ripeté un paio di volte che c'era un caldo infernale, ma a me non sembrava affatto. L'amore, pensai, riesce davvero a fare miracoli.

Poi telefonai a Checco.

- Toh -, esclamò lui, - chi si sente. Buona domenica, piccioncino.

- Ciao, senti, per ieri... Scusa, ti ho fatto aspettare fino a tardi. Mi ero dimenticato del motorino.

- L'avevo capito, che te n'eri dimenticato. Comunque, oggi è un altro giorno, giusto?

Sì, Checco aveva proprio ragione, come al solito. Oggi era un altro giorno. Un *nuovo* giorno. Ed ero emozionato, confuso, ma in fondo così felice. La vita mi sorrideva.

- Mi piace, Checco. Mi piace da matti.

Ci fu un attimo di silenzio.

- Ma lo sai che viene a scuola nostra? -, continuai per scacciare via un filo di disagio. - Io non l'avevo mai vista, e tu?

- Mmh... proprio no. È bella, eh?

- Bella? E basta? -. Sorrisi. - La cosa più incredibile non è la bellezza fisica, ma di contenuto.

- Di contenuto?

- Sì, di contenuto.

- Massa, si dice interiore: *la bellezza interiore*. Una persona non è mica una trasmissione alla tele.

- Va be', comunque hai capito.

- Ho capito, ho capito.

Parlammo ancora un po' divagando, poi il mio amico mi propose di andare al mare, alla spiaggia di Principina.

- Non posso, Checco. Dopo mi vedo con Magghy.

- Ah... capisco. Siamo già arrivati all'appuntamento fisso? -, e nella sua voce colsi una punta di sarcasmo.

- Ma no, ti pare... -, dissi imbarazzato. - Perché non vieni da me, adesso? Ora che ci penso, mamma voleva chiederti una cosa.

- Ah. Okay, allora preparo l'orzo a nonna e arrivo.

Checco e mamma si volevano bene, si vedeva dai saluti che si scambiavano, dai discorsi che facevano. Sono sicuro che lei lo considerasse come un terzo figlio, e lui come una seconda madre...

Quando gli aprì la porta, mamma lo abbracciò e gli chiese subito di seguirla sul terrazzo, c'era una cosa che voleva mostrargli.

- Secondo te, cos'è? -. Mamma gli fece vedere un piccolo vaso. - Ho trovato i semi in un cassetto, chissà dove e quando li ho comprati. Non credevo nemmeno che sarebbe spuntato qualcosa...

Al centro del terriccio spuntava una fogliolina verde. Checco la studiò a lungo, poi gli si illuminarono gli occhi. - Ma certo! È un'orchidea!

Mamma sorrise. - Che bella notizia mi hai dato. Ci speravo proprio. Il mio fiore preferito! Almeno questo...

Lo ringraziò carezzandogli i riccioli. Poi lo baciò sulle guance, e lui arrossì.

Rientrammo, parlammo ancora qualche minuto, infine Checco si congedò.

Un po' mi dispiaceva non andare al mare con lui; le nostre passeggiate in pineta, sovrastati dal baccano delle cicale, valevano sempre la pena.

Be', sarà per la prossima volta, mi dissi. Ci salutammo, ma prima che se ne andasse gli ricordai di tenere bene aperte le finestre. Se fossi passato dal bar, gli avrei dato i soliti tre colpetti di clacson col Benelli arrivato in via Sicilia.

Quel giorno non riuscii a passare dal bar, o meglio, ci passai, ma andavo così di fretta che proprio mi dimenticai di suonare a Checco. Era metà pomeriggio e avevo accompagnato Magghy a casa. Avevo deciso di portarla a cena fuori, ma avevo bisogno di qualche lira extra.

Parcheggiai di fronte al campetto della scuola calcio Invicta ed entrai. Papà stava guardando la Tv insieme a un paio di clienti.

- Aò! -, mi disse. - Ce sta' l'Argentina. Pensa che stanno a giocà de' mattina, là negli *States*.

Lanciai una rapida occhiata allo schermo. La partita? Non me ne poteva fregare di meno. Oltretutto, vederla giocata in uno stadio di football non era emozionante come all'Olimpico.

Osvaldo commentò: - In che mondo siamo finiti! Giocà sull'erba finta! Sintetica! Che mondo ignobile!

Passai di là dal banco e mi avvicinai a papà. Si fissava le scarpe. - Me sa che me devo da comprà un par de scarpe nove. Ve'?

- Se ti ostini a prendere scarpe da quattro soldi, sì. Ti devi comprare le Nike, quante volte te lo devo dire?

- See, bello mio, per le N-i-k-e, come dici te, me ce voijono cento sacchi.

- Ho capito, papà, ma ti durano dieci anni! Si studia anche a scuola, si chiama rapporto qualità/prezzo.

Lui mi guardò arricciando il naso, allungò una mano sotto al banco e si lanciò in bocca una manciata di noccioline. - Dureranno anche dieci anni, ma i cento sacchi spariscono lo stesso in un secondo.

Con questa premessa incoraggiante, mi preparai a fare la mia richiesta: - Ventimila.

Papà sospirò. - Perché?

- Come perché, papà? Mi servono.

- Non ce l'ho.

Che significa? Che gli avevo fatto perché me le rifiutasse? Cercai di scovare qualche indizio utile a chiarire il mistero. Non ne trovai.

- E dai, papà...

- Che ce devi fa'? -, mi chiese senza staccare gli occhi dallo schermo.

- Ho un appuntamento.

- Un appuntamento? Di lavoro? -, rise.

- Dai, papà, non scherzare. Un appuntamento, davvero.

- Allora uguale a me.

- Uguale a te cosa?

- Uguale davvero. Anch'io, *davvero*, non ce l'ho da darti ventimila lire.

Non capivo... Cacchio, solo ventimila lire. Che mai sarebbe stato?

- Quindici? -, provai a contrattare.

- Famo cinque -, rispose papà, e si mise in bocca altre noccioline.

- Cinque? Ma come cinque! Ma che ci faccio con cinquemila lire?

- Ci prendi due coni con doppia panna.

No, cavolo, non poteva farmi questo.

- Papà, ma è importante.

- Mi dispiace, fijo mio, ma oggi proprio nun'è giornata, c'ho le scadenze.

- Cazzo so' mo' 'ste scadenze?! -, mi scappò detto in romanesco.

- Le scadenze, Massimijà! -, rispose lui nervoso.

Maledette scadenze! Ma la mia, allora, non era una scadenza?

Forse non avrei dovuto reagire così, ma insomma, che diamine, ero suo figlio, e quello era il giorno più importante della mia vita, almeno fino a quel momento... Per ventimila misere lire, invece, ora dovevo rivoluzionare tutti i miei piani. Non potevo comprare una rosa a Magghy, portarla nel posto che avevo scelto, non potevo offrirle la cena, nulla, non potevo fare nulla. In due parole, *non potevo* dimostrarle che ero già un uomo...

Provai a racimolare qualcosa qua e là: in un cassetto, nella scatolina degli spiccioli sulla mensola del laboratorio. Con il mio progetto ormai andato a monte, per me era diventata una questione di principio. Alla fine, riuscii a raggranellare appena duemila e seicento lire.

Uscii dal bar incavolato nero.

Mi ero rifugiato al Grande Cipresso, e stavo pensando a come trovare una soluzione. Secondo Checco, il *Cupressus*, come lo chiamava lui, era l'albero più antico di tutta la città. Aveva una circonferenza di quasi tre metri e la chioma svettava alta più di un campanile. Era uno spettacolo, ma a renderlo eccezionale era il fatto di trovarsi alla fine della strada che portava alla vecchia fornace, isolato dalle altre piante, come se stesse lì a indicare qualcosa.

Fissavo l'albero, e mi rendevo conto che il mio bisogno di libertà stava crescendo ogni giorno di più. La presenza di Magghy mi infondeva una determinazione che fino a quel momento non sapevo di avere. Non facevo altro che pensare ai suoi baci, ed era un continuo immaginarmi la forma delle sue gambe, le sue curve.

Mi venne un'idea: avrei chiesto un piccolo prestito a Checco. Lui non mi avrebbe di certo sollevato obiezioni.

Rassicurato da quel pensiero, inforcai il mio *Benellindson* e tornai verso il bar. Mi fermai al portone di Checco e suonai il campanello. In quello stesso istante mi venne un dubbio. Come avrebbe reagito alla mia richiesta? E se fosse stato uno sbaglio?

Non ottenni risposta. Mordicchiandomi un'unghia, provai a suonare di nuovo. Niente. Forse non c'era nessuno. Sarà uscito con la nonna, pensai. Mi sentivo leggermente in colpa.

Aspettai ancora un po', ma alla fine fui costretto a desistere.

Con la testa incassata nelle spalle, deluso e nervoso, non sapendo che altri pesci pigliare, mi dissi che avrei chiesto a mamma almeno diecimila lire.

Non lo facevo quasi mai, perché di solito in cambio mi obbligava a fare sempre un mucchio di cose, ma io non avevo tempo da perdere dietro alle faccende di casa. Che ci pensasse Monica, a darle una mano. Del resto, lo diceva sempre anche mamma, era lei la donna di casa.

Salii al quarto piano. Mamma era in cucina, Monica in camera sua.

Ero ancora indeciso ma alla fine, no, proprio non mi andava di chiedere dei soldi a mamma. Cavolo, se almeno papà mi avesse aiutato!

Mangiai la panzanella in silenzio, rimuginando su come potevo racimolare un po' di denaro. Dopo pranzo mi fiondai nella mia stanza, mi buttai sul letto e, come un fulmine a ciel sereno, mi venne un'idea a dir poco brillante. E se fossi andato al ristorante e avessi lasciato in pegno un oggetto prezioso, con la promessa di saldare il conto non appena mi fosse stato possibile? Perché no? Sbaglio o nell'antichità era così che si facevano gli affari?

Soddisfatto della mia trovata, cominciai a frugare qua e là alla ricerca dell'agognato oggetto prezioso. Passai in rassegna uno Swatch scarico, una penna, regalo della prima comunione, una catenina d'argento con un ciondolo di pietra verde e un portachiavi di corallo. Picchiai il pugno sul palmo. Niente da fare, meglio abbandonare la mia splendida idea. Quel che sarà, sarà, dissi tra me e me. Ero o non ero, oltretutto, uno che amava vivere alla giornata, senza progetti e seguendo il ritmo della natura?

Quando non ci speravo più, nella tasca dei jeans abbandonati in fondo al letto trovai cinquemila meravigliose lire. Più le duemila e seicento facevano la bellezza di settemila e seicento lire. La fortuna aiuta davvero gli audaci. Con quel bottino, dallo Zozzone riuscivo a portar via due cheeseburger con doppia salsa e due bibite.

Potevo concedermi di rilassarmi e misi su un po' di musica aspettando l'ora dell'appuntamento.

Quando arrivò, Magghy era ancora più bella della sera precedente. Le labbra lucidissime. Indossava una gonna bianca di cotone un po' aderente sui fianchi e corta sopra al ginocchio, una camicetta e un paio di sandali rossi; i capelli sciolti, splendenti come il sole di maggio. Due orecchini d'argento completavano l'opera. Camminava con la solita disinvoltura. Era venuta a piedi. Mi raccontò della sua giornata, di Caty che si era voluta comprare *per forza* la sue stesse scarpe. - Sai, quelle che indossavo ieri sera.

La serata era fresca, perfetta.

Il locale in periferia era attiguo a un distributore di benzina ed era famoso per i suoi hot dog. Sembrava un posto per soli camionisti, ma era frequentato da almeno mezza città. Ci mettemmo in fila tenendoci per mano. Lo Zozzone, un ometto baffuto, ci servì in quattro e quattr'otto. Magghy chiese solo patatine fritte. - Adoro *solo* quelle! -, aveva spiegato. Io tirai un sospiro di sollievo, sarei rientrato nel budget alla grande. Mangiammo a un tavolo a pochi metri dall'autolavaggio. Gli ultimi colori del tramonto inondavano quell'angolo cittadino di una luce calma e romantica.

Ero davvero felice.

Quando la sua bocca si posò sulla mia, davanti al portoncino di casa sua, da quelle labbra sottili appena illuminate da un lampione mi fu trasmessa un'emozione ancora più intensa della sera precedente.

Ci eravamo appena salutati e mi accorsi di vedere già le cose da un altro punto di vista: il ricordo della sua voce mi esplodeva dentro alla testa. Il pensiero di lei avvolgeva tutto ciò che avevo intorno.

Prima di tornare a casa decisi di fare una passeggiata per calmare un po' il batticuore. Mi incamminai verso il centro storico passando da Porta Vecchia. Dall'arco si accedeva alla parte più antica della città. Era qui che si apriva la piccola piazza del Sale, con il suo semplice cassero, un tempo luogo di smercio e di affari, da cui una serie di strette stradine svicolava all'interno, verso il teatro e il Duomo. Attraversai corso Carducci, a quell'ora deserto, e proseguii varcando Porta Nuova, costeggiando le mura illuminate dal flebile giallo dei vecchi lampioni. La brezza mi accarezzava, mentre i richiami degli uccelli notturni mi facevano compagnia. Le strade erano sgombre, i marciapiedi tutti per me, poche le finestre illuminate. Passai da via Roma, con le sue villette primo Novecento, svoltai in via Trento e proseguii dritto fino ad arrivare al bar. Com'era diverso osservare la città di notte! Il riposo del mondo, in un tempo separato, sfuggente, calmissimo. La vita, con tutti i suoi imprevisti, non sarebbe tornata finché l'albeggiare sull'orizzonte non ci avesse risvegliato. Appoggiato alla saracinesca del Paradise, mi misi a osservare il cielo, e immaginai che non avesse fine. Come sarà il mio futuro?, pensai.

Quattro

La mattina dopo, mamma mi disse che papà aveva bisogno di una mano. - Che significa? -, le chiesi.

- Significa che lui ha delle commissioni, tua sorella oggi deve uscire con me, e quindi devi andarci tu.

- Ma mamma! Non posso!

- Certo che puoi.

- Ma io c'ho da fare!

- Be', anch'io c'ho da fare, che ti credi! Pensi che sia facile mandare avanti una casa, voi due e un marito che va via alle sei di mattina e torna alle nove di sera? Pensi che mi diverta? E poi oggi io e Monica c'abbiamo da fare. Quindi non fare storie e fa' come ti ho detto.

Rimasi un attimo in silenzio, poi sbuffai. Non esce mai, e proprio oggi c'ha da fare. Che sfiga!

- Uff, però. Va bene, quando devo andare?

- Ti vesti e vai.

- Adesso?

- Sì, adesso.

E io che mi ero fatto lo scrupolo di chiederle un piccolo prestito... Al diavolo!

Non era il lavoro che non mi andava, era piuttosto il fastidio di dover stare dietro al bancone per tante ore consecutive. Mi sentivo come in galera, cacchio. Non la capivo, questa *necessità* di dover guadagnare. Ma non sarebbe stato meglio autogestire i luoghi di lavoro, dove ognuno avrebbe potuto dare il suo piccolo contributo ricevendo in cambio solo ciò di cui aveva bisogno per vivere? Io proprio non la concepivo, questa maledetta economia. Odiavo quelli che parlavano di economia, odiavo gli insegnanti di diritto commerciale, odiavo le società finanziarie... Odiavo tutto, di quel mondo. E per giunta avevo ancora un anno di questa scuola da fare.

Entrai al bar con aria indifferente.

Passai dietro al bancone, posai gli occhiali da sole vicino alla cassa e mi presi il solito succo alla pera.

- Vado a comprarmi le scarpe -, disse papà.

Come sempre Osvaldo borbottava davanti al televisore.

Ormai la mattinata era bell'e che andata. Afferrai la cornetta per chiamare Checco, ma a metà numero riattaccai. Se mi avesse proposto di andare al mare avrei dovuto rifiutare di nuovo. Io e Magghy ci saremmo potuti vedere nel pomeriggio, ma non mi aveva detto di preciso quando. Fortuna che le avevo dato anche il numero del bar, mica potevo non farmi trovare.

Il Paradise, finita la stagione scolastica, sembrava un altro posto. Era la prima volta che lo osservavo così, mezzo vuoto e un po' in disordine. Il mio sguardo si posò sugli oggetti: i bicchieri sulle mensole del retrobanco, i pochi pacchetti di gomme nell'espositore accanto al banco frigo dei panini, conservato bene anche se piuttosto vecchio... Il ventilatore che girava monotono. Ecco, papà aveva fatto un piccolo rifornimento di bibite e gelati. Almeno quello...

Mi misi seduto a uno dei tavolinetti tondi in acciaio della sala, di fronte al bancone. Cinque anni prima, pensando fosse necessario *ammodernare* il bar, papà li aveva comprati abbinandoli a delle sedie di ferro smaltato dal design futuristico, che a me non erano mai piaciute ma che secondo lui invece erano perfette. Sulle pareti, qua e là, aveva poi attaccato stampe di ogni tipo: Coca-Cola, Martini, Sammontana, un paio di foto della «Grosseto di una volta» e, come poteva mancare?, un poster della Lazio ai tempi dello scudetto, proprio accanto al soffietto del laboratorio.

Mi alzai e feci il giro del locale. In fondo al banco, sulla sinistra, c'era un archetto dal quale si accedeva alla saletta interna, dove erano sistemati alcuni tavoli rettangolari muniti di panche, il tutto rigorosamente di formica bianca - papà li aveva comprati usati, però sembravano nuovi. Adesso erano vuoti, ma attorno a loro si erano accalcate frotte di ragazzi bevendo Estathé. Sotto al piccolo lucernaio in fondo alla sala, adiacente alla porta del bagno, il biliardino stazionava silenzioso.

La mattinata passò noiosa, noiosissima. Feci qualche caffè e servii un paio di spume a Osvaldo, che da quando era entrato non la smetteva di imprecare contro il tempo e il governo. - So' tutti *dilinquenti*! Tutti quanti!

Papà tornò all'ora di pranzo. Ai piedi, un paio di scarpe da ginnastica nuove fiammanti, dalle vistose bande rosse. Erano decisamente pacchiane, specie se accostate a pantaloni bordeaux e maglietta bianca a striscine gialle. Mi scappò una risata.

- Papà, ma che ti sei comprato?

Si guardò i piedi, poi di nuovo me, arricciando il naso. - Perché? Mi sono preso le Asisc. Che te ne pare? Guarda. Me le sono messe subito.

- Ma quelle non sono Asics! Ti hanno fregato!

- Come, mi hanno fregato? Le ho pagate cinquantanovemila lire!

- Papà! -, lo sbeffeggiai. - Si chiamano Asics! C-*s*, non *s*-*c*. Hai capito?

- Ma che ne so io! -, reagì un po' indispettito. - Tutti questi nomi strani. Che bisogno c'è de chiamà un paio de scarpe in questa maniera?

Scrollai il capo, pensando a quanto «antico» fosse papà, con quel suo strano modo di abbinare i colori senza dimostrare un minimo di buongusto.

Mi stavo già gustando la libera uscita, quando a un tratto sentii un rombo inconfondibile. Papà mi precedette. - Te l'ho detto che è tornato Vezio?

- Eccolo!

Vezio era uno dei clienti più affezionati del bar. Un tipo sopra le righe: aveva ventinove anni ed era innamorato degli anni '80, «il decennio più bello del mondo», come amava ripetere. La sua divisa era costituita da Levi's 501 strappati, camicia di lino consumata e ai piedi le immancabili Converse. Lavorava come barman stagionale tra alberghi e navi da crociera, e dal momento che abitava da solo, in un appartamento ricavato da un vecchio podere in campagna, vicino Gavorrano, quando tornava passava la maggior parte del suo tempo al Paradise, a chiacchierare e a bere Bellini. Mi sarebbe piaciuto vederla, casa sua, ma con la scusa che stava sempre in giro e non aveva mai tempo di metterla a posto, in tutti quegli anni non mi aveva mai invitato.

A me Vezio piaceva, perché ogni volta mi raccontava delle sue avventure, dei posti dove era stato, delle donne che aveva conosciuto. E poi aveva il ciuffo più figo che avessi mai visto. Gli copriva un occhio, quindi di tanto in tanto lui se lo tirava indietro con una mossa talmente fluida che quasi lo invidiavo. Nemmeno alla tele se ne vedevano di tipi così e io, be', cercavo di imitarlo. Puntualmente, mi regalava una musicassetta con le canzoni di qualche Paese lontano e io la ascoltavo incuriosito, immaginando posti che non avevo mai visto, sapori che non avevo mai gustato.

- Che t'hanno licenziato? -, gli domandai sorridendo.

- Buongiorno, fratellino.

Mi chiamava così da sempre, perché secondo lui avevamo qualcosa in comune. Ripeteva che le anime ribelli si riconoscono a colpo d'occhio: «Siamo della stessa pasta, Massa!». Ne andavo orgoglioso.

Papà gli era affezionato, si vedeva da come se lo coccolava. Gli servì subito un caffè, che lui bevve in un sorso solo. Quindi posò la tazzina sul piattino facendola tintinnare come un campanello.

- Non potevo perdermi questo inizio d'estate maremmana -, proseguì Vezio giocherellando con la collanina hawaiana che portava al collo. - Un giugno così bello non s'era mai visto.

Concordavo in pieno.

Mi raccontò un sacco di aneddoti e, chiaramente, mi disse di tutte le femmine che aveva frequentato. Me lo immaginavo mentre si tirava indietro il ciuffo e faceva battute. In quel momento squillò il telefono.

- È per te -, mi disse papà.

Checco, pensai.

Presi la cornetta: - Ti avrei chiamato -, esordii subito.

- Davvero?

Era Magghy.

- Ah, scusa. Pensavo fosse Checco, il mio amico.

- Avresti preferito lui, per caso? -, domandò un po' risentita.

- Ma no, non scherzare, dai...

- Volevo solo dirti che sto uscendo con mia madre. Puoi venire per cena, saremo noi due da soli. D'accordo?

D'accordo, meglio di così. Aveva fatto tutto lei. Pensai al povero Checco: magari potevo chiamarlo e proporgli di andare a fare un giretto dalle parti del Villaggio Curiel, al cui limitare si estendeva un grande campo di barbabietole altissime.

- Senti un po', fratellino -, fece Vezio aggiustandosi i capelli, - perché non lasciamo qui al Paradise questo vecchietto di Antonio e ce ne andiamo un paio d'ore al mare, soli soletti, io e te? Così mi racconti della scuola e dei tuoi progetti per l'estate.

Guardai papà, papà guardò Vezio, Vezio guardò papà. Sembrava una scena alla Sergio Leone: due cowboy pronti al duello. - Io -, sbottò papà, - prima o poi quel ciuffetto ribelle te lo taijo pe' davero! E andate piano, con quella macchinetta sportiva!

Vezio allungò una mano e io gli battei un cinque, contento di poter trascorrere qualche ora in sua compagnia. Avrei chiamato Checco non appena fossi rientrato. Promesso.

Fuori c'era un caldo infernale, ma ero così emozionato al pensiero del mare e di Magghy che quasi non lo sentivo.

Io e Vezio salimmo sulla sua Opel Kadett 2000 Gsi turbo, decappottabile, con lo stereo Cd a sei altoparlanti, che sparava rimasterizzazioni degli anni '80 e tutte le ultime uscite pop e dance. Vezio si schermò gli occhi dal sole che batteva a picco con la mano, avviò il motore e accese subito lo stereo. Come sempre, aveva le mani rovinate dal brillantante per lavastoviglie del bar, ma stavolta notai anche un vistoso cerotto proprio sul palmo.

- Un cocktail acrobatico riuscito male?

- Colpa dei bordi dei bicchieri troppo taglienti... Ma ora non farmi pensare al lavoro, voglio portarti in un posto dove sicuramente non sei mai stato -, tagliò corto inforcando i suoi amati Ray-Ban alla *Top Gun*.

- E dove?

- Ah, è una sorpresa.

Feci un sospiro, e con un braccio fuori dal finestrino mi lasciai trasportare dal vento. Percorremmo viale della Pace e girammo in via Oberdan. Di fronte alla scuola guida c'era un gruppetto di ragazzi. Per atteggiarmi un po', infilai gli occhiali da sole e cominciai a battere il tempo con la mano sulla fiancata della Kadett. All'imbocco della provinciale, un piccolo gregge di pecore stazionava quasi immobile su un campo recintato a un passo dalla strada. Alla vista della campagna fui preso da un'insolita malinconia. Lì, su due piedi, non me ne spiegai il motivo, o forse sì: era il ricordo della prima estate con Checco, quella del '90, quando con le biciclette ci spingevamo fin lì ad ammirare i girasoli. Lasciai che quell'emozione diventasse la vera protagonista di quel breve viaggio di inizio estate.

Con la coda dell'occhio osservavo Vezio masticare le Vigorsol. mentre lo stereo suonava un Rick Astley davvero lontano nel tempo.

Arrivammo al mare, sulla spiaggia del Parco naturale della Maremma. Vezio tirò fuori dal baule due grandi teli e ci sistemammo tra una duna e l'altra. Era molto affollato, i bagnanti, a giudicare dalla bianchezza della pelle, erano probabilmente turisti del nord Europa. Alcune donne mostravano senza imbarazzo il loro bel seno. Mi soffermai a guardare. Esplorando quel paesaggio, mi accorsi a un tratto di una sfilata di sederi bianchi vicino alla riva. Tutti femminili. Non avevo mai visto niente del genere. Erano belli e sodi, intriganti. Una certa eccitazione s'impadronì di me. Mi sentivo così uomo, o meglio, così *maschio*. Pensai automaticamente a Magghy. Come avrei desiderato baciarla...

- Quante belle signore, vero? -, commentò Vezio.

- Come, scusa?

- Che hai, gli ormoni a mille?

- Macché! -, risposi imbarazzato.

Il mare era uno specchio. Il richiamo dei gabbiani sembrava provenire da un'altra dimensione. Socchiusi gli occhi e assaporai la calma infinita di quel momento.

- Allora la scuola, per quest'anno, è andata? -, mi chiese Vezio dopo qualche minuto. Era abbronzatissimo, e mi domandai come avesse fatto a prendere già tutto quel sole.

- Diciamo. Non è che mi sia impegnato granché, però. Proprio non ce la faccio, non mi piacciono le materie. Giusto scienze, e va be', disegno -, gli risposi sincero.

- Ti manca solo un anno. Ne hai già perso uno, poi.

- Che palle -, dissi abbassando il capo. - Ti ci metti anche tu, ora... A me piace la natura, sentirmi immerso nelle cose *vere*. Tutti quei conti, invece, quelle formule che ti devi ricordare per forza ma non capisci a che servono, io le odio, capito? *Le odio*... È tutto astratto! Chimica, inglese, per non parlare di storia... Che palle!

- Non dire così, fratellino. Non è vero che le cose che studi a scuola sono astratte. Nella vita certe conoscenze ti serviranno. Fidati... Prendiamo inglese. Se vuoi viaggiare, devi conoscerlo. O sbaglio?

- Mmh...

- Per esempio, non ti piacerebbe fare una bella esperienza all'estero, a Londra, magari?

- Ma chi, io? Non ci ho mai pensato...

- Be', e cosa aspetti? Ora sei adulto e puoi, anzi, *devi* decidere della tua vita.

Lo guardai. - Ma sei sicuro, all'estero?

- Altroché! È un'esperienza fondamentale. S'imparano un sacco di cose, sulla vita, sul mondo.

Non avevo mai pensato a questa opportunità. E poi figuriamoci, l'inglese non era proprio il mio forte. - Mah, non saprei... E poi, insomma, a inglese sono davvero uno zero.

Vezio mi rispose con una risata. Con quegli occhiali a specchio e quella collanina al collo sembrava un attore. - E dai, le frasi per sopravvivere le conoscono tutti, no? *Where are you from? I'm from Italy. What time is it?* -. Vezio guardò l'orologio. - *It's two o'clock*. E poi, di cosa ti preoccupi, fratellino? Troverai un sacco di inglesine pronte a darti ripetizioni! -. Era proprio un attore mancato.

Pensai a Magghy. E ne parlai a Vezio.

- Ma è perfetto! -, esclamò. - Partite insieme! In due è più facile. Il mondo è fuori, Massa, ricordatelo!

L'idea cominciava a stuzzicarmi. Non mi ero mai soffermato su ciò che sarebbe successo una volta preso il diploma. Nessuno mi avrebbe costretto ad agire contro la mia volontà, avrei resistito con tutte le mie forze, questo era sicuro.

All'estero... Più ci pensavo, più sentivo che l'idea mi calzava a pennello. Sì, ci sto, mi dissi, ed ero convinto che anche Checco mi avrebbe appoggiato in pieno.

Dovevo festeggiare.

Una volta rientrato al bar, pensai che fosse il caso di chiedere a papà un «contributo» per la mattinata di lavoro. Diecimila lire sarebbero state una paga equa. Avrei portato due pizze e due patatine fritte da Magghy.

Guardai l'orologio. Cavolo, anche stavolta non ce l'avrei fatta a passare da Checco; c'erano così tante cose che avrei voluto dirgli che non potevo concentrarle tutte in mezz'ora. Mi morsi il labbro.

Papà non la pensava come me sul «contributo». - Adesso ce manca solo che me ricatti pure mi' fijo, er regazzino! -, era sbottato in una risata beffarda. A me sembrò una reazione esagerata ma d'altronde, per lui, ero solo un *regazzino*.

Ah! Se solo fossi stato all'estero...!

Cinque

Vezio se n'era appena andato, quando papà tornò sull'argomento. - Perché tu non te ne sei accorto che la scuola calcio è stata trasferita, giusto? -. Mi bucò con lo sguardo.

- Ma adesso che c'entra l'Invicta, papà?

- E certo, che c'entra l'Invicta. Tu stai a pensà a divertitte, che te frega d'a scola calcio.

Ma che voleva dire?

- Insieme alla scuola calcio, se ne so' annati anche tutti gli allievi, i genitori degli allievi e i parenti degli allievi. Capito?

Cominciavo a capire, in quel momento.

- Ma ne apriranno un'altra -, dissi così, tanto per dire. Non mi veniva in mente altro.

- Campa cavallo. Ma l'affitto non aspetta. E non voijo pensà alle scadenze Iva de luglio. Qui semo messi male, capito?

- Che dici, papà?

- Dico, dico. Ne ho parlato pure co' tu' madre. È giusto che lo sappia anche tu, non solo tu' sorella che qui ce lavora. Io sto a cercà de inventamme de tutto, ma... vedemo un po' come andrà a finì, fijo mio -, e s'interruppe, scomparendo nella saletta interna.

Sentii un brivido. Ecco il perché delle trovate che da alcune settimane vedevo circolare al bar: quel cocktail analcolico dagli ingredienti «segreti» e quelle, secondo lui, «squisite» pizze farcite con salame toscano e fettine di banana. Le aveva presentate come la novità della stagione: «Sono meglio del formaggio con le pere, o del melone col prosciutto», aveva detto. Ma i clienti, che già erano pochi, non è che ci andassero pazzi, anzi, alcuni lo avevano pure preso in giro, e io stesso ci avevo scherzato su. Ora almeno capivo il perché di quegli esperimenti, e anche perché Monica, che non era certo tipo da intromettersi nei discorsi altrui, lo aveva difeso in più di un'occasione.

Guardai fuori. La luce del giorno illuminava il campetto proprio dall'altra parte della strada, venando il terreno di striature bianche, mentre due ragazzini in bicicletta passavano veloci, rincorrendosi l'un l'altro.

Me ne andai senza dire altro. Per questa volta Magghy si sarebbe accontentata, mentre il progetto di trasferirmi all'estero stava acquistando sempre maggiore concretezza. Almeno nella mia testa...

Il sole stava scomparendo al di là della ferrovia per lasciare spazio all'umida notte maremmana. Arrivai di fronte al palazzo di Magghy un po' in ansia. Parcheggiai il *Benellindson* e suonai. Nello stesso istante il portone si aprì e ne uscì una ragazza. Era una delle sue amiche. Mi sorrise e si allontanò. Magghy mi aspettava sulla porta e appena mi vide mi stampò un bacio sulla bocca. La casa era immersa in una piacevole e colorata confusione. Si percepiva l'assenza di una figura maschile. I suoi avevano divorziato una volta nata la sorellina di Magghy, che ora aveva dieci anni. In cucina vidi due pacchi di biscotti light aperti sul tavolo e una pila di piatti nel lavello. La camera di Magghy era a dir poco femminile: un mega poster dei Take That campeggiava a tutta parete, mentre una serie sterminata di scarpe col tacco correva lungo il battiscopa.

Mi eccitai, e un leggero velo di sudore mi imperlò la fronte. Con due dita mi scostai la maglietta dalla pancia. Mi sentivo un po' in sovrappeso, e un po' me ne vergognavo. Speravo tanto di piacerle lo stesso.

Una volta terminato il giro delle varie stanze, finimmo sul divano del piccolo salotto. Magghy aveva acceso la Tv, sullo schermo le immagini del videoclip di *Serenata rap*, di Jovanotti.

- Che caldo... -, fece lei a un tratto. Io avevo il cuore a mille, ma che dico, a diecimila.

- Togliti questa -, le proposi aiutandola a sfilarsi la canottierina bianca. Sotto non portava nulla. Le guardai il seno per un attimo, e poi la baciai di nuovo. Un fremito mi salì lungo tutta la schiena.

L'ombra e la luce che si diffondevano contemporaneamente creavano giochi di colori d'oro e d'argento sopra al suo corpo sinuoso. Il suono del televisore arrivava attutito, e sembrava avvolgere gli oggetti intorno, immobili.

Io pensavo a tante cose, ma frullavano così alla svelta che non riuscivo a fissarne nessuna. Mi sentivo come in un sogno, il sogno più incredibile che avessi fatto. I miei occhi erano pieni solo delle forme di Magghy, e nella penombra era bellissima: sembrava una statua in carne e ossa, con le dita affusolate, i capelli come seta, e le sue labbra che si muovevano, e il suo respiro che mi avvolgeva.

- Ma tra poco torna tua madre -, dissi in preda all'agitazione più totale.

- Zitto, e vieni qui... -, fece lei accarezzandomi la testa, infilandomi la mano tra i capelli, nel ciuffo.

Fu così, grazie a quelle ultime due parole, che dentro me affiorò una sensazione piacevolissima, come un lampo che illumina la notte in un attimo indimenticabile.

Con un gesto improvviso, Magghy mi afferrò per i jeans e li tirò a sé, convulsamente. Io ingoiai la saliva tirando in dentro la pancia. Lei aveva indosso solo gli slip. Mentre ci accarezzavamo tutto diventava ancora più bello, elettrizzante, e io avrei voluto spegnere il tempo e stare lì all'infinito.

Eppure, nonostante la distanza minima che ci divideva, mi sembrava ci fosse uno spazio immenso tra noi, che non riuscivo a colmare.

Poi di colpo le sue mani mi sbottonarono i jeans, e un terremoto interiore mi scosse. Tirai ancora più in dentro la pancia; ormai non c'era più scampo. Avrei voluto sentirmi potente come un re, ma invece, stranamente, mi sentivo come uno schiavo, uno schiavo ai suoi ordini...

Attesi un tempo indefinibile prima di staccarmi da quell'ultimo bacio e tirarmi su. Mi avvicinai al portafoglio che avevo poggiato sul televisore. Era strano, ma in quel preciso istante mi sentii come se dentro me abitasse un'altra persona che agiva in totale autonomia. Ma non potevo né riuscivo a tirarmi indietro. Una vampata di vergogna mi assalì quando mi trovai a stringere fra le dita l'involucro rilucente del preservativo, che a ogni minimo movimento produceva un riflesso quasi fastidioso. Nella stanza calò un silenzio di pulsazioni immateriali. Magghy afferrò rapida un angolo del Control e lo strappò, e l'aria fu inondata da un odore intenso di lattice. Ce l'ho ancora nelle narici, quell'odore.

Poi chiusi gli occhi, e lasciai andare tutti i miei sensi...

- Ma io... -, fu tutto ciò che riuscii a dirle.

Magghy afferrò nervosamente la sua canottierina.

- Io... -, sospirai confuso. - Ma perché fai così...

- Lasciami stare, è una cosa da donne... Non puoi capire.

- Ma come non posso capire?

- Sì, non puoi capire, noi donne siamo diverse -, rispose Magghy, - *non lo sapevi?*

Basta un attimo perché un momento splendido si trasformi in una catastrofe.

Magghy, quella sera, si era innervosita a tal punto da sbattermi fuori casa. Mi accompagnò addirittura al portone, che chiuse così forte da far tremare i cardini. Rimasi fermo, immobile, con la punta del naso a sfiorare la vernice rinsecchita. Non capivo, non riuscivo a capire! Cosa avevo sbagliato per subire un'umiliazione simile? Cosa?! Avevo voglia di piangere, piangere e buttare giù quel dannato portone. Un anziano, seduto a frescheggiare su una panchina poco distante, assistette a tutta la scena. Mi sarei letteralmente sotterrato. Ero deluso, deluso da me stesso, deluso da tutto. Non le avevo nemmeno detto del progetto dell'estero, e mi venne anche in mente che non avevo mangiato niente. Be', male non mi avrebbe fatto.

Inforcai il mio caro *Benellindson* e me ne tornai mestamente a casa.

Quella notte non dormii. Ero troppo giù di morale. Avevo sempre pensato che la mia prima volta sarebbe stata fantastica, e invece, che umiliazione... Chissà se anche agli altri era andata così. E Checco? Come sarebbe stata la sua prima volta, ma soprattutto *quando* ci sarebbe stata...?

Sei

La mattina dopo, come ritornato alla solita routine, preparai la mia colazione preferita: una tazzona di latte fumante da accompagnare con fette biscottate e marmellata. Provai a mangiare, ma avevo lo stomaco chiuso. Mamma tentò di cavarmi di bocca una spiegazione ma io le ripetei più volte «niente». Mi vestii e uscii.

Quando arrivai in via Sicilia e passai davanti alla scuola, vidi un furgone con le portiere aperte. Mi fermai incuriosito. Due uomini stavano scaricando dei distributori automatici. Mi avvicinai. Ne contai sei tra macchinette per caffè, bibite e due con quelle buffe spirali per gli snack. Finalmente, pensai, ci ammoderniamo un po'. L'ultimo anno di scuola si preannunciava meno noioso. Magghy poi, che oltre che per le patatine andava matta per la Coca Light, ne sarebbe stata entusiasta.

Entrai al bar. Papà spazzava a testa bassa. Il manico della scopa, stretto tra le sue mani, sembrava un esile ramoscello.

- A scuola mettono i distributori -, dissi. - Come quelli del cinema.

- Il cinema? -, rispose distrattamente.

- I distributori automatici. Come quelli che hanno al cinema Europa.

- Ma di che stai a parlà? -, chiese alzando il capo, gli occhiali calati fin sulla punta del naso. Se li tirò su col dorso della mano.

- Ho detto che a scuola mettono i distributori! Era ora.

Papà si fermò. - I distributori di cosa, scusa?

- Ma di tutto. Caffè, merendine...

- Ma quando?

- E quando. Ora. Stanno scaricando.

Papà mollò la scopa in mezzo alla sala e uscì di corsa.

Tornò dopo cinque minuti, scuro in volto. Passò nel retrobanco e afferrò il telefono. Parlò con due persone diverse prima che gli passassero quella giusta. Si innervosì ancora di più. Era tutto rosso. - Mi sta dicendo che la scuola non rinnoverà il contratto?

Silenzio.

- Ma insomma, non ci sono mai stati problemi! So' due anni che non alzo de cento lire il prezzo de un panino. E debbo venire a sapere da mi' fijo che la scuola installerà dei maledetti distributori automatici con i panini de gomma! Robba da pazzi! -. Dopodiché ebbe uno scatto d'ira e sbatté con violenza la cornetta. - Maledizione!

Fece un profondo respiro, poi mi disse, con apparente calma: - Capito? Da settembre non porterò più le merende a scola. E tu sei pure contento. *I moderni distributori automatici* -, mi fece il verso.

Io mi sentii piccolo piccolo. Che stupido ero stato a non pensarci prima.

Provavo un senso di pena pensando a papà, e da quel giorno il mio istinto di ribellione e di rifiuto nei confronti del *sistema* aumentò di almeno due tacche.

Mi sentivo ingabbiato, stretto in una morsa insopportabile. Avevo bisogno di sfogarmi, trovare delle *risposte*, e c'era solo una persona con cui avrei potuto farlo.

Quando dall'altro capo del filo arrivò la sua voce, dentro di me scattò come un meccanismo automatico, e i miei occhi si riempirono di lacrime.

- Checco, ti devo parlare.

Lui, per tutta risposta, emise una specie di urlo. Era contento, proprio come me. - Allora oggi -, disse, - per festeggiare, cocomeri!

Ci demmo appuntamento dopo pranzo, alla fine della strada sterrata sulla provinciale della Trappola, verso l'argine del fiume.

Arrivai un po' in anticipo per riordinare le idee.

Allora, pensavo che aspettare fosse sempre meglio che essere atteso. Oggi penso l'esatto contrario. Quando c'è qualcuno che ti aspetta, di certo non si dimenticherà mai di te...

Faceva un gran caldo. Il sole incandescente sopra la mia testa. Tutt'intorno, cicale e altre piccole creature dell'estate se la spassavano tra la vegetazione. Davanti a me, dolci e basse colline coltivate a vite e olivi disegnavano i confini di quel piccolo mondo.

Quell'estate non era solo l'ultima della mia adolescenza, era davvero diversa. Ecco qual era la verità. Non avevo né carta né penna ma una gran voglia di fermare quel momento, di fare un ritratto di me che andasse oltre il mio corpo. Ma sarebbe stato impossibile disegnare i movimenti della mia anima, così decisi di chiudere gli occhi e lasciarmi trasportare dai suoni della natura e dal battito incessante della mia malinconia.

Malinconia. Di cosa? Ancora non lo so...

Avevo fatto l'amore per la prima volta, e anche se era andata com'era andata non avrei mai più dovuto ammettere che ero vergine. Un bel cambiamento, cacchio. Magghy, come dire, speravo di poterla riconquistare, o meglio, di poterla *conquistare*, considerato che fino a quel momento aveva praticamente fatto tutto lei. Vezio mi aveva detto che ero stato fortunato, che ragazze così non se ne trovavano, ma sotto sotto mi sentivo un po' un perdente, per come me l'ero immaginata dovevo essere io a fare il primo passo. Avevo voglia di confidarmi con Checco, ma chissà su quest'argomento come avrebbe reagito. Comunque, c'era anche la situazione di papà a darmi da pensare. Una cosa sola mi era chiara: non volevo seguire le sue orme. Non avrei fatto la sua fine, no e poi no!

A un tratto, sentii lo Zip in lontananza. Riaprii gli occhi uscendo dal torpore interiore. Dall'ultima curva sbucò ondeggiando il familiare casco giallo fosforescente. Checco parcheggiò sul ciglio della strada e mi venne incontro. Portava delle Adidas che non gli avevo mai visto, dai decori talmente strani che faticai a capirne la marca. Con quei riccioli biondi e quella maglietta verde acido un po' aderente sulla ciccia della pancia, poi, non passava di certo inosservato. Era così disinvolto che sembrava davvero mezzo matto, camminava quasi saltellando. Era buffissimo. Si accorse che gli stavo guardando le scarpe.

- Sono da tennis -, precisò. - Se mi allenassi come Jimmy Courier diventerei imbattibile, lo so.

- E allora perché non lo fai?

- Perché io in fondo non sono un tennista, mi sento filosofo! Un filosofo del tennis, magari! Massa, nella vita bisogna *concepire* quello che si vuole, e io ho concepito che i libri mi amano! Figurati, sono appena ai presocratici, hai voglia quanto mi manca!

- Ai preso*che*? -. Sì, forse era matto.

- Beata ignoranza! Santa inettitudine! -, esclamò alzando la testa al cielo.

Non sapevo bene da dove iniziare, ma fu lui a bloccarmi. Ebbe uno scatto, si avvicinò una mano alla bocca: - Schhh... Il momento è topico. Laggiù c'è il campo. Bisogna fare attenzione, però, e strisciare quasi rasoterra per non farsi beccare, vedi la vegetazione com'è bassa? Il cocomero, *Citrullus lanatus*, è una pianta dal fusto sdraiato, e poi bisogna stare attenti alle tagliole.

- Le tagliole? -, domandai.

- Sì, le tagliole. Ma parla a bassa voce. Il contadino cerca di aggirare il naturale processo di decadimento sensoriale del suo organismo con queste trovate bastarde. A uno che conosco, una canaglia di quelle serie, l'anno scorso uno di quegli arnesi ha mozzato un dito del piede, addirittura. Dall'analisi della ferita, secondo il mio modesto punto di vista, poteva trattarsi di una grossa tagliola per la selvaggina tipo lepri o *coniglioli* selvatici.

- Ma dici davvero? -, chiesi sconcertato.

- Davvero sì, te l'ho detto, al giorno d'oggi succede un po' di tutto. Bisogna stare all'erta.

- Porca miseria! -, esclamai con una nota di tensione nella voce. - Ma siamo sicuri di quello che stiamo facendo?

- Stai rilassato, amico.

Ci avviammo lungo quella strada di campagna. Due profonde scie di pneumatico ne segnavano il percorso come un binario storto. Nei passanti dei pantaloni, Checco aveva fissato un astuccio con un coltellino e da una tasca vedevo spuntare delle forbici.

- Amata tranquillità -, dissi.

- Guarda -. Checco mi indicò in lontananza la vetta del Monte Amiata che si stagliava scura e limpida nel cielo mattutino.

- Ci pensi -, continuò lui, - a quando era un vulcano?

- Tipo un milione e mezzo di anni fa.

- Chissà che razza di uomini poteva abitare un territorio del genere. Sul manuale di paleontologia umana non ho trovato molte indicazioni. Sicuramente c'erano già le paludi. Ma chissà le zanzare?

- Mah... chi lo sa.

Continuammo a camminare e, dopo una piccola curva, ci imbattemmo in un appezzamento di girasoli. Le piante erano quasi più alte di noi. Due trattori e alcune vecchie automobili erano parcheggiati davanti a un annesso agricolo. Checco sospirò.

- Ho fatto l'amore, ieri -, dissi tutto d'un fiato.

Checco si fermò. Spalancò gli occhi. - Cooosa? E me lo dici così?

- E come te lo devo dire?

- Caspita... Be', come dire, congratulazioni.

Ma io non ero contento. Proprio no. E poi quella sua reazione distaccata mi fece sentire ancora peggio. Alla fine gli confessai tutto.

- Allora sei umano anche tu! -, fu la sua risposta, che non mi aspettavo. - Ma sai, caro Massa, sono cose che capitano...

Cose che capitano? Aveva detto proprio così? Non era certo da Checco.

- Checco! Ma come, cose che capitano?

- Perché ora ti scaldi?

- Ma perché sì, scusa. Che risposta è «sono cose che capitano»? La mia prima volta è andata una merda e te, il mio migliore amico, sai dirmi solo questo?!

- Ma Massa, è la verità. Sono-cose-che-capitano.

- No! Non a me! -, gridai dando un calcio al vento.

Era la prima volta che reagivo così davanti a lui, ma non riuscii proprio a trattenermi. Ero oppresso da una forza invincibile. Il cuore mi cavalcava nel petto. Una tristezza che non avevo mai provato s'impadronì di me. Mi sentivo inutile, mi sentivo sbagliato.

Checco aveva abbassato la testa senza dire niente. Strappò un lungo filo d'erba dal ciglio del viottolo e se lo mise in bocca. Poi sputò a terra un paio di volte. Dopo cinque minuti riprese: - Almeno tu, Massa, almeno tu l'hai fatto...

In quel preciso istante, capii tante di quelle cose che ci vorrebbe un'ora a elencarle tutte. Mi sentii uno stupido. Ecco perché aveva reagito così alla mia confidenza, allora era questo il problema.

- Checco, ma che dici? -. Mi si strinse il cuore.

Fu così che alla fine mi ritrovai io, a consolarlo. Decise di fare il giro largo, per avere ancora qualche minuto di tempo per parlare. Mi disse che per lui la cosa più importante era trovare la persona autentica, ma non poteva cercarla, il problema era tutto lì. Io gli chiesi cosa intendesse, e lui mi spiegò: - C'è già un filo che ci lega, lei a me e me a lei, ma solo quando questo filo sarà teso potremo vederci. Certo, può darsi che io ne conosca anche altre, di ragazze, ma spero di non cadere nella loro trappola con tutte le scarpe! -, concluse sorridendo. - Quella giusta, comunque, prima o poi arriverà, a me non importa quanto ancora dovrò aspettare. D'altronde, la cometa di Halley passa una volta sola, nella vita. No?

Rimanemmo in silenzio. Riflettei su quelle parole. Checco era davvero speciale.

Una volta assorbita l'emozione, gli raccontai di papà.

- Il bar è in crisi.

- Il bar? Ma che dici?!

- Purtroppo sì. C'è crisi, te l'ho detto.

- Crisi... che parola infame, sembra senza fine -. Checco si mise a riflettere. - In fondo, tutte le società vivono dei cicli di avanzamento e di regressione, anzi, di sviluppo e di imbarbarimento, e ora, be', siamo nella curva discendente della parabola. Il decadentismo non è affatto finito.

Io non lo sapevo che cos'era questo decadentismo, o forse non me lo ricordavo, ma ero d'accordo con lui. Cacchio, il lavoro era sempre più difficile da trovare, la benzina, per esempio, in pochi anni era aumentata del 40%. Ma dov'era il futuro? Forse Vezio aveva davvero ragione. Il mondo è fuori. All'estero.

Poi Checco, dopo aver tenuto per un bel po' il muso lungo, fece finalmente un largo sorriso. - Ho la soluzione.

- Che soluzione?

- Per il bar.

- Cioè?

- Mmh... Non fare domande. Segui il mio consiglio: domani vai al Paradise e cerca di far sloggiare Antonio almeno per un'oretta. E vedrai che con l'aiuto del tuo Checco...

Non riuscii a scucirgli altro.

Alla fine, arrivammo all'entrata di un vecchio podere. La strada terminava lì. Si aprì una finestra al primo piano e una vecchia signora piuttosto in carne si affacciò sbattendo fuori quello che sembrava essere uno scendiletto. Il sole le picchiava dritto sul viso, e quando alzò lo sguardo verso di noi si schermò gli occhi con una mano. Poi rientrò nell'oscurità.

- Ma i cocomeri? -, chiesi a un tratto.

Checco si fermò. - Dannazione, non ci pensavo più. Li abbiamo superati. Forza, torniamo indietro.

Ora il sole risplendeva davanti ai nostri occhi. Checco guardò l'ora: - Mancano venti minuti a mezzogiorno. Meglio così, il contadino ora torna a casa per pranzo.

Arrivati al campo, il mio amico prese le forbici e sfilò il coltello dall'astuccio. Aguzzò la vista. - Non ci sono problemi, e stai un po' rilassato, amico.

- Come si fa a entrare nel campo? -, chiesi un po' nervoso.

- E come pensi di fare? Ci entri e via, con le gambine -, rispose.

Gli sembrava facile, a lui. - Ma se ci beccano?

- E se ci beccano e se ci beccano! -, ripeté Checco. - Ma secondo te il ladro può permettersi pensieri come questi? È normale che se ci beccano siamo fottuti, ma la vera impresa del ladro non è tanto quella di rubare, quanto quella di farlo senza che nessuno se ne accorga. Lo dice anche Sherlock Holmes. Capito?

Se lo diceva lui... - Dai, su, andiamo... -, mi convinsi.

Checco si bloccò un attimo e si girò verso di me: - Grazie, Massa. Per prima. Mi dispiace di aver monopolizzato l'argomento, alla fine...

Gli diedi uno scappellotto amichevole e ci inoltrammo nel campo. Era leggermente in discesa, con una serie di file di cocomeri verdognoli sdraiati sulla terra. In effetti, non c'era molta vegetazione per nascondersi, anzi, non ce n'era affatto. Checco si fermò da una parte accovacciandosi e io gli arrivai proprio dietro le spalle. Si mise a trafficare con i suoi arnesi.

Infine si sentì un colpetto secco. - Tiè! Guarda, bello -, disse voltandosi con un cocomero di circa tre chili.

- Grande, Checco, è bello davvero...

Ammirammo per qualche secondo il cocomero, poi udimmo un rimbombo spaventoso. Una specie di esplosione sopra alle nostre teste. Sussultai improvvisamente, Checco per reazione strinse il cocomero tra le braccia e si voltò con un salto.

- Ma che cazzo è stato? Checco!

Lui scrutò un secondo dalla parte della vecchia casa, poi mi guardò. - Il contadinooo!

In un batter d'occhio eravamo già sulla strada e correvamo a gambe levate. In lontananza il contadino, a tracolla un fucile caricato a salve.

- Ma non avevi detto che non ci vedeva!? -, gridai respirando veloce come un cane.

- Caspiterinaaa! L'imprevisto! C'è sempre un imprevistooo! -. Un secondo rimbombo si propagò nell'aria. - Corri, Massa, corri! Quello ci sparaaa! Quello ci buca il culooo!

Sette

Papà aveva approfittato subito della mia insolita disponibilità, e ora ero dietro al bancone del bar con penna e foglio millimetrato a buttare giù il disegno del nuovo Paradise. Checco, armato di cartellina, metro estensibile e matitona da falegname, faceva da direttore dei lavori. Per l'occasione, si era messo anche un cappellino con la scritta «Caterpillar». Me l'aveva fatto notare subito, appena entrato.

Era proprio mezzo matto. Eppure, dimostrava così tanta sicurezza che alla fine il matto quasi quasi sembravo io. Io, che non mi ero mai impegnato più di tanto e facevo solo lo stretto necessario. Io, che perdevo ore a disegnare paesaggi immaginari e provavo il *moonwalk* di Michael almeno due volte al giorno, non riuscivo a sfogliare più di tre pagine consecutive di un libro, specie quelli di scuola. Mamma e papà a volte mi rimproveravano, ma la mia fortuna era che in fondo non avevo mai dato loro grane. Checco, invece, un papà non ce l'aveva mai avuto, e da quando l'anno prima che ci conoscessimo un brutto male gli aveva portato via anche la mamma, era rimasto solo con la nonna, che ora era anziana e lui accudiva con assoluta dedizione. Era questo a renderlo speciale ai miei occhi: dietro a quella sua apparente stravaganza e a quella sua aria svagata, nascondeva un cuore grande così.

Diceva che nella sfortuna era stato comunque fortunato, perché grazie a sua mamma, che era notaio, si era ritrovato una casa grande e un bel gruzzolo in banca. «Pensa a chi non ha nemmeno da mangiare», mi diceva.

E aveva ragione, santo cielo.

Secondo il progetto preliminare da lui stilato, buttando giù una parete e cambiando la disposizione dei tavoli, il Paradise sarebbe diventato la paninoteca più figa della città. Sì, a Magghy sarebbe piaciuto moltissimo.

Checco lavorò tutta la mattina tra ipotesi e calcoli. Quando risbucò dalla saletta interna era completamente sudato, gli occhiali gli erano scivolati sulla punta del naso e i riccioli gli si erano increspati, inumiditi dalla fatica. Mi mostrò i suoi appunti, zeppi di numeri e punti esclamativi.

- Non ci capisco niente -, dissi.

- Uff, Massa, sei sempre il solito. E io e Antonio che ci illudiamo che tu possa diventare commercialista! Usa un po' il cervello, no? Questa è trigonometria! Trigonometria filosofica. È una disciplina che ho elaborato io medesimo. Non abbiamo tempo di stare qui a dilungarci, ma è molto semplice. In ogni calcolo, devi sempre tener conto di due variabili: le triangolazioni e la speculazione filosofica. La prima non ammette errori, per questo è perfetta; la seconda è infinita, perciò libera di scegliere. Il sistema si può applicare a qualsiasi cosa, anche al tennis, e infatti ne ho spedito un sunto fino in America a Jimmy Courier, per aumentare ancora la potenza del suo servizio, e pure ad Andre Agassi per il rovescio a due mani.

- Ah... E ti hanno risposto?

- Ancora no, ma confido entro l'anno. La dovranno sperimentare prima, no?

Annuii.

- Tanto è inutile parlare con te di argomenti seri. Il fatto è che, organizzando così il Paradise -, e mi indicò sulla carta dei geroglifici incomprensibili, - mettendo in conto le variabili della teoria del caos, e figuriamoci se sto qui a elencartele, i miei computi sono illuminanti. Se entriamo in una cooperativa di consumo, il gioco è fatto. Ho già fatto una simulazione con le tabelle di Fra' Pacioli.

- Fra' che?

- Pacioli. Pi-a-ci-i-o-elle-i. Mai sentito parlare di «partita doppia»?

- Ah, sì, certo.

- Allora saprai che se l'azienda risparmia sull'acquisto dei beni, è scontato che i ricavi saranno maggiori. Dico bene?

- Benissimo.

- Secondo altre operazioni statistiche, densità della popolazione, attività concorrenti eccetera, ho calcolato che potremmo avere un afflusso di quarantuno virgola due persone a sera. E sto parlando solo della paninoteca, escluso il servizio bar!

- Virgola due, giusto?

- Esatto. È un dato *statistico*. A scuola dovresti averle studiate anche tu, certe cose... Ma lasciamo perdere. Se invece vuoi sapere quanti caffè sfornerai -, disse sfogliando il suo blocchetto arancio ANAS, - dovrebbero essere circa...

- Okay, okay! Basta, ti prego! -, esclamai. - Ho capito benissimo.

Checco si asciugò il sudore dalla fronte con aria soddisfatta.

Paninoteca Paradise. L'idea non mi dispiaceva. Se il progetto fosse andato in porto, però, addio viaggio all'estero.

- E le tasse? -, chiesi a Checco.

Lui cominciò a rovistare nervosamente tra le sue scartoffie, che alla fine gli caddero di mano sparpagliandosi ovunque.

- Oh, no! -, esclamò. Si buttò per terra a raccoglierle. - L'esperienza insegna -, proseguì, - che in questo caso c'è bisogno di un buon commercialista.

Sarà. Il solo pensiero di rendermi economicamente libero, comunque, mi faceva sentire leggero. A una condizione, però. Papà e Monica non avrebbero messo piede nel *mio* locale.

Chissà, sarei anche potuto diventare famoso. E se poi gli affari fossero andati davvero bene magari sarei riuscito pure a comprarmi una Ferrari.

- Mi è venuta un'idea -, dissi all'improvviso. - Potremmo assumere Vezio come barman del locale!

Checco, però, non sembrava molto convinto.

- Perché no?

- Ma perché lui è un... *professionista*, guadagnerà almeno due milioni al mese. Non ce lo possiamo permettere.

Non aveva tutti i torti.

Il pomeriggio, quando con l'andatura che lo contraddistingueva Vezio arrivò al bar, avevo appena smesso di litigare con Monica. In un eccesso insolito di fratellanza, perché io e lei non andavamo affatto d'accordo, avevo buttato là il discorso su un'ipotetica ristrutturazione completa del Paradise. Lei, senza darmi troppe spiegazioni, disse e ripeté che le sembrava irrealizzabile, che era troppo complicato e non avevo la minima idea di quanti problemi avrei dovuto affrontare. Sarebbe stato un inutile spreco di energie, tanto più che ero un tipo inaffidabile! Io allora le avevo dato della stronza. Vezio entrò sistemandosi il ciuffo con un colpetto di testa, poi allargò il sorriso masticando incessantemente le solite Vigorsol. I Ray-Ban erano ormai entrati in simbiosi con la sua faccia. Attaccò a leggere la «Gazzetta».

- Un Bellini a regola d'arte, grazie. Con un goccetto di gin, magari... -, disse rivolgendosi a Monica, che ora stava silenziosa dietro al banco. Quindi si alzò dallo sgabellino, prese bicchiere, succo alla pesca, spumante, e per ultimo la bottiglia di gin dal mensolone sospeso sopra al banco.

Mi faceva proprio incavolare, quella. Eravamo davvero agli antipodi. Non aveva amici ed era già vecchia dentro, sempre casa, lavoro, lavoro, casa. Quando parlava con papà aveva in bocca il bar come un disco rotto, «ordinare quello», «pagare quell'altro», e basta. Lei, chiaramente, non la rimproveravano mai. E poi si vestiva continuamente di nero e a me il nero dava un senso di cimitero, sempre con quel muso lungo come se tutti ce l'avessero perennemente con lei. Per provocarla le dicevo che se avesse continuato così, alla fine quel musone le sarebbe arrivato ai piedi. E poi, solo perché aveva quattro anni più di me spesso si sentiva in diritto di comandarmi: «Mamma ha detto che devi fare questo, papà mi ha detto di farti fare quest'altro», e io purtroppo, almeno finché non mi fossi reso indipendente, dovevo darle retta, almeno qualche volta. Soffriva di asma e ogni tanto tirava fuori l'inalatore e se lo spruzzava in bocca. Per infierire, le dicevo che aveva l'asma perché era stitica di parole, che se avesse allenato un po' di più la voce le sarebbe andata via. Ma io sapevo che già lo faceva. A casa, mi era capitato un paio di volte rientrando di sentirla cantare Madonna in camera sua. Si capiva che le piaceva da morire, ma non l'avrebbe mai ammesso con nessuno.

Però era bella, e aveva gli occhi verdi, come me. Dicevano che eravamo l'uno la fotocopia dell'altra, e a me un po' faceva piacere, perché era la prova tangibile che io non facevo schifo...

Monica servì da bere a Vezio e gli diede un buffetto sulla testa. Ci avrebbero potuto scambiare benissimo per tre fratelli.

Otto

Due giorni dopo, ero di nuovo solo al bar. Ero nervoso, cavolo, mi avevano mollato lì un'altra volta! Provai a telefonare a Magghy. Mi rispose sua madre. Paralizzato dall'imbarazzo, non mi uscì nemmeno una parola e riattaccai. Il suo tono di voce così squillante e perentorio aveva smontato il mio - già incerto - tentativo di rappacificazione con Magghy. Poi, a un tratto, me la vidi sbucare davanti alla porta del bar, lo sguardo tagliente.

- Sei proprio uno stronzo -, esordì.

L'unico cliente, un signore che stava consumando un caffè al banco, si girò di scatto. Io diventai rosso come il mio *Benellindson*.

- Io? -, fu l'unica risposta che mi venne in mente da dire.

- «Io» un corno! Ti sembra un bel modo di comportarti? Andare via così, senza dire niente?

- Ma... veramente -, farfugliai. - Ti ho telefonato giusto due minuti fa ma non c'eri.

- Bugiardo, bugiardo e ancora bugiardo. Oltre che stronzo.

Detto questo, girò i tacchi e sparì.

- Bel tipino, eh? -, osservò il signore all'ultimo sorso di caffè.

Io feci un mezzo sorriso tra i denti e le corsi dietro nel tentativo di chiarire l'equivoco. Non ebbi il tempo di superare la soglia che mi sentii afferrare un braccio, e una lingua affondare nella mia bocca. Magghy!

Il cuore mi saltava su e giù come un puledro impazzito.

- Pensavi davvero di poterti liberare così presto di me? -, disse languida.

Oh, no...

Magghy aveva la straordinaria capacità di farmi fare tutto quello che voleva. Era così bella, così passionale, così... insomma, io mi sentivo innamorato. *Ero* innamorato. Mi teneva in pugno.

Avevo davvero gli ormoni a mille. Mi serviva aiuto. Chiamai Vezio, che si precipitò.

Mi aveva già raccontato certe storie di famose ballerine brasiliane dal culo a mandolino, che facevano l'amore in modo divino. E poi le francesi: «Ah, le *fvancesi...*», diceva. Lui le donne le conosceva, era proprio la persona giusta a cui chiedere consigli per non collezionare altre brutte figure.

Col bicchiere in mano, Vezio espresse ottimi apprezzamenti in favore di Magghy, arrivando addirittura a considerare «una manna del cielo» la sua notevole intraprendenza e decisione. - Fossero tutte così, le donne! -, disse. - Per noi maschietti il mondo sarebbe un grande balocco.

Nemmeno io ero arrivato a pensare a tanto.

Comunque, a quel punto mi propinò una sfilza di consigli così chilometrica che avrei dovuto annotarli per non fare confusione.

- Secondo me -, concluse, - la cosa più intelligente che puoi fare resta una bella esperienza all'estero. Magari potreste fare i ragazzi alla pari.

- Cioè? -, chiesi con un certo imbarazzo. - Dobbiamo pagare il viaggio in... natura?

Vezio si fece una bella risata e si spostò il ciuffo con la mano. - Ma che ti viene in mente, fratellino! I ragazzi alla pari! Voi e dei vostri coetanei stranieri vi scambiate la casa. Tu e Magghy andate a stare dalle loro famiglie e loro vengono dalle vostre.

- Mmh... Un'altra famiglia? No, grazie. Non fa per me.

- Va be' -, fece Vezio, - mettila come vuoi, ma vacci, all'estero. Potreste andare a raccogliere fragole in Inghilterra. Libertà, Massa, nuove esperienze e libertà. Ah! Se solo potessi tornare indietro!

Quella dei campi di fragole in Inghilterra non la sapevo, ma il pensiero era emozionante. Mi immaginai là in mezzo, con le nuvole sopra la mia testa a solcare il cielo basso del Nord. Una scogliera altissima battuta dal vento, il mare che si infrangeva contro la roccia. Avrei potuto imparare bene l'inglese, frequentare una scuola di disegno e magari, chissà, qualcuno mi avrebbe preso veramente sul serio!

Forse Vezio aveva proprio ragione. È la libertà il bene più prezioso. La nuova attività con Checco, gli orari di lavoro, la gestione commerciale, le scadenze... E poi gli scontrini da conservare per dieci anni, e la bestia nera di papà, l'Iva... Erano solo altre catene e una volta che ti avevano stretto... In due parole, accantonai il progetto della paninoteca e immaginai il mio futuro lontano da via Sicilia, dai miei, da tutto quello che avevo conosciuto fino a quel momento. Per prima cosa, mi consigliò ancora Vezio, poiché il mondo era grande, dovevo sbrigarmi a prendere la patente.

La patente. Diavolo, è vero. Avevo diciotto anni e ancora non ci avevo pensato. Fu come un'illuminazione. Da questa nuova prospettiva, il Benelli mi apparve ormai come un vecchio compagno di giochi da salutare.

Non persi tempo e appena rientrò papà glielo comunicai.

- A una condizione -, precisò lui riguardo la scuola guida, - non farmi sganciare soldi.

Che palle, pensai.

- Soldi, soldi, qui vogliono tutti soldi! -, dichiarò Osvaldo varcando la soglia del bar.

Fu allora che mi ricordai di avere un libretto di risparmio alle poste. - Ho i risparmi alle poste, no? Utilizzerò quelli.

Fortuna che per la cresima i nonni mi avevano regalato quel libretto. Non l'avevo mai usato. Tornai a casa e chiesi a mamma di farmelo vedere. Capitale: cinquecentosettantamila lire. Alla grande. Però mi accorsi anche che negli ultimi sei mesi qualcuno aveva prelevato, prima centoquarantamila, poi altre duecento. Sarà stato papà, pensai. Ma non avevo voglia di farmi altre domande.

Montai sul Benelli e mi precipitai alla scuola guida in via Oberdan. Papà mi aveva già fatto guidare qualche volta nelle stradine deserte, e poi mi sentivo portato, al contrario di Checco... Mi sarebbero bastate pochissime lezioni. Caro *Benellindson*, presto per te arriverà la pensione, dicevo tra me e me.

Nove

Le due settimane successive erano trascorse tra Magghy e le lezioni di guida, oltre ai soliti brontolamenti in famiglia.

La madre di Magghy usciva quasi ogni sera e una volta che la sorellina si era addormentata, entravo in scena io.

Dopo l'umiliazione della prima volta, adesso le cose andavano decisamente meglio. Dal momento che la mia attenzione era rivolta esclusivamente a Magghy, Vezio mi aveva raccomandato di concentrarmi anzitutto sui *segnali* che mandava il suo corpo: fremiti del bacino, delle spalle, compresi gemiti dalle particolari melodie... e poi mi aveva detto che durante il rapporto dovevo «pensare a tutt'altro»: una scena di un film d'azione con Rambo, un cavallo selvaggio che corre nella prateria... Insomma, non era mica un'interrogazione. All'inizio mi sembrò assurdo: - Ma come faccio a pensare a Rambo con il mitra in mano mentre...? -, avevo obiettato, e anche un po' schifato, ma alla fine la tattica risultò vincente.

Domenica tre luglio, a metà mattinata, eravamo nudi sul letto di Magghy, esausti, con gli occhi chiusi. Da fuori ci arrivava una leggera brezza che ci accarezzava la pelle, e io mi sentivo un concentrato di emozioni: le mani mi tremavano e il cuore batteva all'impazzata, il fiato sospeso. Era la prima volta che provavo un *vero* orgasmo. Avevo sentito una parte di me andare oltre, fuori da me stesso. Forse era la mia anima. Ero riuscito a sentire il suo corpo, in ogni suo movimento, in ogni impercettibile contrazione, e i suoi respiri erano diventati i miei, e miei i suoi sussulti. Mi ero dimenticato di ogni paura, di ogni giudizio. Avevamo fatto l'amore, quello vero, quello che fanno i grandi. Magghy sembrava appagata e finalmente serena, distesa accanto a me in tutta la sua femminilità. Il seno sodo si muoveva su e giù seguendo il suo respiro, mentre le mani mi accarezzavano dolcemente. Anch'io mi sentivo tranquillo e con la mente sgombra da ogni dubbio.

Rimanemmo così almeno venti minuti, finché non ritornai sulla Terra e l'anima, che sa da sola come orientarsi, decise di ricongiungersi al mio corpo.

Oggi, dopo così tanti anni, posso dire che tutto quello non era davvero il paradiso, era semplicemente *vivere*, spegnere la mente ed *esserci*. Sono sicuro che, quel giorno, le nostre anime hanno percorso la stessa strada, mano nella mano. Così, da quel momento in poi, iniziammo ad avere fame di noi e dei nostri corpi uniti, l'uno nell'altra. Non importava né dove né come, né che ora fosse. Era bello sentire il sangue infuocarsi, prendersi e lasciarsi andare, senza limiti, senza paura. Da quel giorno Magghy iniziò a chiamarmi «amore».

Di tutto il resto, non me ne importava un fico secco.

Al tramonto, montai sul *Benellindson* e partii. Ero esaltato.

Il vento sulla faccia mi asciugava le ultime gocce di sudore, mentre la maglietta svolazzava facendomi il solletico sulla schiena. Viaggiavo spensierato, passando per le vie che mi piacevano di più. Improvvisamente, mi resi conto di essere finito in mezzo al giallo intenso di un campo di girasoli. Mi girai e vidi l'albero.

L'istinto mi aveva portato al Grande Cipresso. Pensai a Checco, e mi accorsi che erano giorni che non lo chiamavo, me ne ero completamente *dimenticato*. Per un attimo rividi come in un film tutta la storia della nostra amicizia, e mi sentii come se fosse finito un capitolo, come se un cerchio si fosse chiuso.

Qualche anno prima, proprio in quel posto, ci eravamo promessi che niente e nessuno ci avrebbero mai diviso. Adesso, io ero appena diventato *uomo* e lui, il mio migliore amico, nemmeno lo sapeva... Mi sentivo in colpa. Il giallo dei girasoli iniziò a infastidirmi. Feci inversione e me ne andai.

Dieci

La mattina successiva, mentre stavo bevendo il mio latte fumante, mi accorsi di un biglietto sul tavolo. La scrittura era quella di mamma.

Sono fuori con Monica, non torniamo per pranzo. Dài da mangiare a Mila e quando esci chiudi con due giri di chiave.
P.S.: ieri sera ha chiamato Checco, ha detto di sbrigarti ad andare da lui che ti deve dire non so che cosa di un qualche teorema.
TVB Chicco,

Mamma

TVB... Mamma me lo scriveva sempre. Per la verità, me lo diceva, anche. Me l'aveva sempre detto. Io, invece, per certe smancerie non ero affatto portato, e lei me lo rimproverava ogni volta: «Quanto sei scorbutico», mi diceva. Al contrario, Monica, che con gli altri teneva quel musone, con mamma era sempre affettuosa, sempre piena di piccole attenzioni. Me ne ero chiesto il motivo. Forse tra donne si capivano di più, chi può saperlo. Era anche vero che mamma, comunque, non aveva amiche. Forse era per questo che stavano sempre insieme, loro due. A volte ci pensavo, al fatto che mamma non facesse niente, a parte starsene a casa e fare la spesa.

Mi venne in mente che qualche settimana prima, stendendo i panni sul terrazzo, l'avevo sentita confessare a Mila che si sentiva stanca. Forse, pensai, voleva dire che si annoiava. Cavolo, perché non si rimetteva a dipingere? Erano almeno due anni che non prendeva più un pennello in mano, e mi dispiaceva; avrei voluto di nuovo condividere quel momento, osservarla e carpire qualche altro suo segreto, come quando ero piccolo e mi sedevo sul pavimento, nello sgabuzzino di Albinia. Mila entrò in cucina miagolando pigramente, per poi nascondersi sotto una sedia.

Ma ora c'era Checco. A quanto pareva lui non si era dimenticato di me. Dovevo fare qualcosa.

Il progetto della paninoteca continuava a non convincermi fino in fondo, ma insomma, se con Magghy le cose avessero continuato ad andare così, un lavoretto poteva sempre tornarci utile.

Chiamai il mio amico, che mi diede appuntamento proprio lì, al Grande Cipresso.

Secondo lui in quel punto, sottoterra, passavano dei flussi di energia particolarmente intensi, forse gli stessi che avevano attirato pure me il giorno prima. Il mio amico ci andava spesso anche a studiare e insisteva perché lo seguissi, ma io, chissà perché, trovavo sempre una scusa per evitarlo...

Checco arrivò vestito in modo così bizzarro che mi scappò un po' da ridere. Si tolse il casco e il cespuglio di riccioli biondi esplose come fanno i pupazzi dalle scatole. Sembrava Doc, lo scienziato pazzo di *Ritorno al futuro*.

- Ci siamo, Massa, ci siamo! La CEE offre dei finanziamenti a fondo perduto per i giovani imprenditori -. Era su di giri.

Mi disse che l'aveva scoperto sfogliando la «Gazzetta Ufficiale» in biblioteca, e mi spiegò le modalità di presentazione della domanda per il bando nei minimi dettagli. Mi sembrava incredibile che fosse riuscito a raccogliere tutte quelle informazioni.

- Te l'ho detto, è fatta!

A me, tutti quei documenti da preparare e tutte quelle carte bollate facevano venire l'orticaria, e in fondo in fondo mi mettevano ansia. Checco, invece, era davvero convinto di questo diceva. Tutto infervorato, citava esempi di persone che ce l'avevano fatta:

- Con un po' di fortuna, potremmo diventare famosi, Massa. Seguire le orme dei grandi locali di Berlino, o Parigi. Organizzare eventi, mostre d'arte, chiamare musicisti.

«Diventare famosi»: magari. Ne avevamo parlato varie volte. Mi immaginai i titoli dei giornali: *Giovanissimo imprenditore risolleva l'attività in crisi del padre e rivoluziona il mondo delle paninoteche.*

Parlando con Checco mi accorsi che forse la scelta più sicura tra il trovare la mia strada all'estero oppure a Grosseto, era proprio quest'ultima. La strategia rivoluzionaria ancora non l'avevo ben chiara, ma presto l'avrei messa a punto.

Checco mi annunciò che sarebbe tornato subito a casa a studiare altre carte, e che io avrei dovuto pensare a tutto il resto: stile, arredamento del locale, organizzazione degli eventi, promozione.

Undici

Avevo deciso di buttarmi a capofitto in quell'impresa, ma ancora non sapevo da dove partire. Mi ero interrogato sul da farsi per un intero giorno e alla fine, per cercare una qualche ispirazione, ero andato al bar e mi ero messo a leggere la «Gazzetta».

Entrò Vezio. Ordinò il solito Bellini, ne bevve un bel sorso senza smettere di masticare le Vigorsol e si mise a guardare una partita dei mondiali in Tv.

Arrivò anche Checco.

- Ricciolo -, lo apostrofò Vezio. - Allora?

- Sessanta minuti -, rispose lui. Poi si avvicinò a me. - Massa, ma cosa stai facendo? Qui bisogna sbrigarsi, il bando mica aspetta noi, non ci possiamo permettere ritardi. Hai fatto quello che ti ho detto?

- Che bando? -, s'intromise Vezio.

- Ma niente, un progetto extrascolastico -, tagliò corto Checco.

Io mi sentivo un po' nervoso. Secondo me, avremmo dovuto comunque provare a chiedere un consiglio a Vezio. Insomma, lui era un professionista.

Dissi a Checco che l'avrei fatto il prima possibile. Lui sbuffò, mi salutò con un «okay» rassegnato, e uscì.

- Nervoso, il ricciolone? -, domandò Vezio.

- Mah, è solo un po' in apprensione per questa cosa. Ai secchioni succede.

- Ma cos'è questo bando?

- Cosa?

- Il bando. Di che si tratta? Ho come l'impressione che non vogliate dirmelo.

- Ma no, è solo una cosa di scuola, davvero... -, risposi vago.

Finì il suo Bellini senza dire altro. Monica era scomparsa nel laboratorio a preparare non so cosa. Allora mi venne in mente di fargli una domanda. Cercai le parole giuste: - Senti, Vezio. Una curiosità, legata al bando. Ma te, quanto guadagni?

- In che senso, scusa?

- Così, hai visto, con quella dannata contabilità io già non ci capisco niente, dobbiamo presentare un progetto commerciale e ci stiamo informando su certe cose.

- Ho capito. Be', allora, vediamo un po', quanto guadagno... -. Ci pensò a lungo.

- All'anno? -, chiese dopo qualche minuto.

Che ne sapevo? - Sì.

- Dunque... Allora... Vediamo... -. Si sistemò i Ray-Ban.

Doveva guadagnare tanto, pensavo. Attesi ancora un po'.

- Mah... Di preciso non riesco a calcolartelo, su due piedi. Dipende. A volte guadagno di più, a volte guadagno di meno.

Detto questo, si avvicinò al bancone rivolgendosi a Monica: - Un panino al prosciutto a un povero affamato? Ah, e mi raccomando di togliere la mollica, che appesantisce! E un altro Bellini fresco fresco!

Poi si voltò di nuovo verso di me e aggiunse: - Ecco, mi stavo già dimenticando. Mi hanno chiamato per un lavoro extra, parto tra pochi giorni. Starò via un paio di settimane. Vedi? Non sai mai quanto guadagni!

La testa di Monica spuntò dal laboratorio. - Voi sì che siete uomini duri. Vero, Vezio? -, e sparì.

Solo che notai una rapida intesa tra loro. Lo sguardo di Monica, almeno per un attimo, tradì una specie di complicità. Quando mi rivolsi di nuovo a Vezio, ritrovai il suo solito ghigno.

- Ma te l'ho detto, amore! Abbiamo tutto ciò che ci serve. Sarà la nostra casa, capito?

- Al campeggio? Ma Magghy, sei proprio sicura che possiamo?

- Certo che sei duro, sì che possiamo! La roulotte non si muove mai da lì, e mamma e la mocciosa quest'anno non verranno, possiamo stare quanto ci pare, te l'ho detto!

Mi sembrava un sogno, un sogno a occhi aperti. Mi sentivo come su una barca che mi stava trasportando dritto in paradiso.

Che problema c'era?

In camera mia, dopo aver leggiucchiato qua e là sul manuale di guida i capitoli sulla segnaletica verticale e i limiti di velocità, rimuginavo sull'idea del campeggio, e mi sembrò fattibile. E il bando? Ci riflettei un po' su. In fondo, Checco era così bravo che avrebbe potuto pensare a tutto lui, e poi per programmare le attività c'era ancora tempo...

Il campeggio, invece, non poteva proprio aspettare. Non sarebbe stato troppo complicato. Bastava portarsi un po' di roba da mettersi addosso e il grosso era già fatto. Magari avrei potuto lavorare qualche ora nel bar interno e chissà, a settembre mi sarei anche potuto comprare una macchina, usata s'intende.

Per una giornata di lavoro avrei potuto guadagnare forse trentamila lire, in piena stagione. Nella mia testa cominciai a fare un elenco delle varie spese che avrei dovuto sostenere, almeno all'inizio. Il Benelli, se fossi rimasto al campeggio, mi sarebbe servito solo per andare ogni tanto alla scuola guida a Grosseto. Calcolai perciò una spesa di mille, milleduecentocinquanta lire giornaliere. La questione trasporti poteva già considerarsi chiusa. Per quanto riguardava l'abbigliamento, tre paia di jeans, una dozzina tra canotte e T-shirt e un paio di camicie mi potevano bastare, più sei paia di mutande, qualche paio di calzini e tre pantaloni corti. Tre cappellini da baseball e due paia di scarpe, le Converse e le Nike bianche. Cos'altro? Cavolo, la scorta di gel! Era un bel po' di roba, comunque, ed era solo quella estiva. Pensai ai miei maglioni riposti sotto naftalina nei cassetti, alla scarpiera, ai miei prodotti nel bagno. - Per il momento -, dissi ad alta voce, - mi porterò l'indispensabile. E poi il freddo è ancora lontano a venire, quando arriverà sarò pronto per il mio nuovo guardaroba.

Mi sentivo adulto, e decisi di affrontare quella nuova situazione con coraggio e determinazione.

Andai in cucina. Mamma stava stirando. Il frigorifero ronzava e mi ritrovai a pensare alle spese correnti. La luce, per esempio: quanto pagavamo in casa di luce? Non lo sapevo. Senza dare nell'occhio andai in corridoio e iniziai a rovistare nei cassetti della libreria sperando di scovare la cartellina dove mamma conservava le bollette. Sapevo che c'era, ma non mi ricordavo dove diavolo stesse. Li aprii tutti. Niente da fare. Mi spostai nell'ingresso e cercai nel mobiletto anni '70 verde acido sotto allo specchio. Trovata. La presi e andai in camera. L'aprii. Rata del condominio, aprile-maggio 1994, trentatremila lire. Quasi la paga di un giorno di lavoro, pensai, ma tanto al campeggio il condominio non c'è. Bolletta del gas, trimestre aprile-maggio-giugno, sessantasettemila lire. Al campeggio Magghy ha la bombola, il risparmio sarà assicurato. Passai in rassegna tutte le altre bollette, poi richiusi la cartellina e la rimisi al suo posto. Le duecentomila lire che avevo ancora sul libretto mi sarebbero bastate almeno per un mese. Per mangiare calcolai una spesa di circa quattromila lire al giorno. Poteva anche scapparci una capatina in pizzeria ogni tanto, pensai alla fine.

Avevo preso la mia decisione.

Mamma era davanti allo specchio del bagno.

- Vado a vivere da solo -, le annunciai dal corridoio.

- Dov'è che vai?

Rientrai in camera e provai il *moonwalk*. Ero teso ed eccitato, tanto che inciampai e caddi sbattendo il sedere sulla sponda del letto. - A vivere per conto mio! Lavorerò per mantenermi -, risposi massaggiandomi la natica e maledicendo le sponde dei letti.

Mamma non rispose.

- Ma'? Hai capito?

Apparve all'improvviso, appoggiandosi alla porta. Aveva il viso segnato dalla stanchezza. - E questa splendida idea quando ti è venuta?

Mi sedetti sul letto.

- Sono maggiorenne. Non potete impedirmelo. Posso fare ciò che voglio.

- E perché sei così nervoso? -, chiese mamma. - Sentiamo un po'. Dov'è che pensi di andare? E la scuola?

- Che c'entra la scuola?

- Che c'entra la scuola? Ma va'... Quando ti sarai diplomato ne riparleremo... -, disse mamma, e fece per andarsene.

Rimasi un attimo in silenzio. Poi mi alzai e raggiunsi la finestra.

- Io vado lo stesso! -, dissi.

Mamma tornò indietro: - Ma mi spieghi dove vuoi andare?

- Sono grande abbastanza per prendere le mie decisioni. Non potete costringermi a fare quello che non voglio.

- Ah, è così, eh? E allora sentiamo, cos'è che *non* vorresti fare?

- Ho bisogno anch'io della mia libertà.

- Ma senti mo' che me viene a dì er pischelletto -, disse in romanesco mamma con le mani sui fianchi. Non parlava mai in dialetto, tranne quando era veramente arrabbiata. - Te sembra de non esse libero? Per caso t'ha dato de vorta er cervello? Me sa proprio de sì, ah... quella ragazza.

- Ma che dici? Che c'entra lei, ora?! È una scelta mia, autonoma. Capito?

- Sarà...

Ma io volevo andare fino in fondo.

- Sarà cosa? -, la provocai. - Pensi che non sia in grado di badare a me stesso? Guarda che so come vanno le cose, non ho bisogno di imparare altro!

Mamma uscì dalla stanza, convinta che fosse solo uno sfogo passeggero. Ma io ci credevo davvero, dannazione, volevo andare a vivere con Magghy, al campeggio.

- Fai come ti pare -, gridò mamma dal corridoio.

Quel suo modo di fare mi dava ai nervi.

- Che vuol dire «fai come ti pare»? Non ho mai fatto niente di male, io... Che ci posso fare se i professori sono bravi solo a dare compiti e stare attenti a come vai vestito in giro? Io voglio fare quello che sento, trovare la mia strada, vivere a contatto con la natura, e la scuola col cavolo che mi aiuta... Ma tu cosa ne vuoi sapere! E io perdo anche tempo a dirtelo!

- Ah, davvero? Vuoi trovare la tua strada e vivere a contatto con la natura? E dove vorresti andare a vivere, in una bella villa in campagna? Magari pure con l'orto, così ti coltivi le zucchine e l'insalata da solo?

- Al campeggio. Nella roulotte di Magghy, per ora...

Mamma fece una risata amara. - In un campeggio? Be', me pare proprio un'ottima idea, per ora... Ma lèvate...

- Ma come lèvate! Mamma! Ma perché mi ostacolate in tutto? -, strillai.

- Ostacolare in tutto? Ma cosa stai dicendo? Mi piacerebbe sapere che ne pensa Checco. Ma lo conosco troppo bene, e non credo proprio che ti abbia incoraggiato, vero?

Rimasi in silenzio.

- Ancora non ti rendi conto di cosa significa badare a se stessi...

- Io lo so benissimo come badare a me stesso! -, esclamai.

- Allora sentiamo. Come?

- Con il senso di responsabilità, e con un lavoro, che forse ho già trovato. Ecco in che modo bado a me stesso!

- Che forse hai già trovato? Bene. Sei fiducioso. E sentiamo, de che lavoro se tratterebbe?

- Al bar del campeggio.

Mamma corrugò la fronte. - Ma benissimo! Tu' padre sta a fa' i sarti mortali pe' arrivà a fine mese e tu invece de aiutallo pensi de annà a lavorà ar bar de n'antro! Ar campeggio! Bravo, bravissimo... Complimenti.

- Ve la siete scelta voi, questa vita -, dissi d'istinto.

- Ah, sì? -, replicò lei. - È questo che pensi? E secondo te la nostra che vita sarebbe? Una vita miserabile? Perché se è così di cose da imparare ne hai molte, fijo mio... credimi, molte -. Poi si toccò le tempie. - M'hai fatto venì er mar de testa. Famme andà a sdraià che è meijo.

Per un attimo avevo pensato di dirle del progetto della paninoteca, ma poi avevo rinunciato. Alzai le spalle, cos'altro potevo aggiungere? Mi dispiaceva, ma io mi sentivo nel giusto e poi, pensavo, sarebbe stato solo per qualche mese. Che male c'era? Se il lavoro al campeggio andava bene avrei anche portato qualche soldo a casa. Promesso.

Dodici

La mattina dell'esame di teoria, come accadeva ormai da sette notti, mi svegliai accanto alla mia Magghy. La nostra roulotte era un perfetto nido d'amore. La luce che filtrava dalle finestrelle aveva una sfumatura bianca e dorata. Le lenzuola candide spiccavano sulle plastiche dell'arredamento, e l'ambiente era così raccolto e grazioso da far venire voglia di rimanere a letto ad ammirarlo per tutto il giorno.

Al mare ci andavamo ogni mattina; al ritorno ci riposavamo, facevamo l'amore, cenavamo e andavamo un po' in giro per Principina. Quella frazione di Grosseto era così tranquilla, perfetta per una coppia di innamorati come noi. A parte il minuscolo centro commerciale con qualche negozio, il bar e la gelateria, lì c'erano solo villette immerse nella pineta. A volte passeggiavamo mano nella mano per quei sentieri, ascoltando il frinire delle cicale e raccogliendo pinoli. Poi compravamo un gelato, rimontavamo sul *Benellindson* e via al campeggio, dove facevamo di nuovo l'amore e, mai sazi, replicavamo anche sotto la doccia nel minuscolo box della roulotte. Un giorno lo facemmo perfino tre volte di seguito.

Il bar del campeggio, però, ancora non mi aveva chiamato, anche se contavo di ricevere una risposta nel giro di qualche giorno. I miei calcoli di spesa si erano rivelati piuttosto sballati, e in otto giorni avevo dato fondo a quanto previsto in due settimane. La sera prima, oltretutto, era successa una cosa spiacevole. I vigili urbani avevano beccato me e Magghy in due sul Benelli. Quarantamila lire di multa. - Che fa, concilia? -, mi aveva chiesto il vigile da dietro i suoi occhiali a specchio.

- Conché? -, avevo ingenuamente domandato io. Lui mi spiegò che avrei potuto pagarla subito, e alla fine mi toccò conciliare. Avevo tirato fuori quattro pezzi da dieci e saldato seduta stante quel dannato verbale. Magghy era dispiaciuta, ma non aveva nemmeno accennato a smezzare la multa.

Pazienza, pensai, mi rifarò con il lavoro al bar del campeggio. Quella mattina, comunque, ci alzammo verso le undici perché alle due avevo l'esame, e volevo essere in forma. Facemmo colazione con due croissant che lei aveva «gentilmente offerto» in segno di buon augurio, io avevo bevuto il mio solito latte fumante per poi sdraiarmi sull'amaca, all'ombra. Iniziai a fantasticare sulla patente. Avvisai Magghy che facevo un salto all'edicola del campeggio. Comprai una rivista di motori e mi misi a sfogliarla sul tavolo di plastica. Mi vedevo alla guida di ogni modello, con i finestrini aperti e il vestitino verde di Magghy che si sollevava mostrando le sue bellissime gambe. Fu un pensiero nitido, avvolgente. Sentii quasi l'ebbrezza di stringere il volante della mia futura auto. Doveva essere emozionante, guidare. Immaginai che saremmo stati insieme per sempre, e avremmo viaggiato in lungo e in largo per ogni dove.

Posai la rivista e rientrai nella roulotte. Magghy era sdraiata sul letto, a pancia sotto, gli occhi socchiusi. Aveva mezzo sedere scoperto, e mi fermai a guardarlo.

Volevo vivere con lei, per sempre. Mi sciacquai a lungo il viso con acqua fredda per attenuare il gonfiore della stanchezza, aggiustai bene il ciuffo e baciai Magghy su una spalla, bevvi il latte rimasto nella sua tazza e uscii. Era davvero una giornata di svolta.

Con il vento in faccia, pensai a mamma, con cui avevo parlato un paio di giorni prima nella confusione del telefono pubblico vicino alla gelateria, a papà e a come se la stava cavando; e poi a Checco, che non vedevo né sentivo da più di una settimana. Mi sembrava incredibile. Come erano cambiate le cose!

Quella prima settimana lontano da casa era volata così in fretta che non me ne ero quasi reso conto, ma adesso che mi avvicinavo alla città sentivo un nodo stringermi la gola. Ero come in un limbo: una metà di me era già in preda a quella strana malinconia, l'altra metà aveva voglia di libertà. Mi vennero in mente Vezio e la natura selvaggia dell'Alberese.

Nel bel mezzo di queste riflessioni, sulla provinciale della Trappola che tirava dritta fino all'ippodromo, non lontano dalla città, il mio *Benellindson* a un tratto perse forza e nel giro di un attimo si spense. Trasalii. Pensai subito ai fili. Sì, li avevo presi. Scesi e mi guardai in giro: l'asfalto ribolliva al calore del sole, intorno solo campagna e sul ciglio della strada papaveri rossi che ondeggiavano all'aria. Alzai la sella, poi abbassai istintivamente lo sguardo. C'era una pozzanghera. Osservai meglio. Ma cos'era? Oh, no! Era olio! Il Benelli stava perdendo olio! Sconcertato, cercai di capire da dove fuoriuscisse, ma tutta la parte del «motore» non l'avevo studiata un granché, non sapevo nemmeno da dove iniziare. Per scrupolo, provai a dare una mandata con la pedalina. Ovviamente non successe un cavolo. E adesso?

Guardai l'orologio: l'una e venti. Avevo una mezz'ora abbondante. Spostai il Benelli su una rientranza della strada, quindi iniziai a correre. Quando mi fui scaldato, aumentai la velocità, le mie Nike erano fatte apposta. Sporcarle era l'ultimo dei miei pensieri. Correvo veloce, alcune automobili mi superarono, altre mi incrociarono nella direzione opposta. Con un fiatone incredibile, il sudore che praticamente mi ricopriva il viso e le braccia, mi fermai un attimo appoggiando le mani sulla ginocchia piegate, a testa bassa. Respirai più volte prima di riprendermi un minimo, poi mi girai verso la città. Non mancava molto, un chilometro, forse un chilometro e mezzo. Ripresi la mia galoppata. Corsi più veloce che potevo, mantenendo un ritmo regolare, e dopo altri dieci minuti abbondanti raggiunsi le porte della città. Mi fermai. Ero distrutto e avevo una sete pazzesca, ma ce l'avevo fatta. Al Benelli avrei pensato in un secondo momento...

Con i classici tre errori, me la cavai alla grande. Ero felice, ma anche un po' preoccupato per il mio obbligato rientro a casa. Col Benelli rotto non avrei potuto certo tornamene al campeggio. Come avrei fatto a sistemarlo da là? E con quali soldi, soprattutto...

Mi feci coraggio e mi incamminai verso il Villaggio Azzurro. Raggiunto il portone di casa, suonai. Rispose mamma, che quando sentì la mia voce disse solo: - Ah, sei tu -, e aprì. Aspettai l'ascensore battendo ritmicamente un piede e mangiandomi le unghie. Premetti il tasto «4» e mi guardai allo specchio. Avevo dei capelli assurdi, il ciuffo... al diavolo il ciuffo. Ero talmente in tensione che quasi non mi accorsi che l'ascensore si era fermato.

Quando entrai in casa venni accolto da Mila. Miagolò. Mi sembrò di buon augurio. Invece...

Dopo aver appreso la seconda notizia, quella riguardante il Benelli, mamma si arrabbiò di brutto. Erano anni che non mi prendevo un cazziatone del genere. L'ultimo, forse, risaliva a quando, da ragazzino avevo arrotato con la bici un bambino di fronte a casa, ad Albinia. Fu irremovibile: il motorino era mio, ed era mio dovere controllarlo.

Per giunta, volle sapere del lavoro, se l'avevo trovato. Cercai di darle una risposta rassicurante, ma non dovetti risultare molto convincente perché la sua irritazione salì alle stelle. Avevo fatto il saputello, avevo parlato di responsabilità, ed ecco il risultato, disse. Sperava solo che avessi i soldi per sistemare il Benelli.

Che stupido, che stupido!, continuava a risuonare dentro alla mia testa. E meno male che Monica non aveva assistito alla scena, altrimenti sai che figura anche con lei...

A quel punto avevo solo un'ancora di salvezza: Checco. Non gli avevo detto nemmeno del campeggio. Mi dispiaceva, cavolo se mi dispiaceva... Senza pensare troppo a come farmi perdonare la mia «sparizione», schiacciato nella morsa del bisogno, lo chiamai.

Mi rispose dopo cinque o sei squilli. Sembrava affaticato.

- Chi non muore... si rivede... -, disse respirando affannosamente.

- Scusami, ti ho disturbato?

- Sai, al contrario di qualcun altro è difficile che me ne stia con le mani in mano.

- Scusa -, ripetei. Ero sinceramente imbarazzato.

Non sapevo se per me era più umiliante aver fatto una brutta figura la prima volta della mia vita, oppure sentirmi rivolgere quel tono gelido dal mio migliore amico che, colpa mia, non chiamavo da più di una settimana. Per allentare la tensione gli dissi dell'esame di teoria, ma lui non fece commenti se non un «Ah». Quindi gli riferii del Benelli e lui ci rise su.

- Luisa che ti ha detto?

- E che mi ha detto, s'è incacchiata peggio di una scimmia. Ma ora ho il serio problema di come recuperarlo, è sulla Trappola, saranno quattro o cinque chilometri da Grosseto.

- Come sei venuto?

- Di corsa.

- Di corsa? -, domandò Checco. Forse non si aspettava che potessi arrivare a tanto.

- Sicuro, di corsa. Era l'unico modo.

Ci fu un attimo di silenzio.

- E *lei*?

- È al campeggio.

- Ah, già -, fece lui, - il campeggio. Saltiamo a rana l'argomento. Gliel'hai detto che sei bloccato a casa?

- Eh no, come facevo a dirglielo?

- Mmh... -, rifletté Checco. - Tra mezz'ora passo da te, ci vai con lo Zip.

- Come, con lo Zip?

- Con lo Zip. Te lo presto.

- Ma no, dai. Non ti ho chiamato per questo.

- Ho capito, ma non ti vede tornare, almeno vorrai avvisarla di ciò che è successo?

Ci pensai su. - Ma no...

- Ma come no? Almeno telefonale.

- Eh sì, e dove?

- Ma come dove, Massa?! Al campeggio. L'avranno pure un telefono, alla reception, al bar...

- Ma non mi va di telefonare al campeggio. Dai...

- E allora vacci, t'ho detto. Non vuoi lo Zip? Okay, fatti accompagnare. Dal tuo amico Vezio, per esempio?

- Non c'è, torna la settimana prossima...

- Ma allora lo vedi che è lo Zip che ti cerca! Dai, coraggio! Dov'è il problema, scusa? In mezz'ora vai e torni.

In effetti, problema non ce n'era. Ripensai a quando Checco si era messo a piangere sulla strada della vecchia fornace. La sua sì che era generosità pura, senza chiedere nulla in cambio. Me ne ero fregato di lui per un'intera settimana, ma come niente fosse era pronto a prestarmi il suo Zip. Lui che diceva di aspettare fiducioso il vero amore, che trovava nelle leggi naturali il vero significato magico della vita. Lui che non voleva avere a che fare con le ingiustizie degli adulti, lui che stava cercando *davvero* la propria strada.

E io, invece? Credevo di aver trovato la ragazza della mia vita, eppure da quel momento mi erano capitati mille problemi, anzi, me li ero creati da solo. Cosa mi stava succedendo? Vivevo nell'illusione di una realtà che vedevo solo io, o nella realtà di un'illusione che continuavo a coltivare, nonostante tutto?

Per cominciare, forse dovevo seguire il consiglio di Checco e avvisare Magghy: almeno finché non avessi risolto il problema del Benelli, sarei dovuto rimanere in città.

Presi un profondo sospiro, mi feci coraggio e accettai la proposta.

Dopo venti minuti il mio amico era già sotto casa mia. Dissi a mamma che andavo a recuperare il Benelli. Checco avrebbe aspettato al bar fino al mio ritorno.

Inforcai lo Zip verde pistacchio e partii per il campeggio. Dopo circa dieci minuti ero a destinazione. Mi pizzicava il sedere come se fossi stato seduto su un letto di chiodi. Poi capii perché: con la mia famosa posizione *alla Benellindson* mi ero spinto talmente all'indietro che non mi ero accorto di essere finito col sedere sul portapacchi di ferro dello Zip. Non ricordavo di essere mai stato così nervoso in sella a un motorino. Da una parte il Benelli, dall'altra Magghy; e poi c'erano Checco e i nostri progetti, ma anche papà e il destino del bar.

Parcheggiai lo Zip e mi diressi verso la piazzola. Erano quasi le cinque del pomeriggio e al campeggio regnava un silenzio surreale. Un vecchietto russava su una sdraio, due bambini giocavano a rincorrere lucertole, mentre l'immancabile signore in accappatoio si grattava il didietro e mi lanciava uno sguardo da maniaco. Sembrava proprio che ce l'avesse con me.

Magghy mi vide e si alzò di scatto. Indosso aveva solo il costume. - Ma che fine hai fatto, amore? -, chiese buttandomi le braccia al collo.

Quando le raccontai la mia disavventura, però, s'innervosì. Subito dopo le dissi che l'esame era andato bene, ma a quanto pareva la notizia non le interessava molto. Strano, pensai. Montò poi letteralmente su tutte le furie quando le ripetei che non avrei potuto recuperare il Benelli prima di qualche giorno e che fino ad allora, per questioni logistiche, avevo deciso di tornare a casa. Era stato un imprevisto. Capitano, nella vita, provai a farle capire. Tre settimane prima, con il mio amico Checco, ci avevano anche sparato in un campo di cocomeri, buttai là. Insomma, le spiegai bene la situazione, i soldi, mamma eccetera, ma, come si dice, feci un buco nell'acqua. Rispose che non si sarebbe mai aspettata un comportamento del genere da me, come se il Benelli l'avessi rotto apposta. Aggiunse che la roulotte era la nostra casa e che non potevo andarmene così, su due piedi, e lasciarla da sola.

Ma come le saltava in mente una cosa del genere? Dopotutto, eravamo in vacanza e poi, santo cielo, qualche giorno separati non sarebbe stato certo la fine del mondo. Si scaldò anche di più quando provai a dirle che in fondo, dal momento che non voleva stare da sola, anche lei avrebbe potuto tornarsene a Grosseto, con me. Niente da fare, come parlare al vento. Ma non era finita: Magghy se ne uscì con il discorso che era come se avessi fallito la prova decisiva.

Questo proprio no, non potevo accettarlo.

- Ma cosa stai dicendo?

- Sì, è così. Per me venire qui era come una prova.

- Una prova?

- Sì. Io volevo *vivere* con te, capito? E invece... te ne vai così, dopo otto giorni. Otto miseri giorni! Sei proprio uno stronzo! Ma che ti ho fatto?!

Dire che rimasi scioccato è troppo poco. Passai in rassegna un po' tutte le ipotesi: forse si era drogata o, che ne so, un colpo di sole le aveva giocato un brutto scherzo.

Cercai di spiegarle un'altra volta per filo e per segno cos'era successo, ma era come parlare con un muro di gomma. Si rifugiò nella roulotte sbattendo la piccola porta di plastica. Mortificato, senza parole, tornai sui miei passi e montai sullo Zip.

Durante il viaggio di ritorno volevo piangere, ma ero così amareggiato che non mi uscì nemmeno una lacrima.

Arrivai al bar scuro in volto. Papà mi guardò, si tirò su il ponticello degli occhiali e disse: - Sempre per il rotto della cuffia, tu, eh? C'hai un culo, fijo mio, nun te smentisci mai... -, riferendosi evidentemente ai tre errori all'esame. - Mo' che te manca l'ultimo anno de scola sarebbe er caso da studià un po' de ppiù, nun trovi? -. E si lanciò in bocca qualche nocciolina arricciando il naso.

Papà non rompeva tanto, con la scuola. In fin dei conti, a parte l'anno perso per via del trasferimento e a volte qualche materia rimandata a settembre, ero sempre stato promosso. Era stato lui a insistere per il commerciale, perché pensava che la professione del futuro fosse il commercialista. A me, invece, non importava un fico secco. E poi c'erano tutta quella matematica, e gli esercizi di ragioneria che non mi tornavano neanche a copiarli dal fondo del libro! Dare, avere, avere, dare... Come sempre, alla fine mi salvavo grazie a Checco, che ogni tanto mi passava un biglietto con le soluzioni. Ora il mio amico se ne stava lì in sala, a osservare le pale del ventilatore. Lo ringraziai e gli passai le chiavi dello Zip.

Chiesi a papà se Checco gli aveva comunicato del Benelli. - Sì, e io j'ho detto de ditti de arrangiatte -, rispose semplicemente. - Ah, e poi sia chiaro -, ribadì, - nun ne voijo sapè niente...

Evidentemente quello che più gli importava erano i dannati soldi. Ultimamente, o mi rimproverava trattandomi come un bambino, oppure mi negava anche il minimo contributo economico. Dovevo proprio rendermi indipendente. Fargli vedere che ero un uomo, ormai...

- Non ti preoccupare -, mi rassicurò Checco. - Prendiamo una corda e lo trainiamo fin qui dal meccanico con lo Zip.

Per fortuna c'era lui, la mia «manna», altroché. Tra di noi, evidentemente, vigeva come un accordo che non aveva bisogno di tante chiacchiere, capace di resistere a ogni prova. A tutto. Forse c'era davvero un filo invisibile a tenerci uniti.

Per evitare possibili multe, aspettammo che facesse buio. Erano le nove e mezza di sera quando montai dietro sullo Zip e partimmo. Ogni tanto battevo una testata sul casco di Checco, in effetti non è che fosse un ottimo guidatore, tutto scatti e ondeggiamenti. Fortunatamente il viaggio durò pochi minuti. La notte era calata sulla Maremma. Scendemmo. Dissi a Checco di illuminare bene il punto dello slargo dove avevo sistemato il Benelli, un punto piuttosto nascosto.

Mmh, curioso... Il Benelli non c'era. Come cambiano le cose di notte, pensai. Allora indicai a Checco un altro punto, quello sicuramente giusto. Il faro, però, illuminò ancora solo vegetazione. Lo Zip fece il giro a 360 gradi... niente. Oh, no... Il Benelli era sparito!

Non c'era più!

- Ma com'è possibile! Comeee?! -, urlavo.

Iniziai a muovermi in cerchio come un cane che si morde la coda.

Checco si sfilò il casco e rimase in silenzio finché non scoppiai a piangere.

- A questo punto -, disse, - la questione Benelli mi sembra *definitivamente* chiusa.

A quelle parole, il mio pianto divenne dirotto.

Non potrò mai dimenticare quel momento. Completamente al buio, con il motore dello Zip che borbottava e un fascio di luce a illuminare gli arbusti. Qualcuno aveva rubato il mio caro, adorato *Benellindson*!

- Dannazione! -, esclamai con tutta la rabbia che avevo in corpo. - Se lo becco, quello stronzo, giuro che lo ammazzo! Capito? Lo ammazzooo!

- Stai calmo, Massa, ti si alza la pressione. Piuttosto, nascosto com'era, chi lo ha preso deve essere qui della zona.

Alzando il capo, vidi delle luci accese nei poderi vicino.

- Andiamo a sentire -, propose Checco.

Ero così nervoso che avrei distrutto qualsiasi cosa mi fosse capitata a tiro.

- Nooo... -, dissi, - questo proprio no...

Checco provò a consolarmi.

- Ma ti rendi conto, Checco?! Il *Benellindson*! E adesso, cosa racconto ai miei? Che figura da bambino! Da stupido! Mi romperanno da morire, già lo so! Diranno che ho voluto fare di testa mia pensando di essere responsabile, e invece mi sono fatto fregare il motorino. Porca miseria!

- Lo sai, che ci sono gli imprevisti...

- Imprevisti? Ma questa è una tortura, una punizione divina!

- Forza, non stiamo qui a piagnucolare, andiamo a sentire.

Mi asciugai le lacrime e montai dietro sullo Zip.

- Scusate l'ora -, disse Checco alla signora che ci aprì al primo podere, - ma è successo un guaio. Il mio caro amico Massa, qui, che purtroppo è sconvolto e non riesce a mettere in fila due parole dico due, oggi pomeriggio ha lasciato proprio in fondo allo sterrato, vicino alla provinciale, il suo motorino marca Benelli s50 rosso Ferrari, che si era rotto. Siamo tornati a prenderlo, ma qualcuno lo ha portato via. Non è che per caso, pensando che fosse stato abbandonato volontariamente, è stato prelevato da qualcuno del podere?

La signora, dalla facciona piena, ci guardava un po' allibita. Sarà stato per la capigliatura di Checco, pensai.

- No capire, no 'taliana io. Albània. Vèni 'talia lavoro. Grazi -, e fece per chiudere la porta.

Checco la fermò e le chiese se c'era qualcun altro in casa. - Qualcuno italiano, signora.

- No 'taliana, Albània! Vèni 'talia lavoro.

- See, vabbè, veni 'talia veni... -, le feci il verso. - Dai, Checco, leviamoci da qui.

Ci dirigemmo verso l'altro podere.

Dall'interno proveniva il rumore di un televisore. Checco si avvicinò e suonò alla porta. Dopo qualche secondo ci aprì un tipo grosso e peloso.

- Chi siete? Mica testimoni di Geova? -, domandò aggressivo.

- Ma no, signore.

- Meno male, perché io 'un capisco che ci vengano a fa', qui in Maremma. Noi siamo gente normale. E allora, se 'un siete testimoni di Geova, che volete?

Mi guardò, e io guardai Checco, che attaccò: - Il fatto è che è successo un guaio. Un grosso guaio. Il mio carissimo amico Massa, questo ragazzo qui -, e mi toccò una spalla, - che come vede è purtroppo molto sconvolto e non riesce a mettere in fila tre parole dico tre, oggi pomeriggio ha lasciato proprio in fondo allo sterrato, adiacente alla provinciale, il suo motorino di marca Benelli s50, colore rosso Ferrari, che purtroppo si era rotto. Siamo tornati a prenderlo ma qualcuno lo ha portato via. Non è che per caso, pensando che fosse stato abbandonato volutamente, qualcuno del podere lo ha prelevato e lo ha portato da qualche altra parte?

Il tipo seguì il discorso con aria interessata. - Davvero?

- Signore, scusi, davvero cosa? -, domandò Checco.

- L'hanno portato via? Io l'ho visto, oggi, un motorino rosso.

Mi venne di nuovo da piangere. L'aveva visto. E forse era stata l'ultima persona a vederlo. L'ultima.

Checco, investigando un po', cercò di farsi dare quanti più elementi possibile, ma il risultato fu piuttosto deludente.

- Ve l'ho detto, ragazzi, alle due c'era, poi 'un ci so' più passato sicché 'un lo so quando l'hanno portato via. E 'un so nemmeno chi lo po' avè pigliato. Qui 'e siamo du' poderi, ma a quell'altro c'è du' vecchi e 'na straniera che li guarda, 'un pole mica esse stata lei! Vedrai che sarà stato qualcuno di passaggio.

Insomma, non riuscimmo a cavarne un ragno dal buco. Checco ringraziò anche da parte mia, e tornammo indietro. Per sicurezza, mi volli fermare a controllare di nuovo, ma non si era verificato alcun miracolo. Poi, all'improvviso, venni assalito dal ricordo peggiore: le chiavi del Benelli, le avevo lasciate attaccate al cruscotto pensando di dover prendere i fili!

Scoppiai in un pianto dirotto, stramaledicendo la mia sbadataggine assoluta. I problemi non facevano che moltiplicarsi! E ora, cosa avrei raccontato a mamma e papà? Cosa?

Checco cercò di rincuorarmi, senza molto successo.

Ero così amareggiato che avrei voluto solo sotterrarmi e aspettare che tutti si fossero dimenticati, soprattutto mamma, di me e della mia irresponsabilità.

Passai una delle notti più tormentate e lunghe della mia vita. Magghy ce l'aveva a morte con me, il Benelli era stato rubato, i miei erano tutti coalizzati contro di me e io, cavolo, io... mi sarei preso a schiaffi per quello che ero riuscito a combinare.

La spensieratezza di poche settimane prima era letteralmente svanita.

Tredici

Erano appena le sei quando mi alzai. Avrei dato non so cosa per levarmi di dosso quella frustrazione ripugnante. I miei erano già in cucina.

Quando mi vide, mamma mi chiese subito del motorino: - L'hai preso?

- No. Ci vado dopo, - risposi d'istinto.

Non ce la facevo a confessarle la verità, così, su due piedi.

- Fai come ti pare. Del resto è tuo, no?

- Infatti, è mio.

Papà mi guardava con aria distratta. Bisbigliò qualcosa sottovoce a mamma, salutò e uscì.

Tornai in camera. Guardai il poster di Michael, la faccia di Freddy Krueger con la sua mano fatta di artigli, la vecchia sciarpa della Lazio. Mi sembrava tutto così stupido, senza senso.

Poi ebbi un'idea: avrei potuto dire che, dal momento che sarebbe stato troppo costoso aggiustarlo, avevo deciso di rottamare il Benelli. È vero, non mi avrebbe comunque evitato un altro cazziatone, ma mettere al corrente mamma e papà del furto era decisamente al di sopra delle mie forze. D'altronde, dovevo pur tutelare la mia reputazione in qualche modo.

Mi girai i pollici per un po', ma quando si alzò anche Monica mi affrettai a uscire di casa.

Arrivato in via Sicilia, mi fermai da Checco in cerca di un sostegno morale. Avevo deciso: l'avrei detto prima a papà. Suonai. Mi rispose la nonna. Checco era uscito, mi disse. Sospirai, cercando di autoconvincermi che il mio piano fosse davvero il migliore, almeno in quel momento.

Mi recai direttamente al bar, dove vidi Checco al banco che parlottava con papà. Meno male, pensai. In due è sempre più facile. Cominciai a sudare leggermente. Sollevai la maglietta tra il pollice e l'indice e la agitai avanti e indietro.

- Dormito bene? -, mi chiese papà tirandosi su gli occhiali col dorso della mano.

- Più o meno come sempre.

Checco si girò verso di me e mi fece un gesto come per dire: «È tutto a posto». Al che ritrovai un po' di coraggio. Magari papà era più tranquillo del solito.

- Bene -, continuò lui. - Sono contento per te.

Guardai Checco, che socchiuse gli occhi come a dirmi: «Non ti preoccupare...».

- Si vede che hai la coscienza a posto -, mi punzecchiò papà.

Cosa stava farneticando? Gli chiesi spiegazioni. Allora si asciugò le mani con uno straccetto e lo lanciò lontano: - Così, mo', avemo fatto pure tredici! -, proseguì. - Te sei fatto fregà pure er motorino! Ma porca miseria! Un mijone e ducentomila lire!

Mi venne un colpo. Quindi sapeva già tutto? - Checco, ma...? Ma gliel'hai detto tu?

- E che pensavi di farla franca? -, mi rimbrottò papà.

- Macché! -, balbettai. - Te lo stavo per dire! È solo che... Ma cavolo, Checco! Davvero gliel'hai detto tu? Ma perché?!

- Perché pensavi de falla franca, ecco perché! Ci mancava solo questo! Uno fa i sacrifici pe' 'na vita, ed ecco er risultato! La ciliegina sulla torta... -, e papà alzò le sue grandi mani al cielo.

Non avrei mai creduto che potesse finire così. Insomma, da Checco no, da lui non me lo sarei mai aspettato. Ma cosa gli era saltato in mente? Voleva rovinarmi completamente? Non capivo, dannazione, proprio non capivo. Perché anche lui si era messo contro di me? Non poteva dirmelo prima? Non poteva *chiedermi* il permesso?

Ero furioso, che figura ci avevo fatto! Dopo quella dell'imbranato, anche quella del bugiardo!

Cercai in qualche modo di rattoppare la situazione, ma ormai la frittata era fatta.

Checco tentò di giustificare la sua mossa dicendo che in fondo la verità ripaga sempre, e papà lo difese.

Io però a quel punto non volli sentire ragioni, e alla fine lo mandai al diavolo. Uscii dal bar senza sapere dove andare.

Vagai senza meta per la città. Avevo bisogno di silenzio e pensai fosse una buona idea rintanarmi in una chiesa. Mi diressi verso il centro, con l'intenzione di trovare un po' di pace in Duomo, ma era troppo affollato, così ripiegai verso il convento di San Francesco.

Lungo la strada, le finestre sulle viuzze sembravano far parte di una scenografia. Camminando, osservavo le persiane di legno, i vasi di fiori colorati agganciati sotto ai davanzali, i panni stesi ad asciugare sui fili. Sembrava un'altra città. Giunsi di fronte alla chiesa. Era piccola, fatta di mattoncini, con un rosone semplice al centro. Erano anni che non ci entravo, e non ricordavo fosse così bella. In fondo, alle spalle dell'altare, un crocifisso dipinto era come sospeso in aria. Mi avvicinai per leggere la targa: «Duccio di Buoninsegna, 1290 circa». Mi allontanai un poco per vederlo meglio. Cavolo, era così antico? Sulla destra, scorsi una piccola cappella affrescata della quale ignoravo completamente l'esistenza. Entrai e mi sedetti su una sediolina di legno. L'aria era fresca e mi guardai un po' intorno. Quell'esplosione di colori, quell'odore di cera e incenso... Era come trovarsi in un altro mondo. Sospirai ripensando a tutto ciò che mi era successo in quelle ultime settimane.

Venni assalito dalla tristezza. Cercai di concentrarmi e di pregare, ma non mi riuscì più di tanto. Ero confuso, e incavolato.

Uscii dalla chiesa con l'intenzione di andare a rifugiarmi tra le stradine deserte del Villaggio Curiel, le mie preferite. Quell'antico e minuscolo quartiere aveva un fascino particolare. I suoi portoncini di legno erano riparati da piccoli tetti fatti di tegole e tutte le casette, colorate di rosa, giallo o celeste, erano circondate da orticelli e pollai. Passando di lì, avevi davvero l'impressione di essere tornato indietro di cento anni.

Il sole era alto nel cielo. Ripensai alle parole di papà, e cominciò a montarmi dentro una sorta di panico. Camminavo nervosamente avanti e indietro, cercando di capire cosa fare. E mamma, pensai? Papà gliel'avrà già detto. Che figura, che figura mi ha fatto fare Checco! Ma perché? Proprio non mi davo pace.

- Accidenti al campeggio! -, sbottai. - Se non ci fossi andato, tutto questo casino non sarebbe successo! Al diavolo, al diavolo tutto!

Dopo almeno mezz'ora che me ne stavo lì a brontolare tra me e me, si aprì una finestra al pianoterra e sbucò il viso di una bambina. Poteva avere sì e no dieci anni. - Ti senti male? -, mi chiese.

- No, no, bambina, non mi sento male.

Ci mancava anche questa.

- Va bene, ciao -, disse, e richiuse la finestra.

Feci un lungo respiro.

Mi sedetti su uno scalino e continuai a rimuginare.

Mi ricordai di quando, qualche giorno prima, mi ero detto che presto avrei mandato in pensione il Benelli. Che beffa... E Magghy? Chissà cosa stava facendo. Chissà se mi stava pensando... Cavolo, avrei voluto davvero saperlo.

Sentii di nuovo aprirsi la finestra al pianoterra. Diedi una rapida sbirciata e riabbassai subito la testa, pesante come un masso per i troppi pensieri. Che guardasse pure, la bambina.

Dopo un minuto o due sentii una voce: - Ehi, tutto bene?

Mi voltai. Non era la bambina. Era una ragazza, e pure carina. Avrà avuto sedici anni, gli occhi smeraldo e lucenti come il mare. Mi osservava con uno sguardo che andava dritto nel profondo.

- Diciamo di sì -, dissi distrattamente.

- Però è no. Giusto?

- Però è no...

- La mia cuginetta mi ha detto che è da più di un'ora che sei qui.

- Non mi sembra di dare fastidio a nessuno -, mi giustificai allargando le braccia.

- Oh no, a noi non dài fastidio per niente. Anzi, se vuoi qualcosa, che so, un bicchiere d'acqua, chiedi pure.

- Grazie, non voglio niente -, e mi girai dandole le spalle.

- Okay. Allora non ti disturbo più. Ciao...

Sentii la finestra chiudersi, e soltanto allora mi voltai a guardare.

Rimasi lì un'altra mezz'ora.

A quel punto mamma aveva sicuramente saputo del furto. Inutile ormai scervellarsi più di tanto su come affrontare la faccenda. Feci spallucce e mi incamminai senza sapere dove andare. L'unica certezza era che volevo stare solo.

Superai l'ultima casa del quartiere e proseguii sullo sterrato costeggiando il grande campo di barbabietole. Mi trovavo in campagna. A Grosseto era così: un attimo prima eri in città, poi facevi un passo e ti trovavi in campagna. La natura mi faceva compagnia. Il ronzio degli insetti risuonava tutto intorno, con il fruscio del vento che passava sulle foglie. E c'era quell'odore inconfondibile di terra rossa e di fieno racchiuso nelle presse, che come ruote immobili disegnavano il paesaggio dell'estate toscana.

Ero fiaccato dal caldo, insonnolito, e avevo voglia di chiudere gli occhi. Trovai un piccolo spiazzo erboso e decisi di sdraiarmi. Com'era rassicurante e piacevole! La natura era davvero come una madre accogliente. Cercai di rallentare il respiro e di farmi invadere da quell'armonia. E alla fine mi addormentai.

Sognai che Checco telefonava a casa mia e raccontava tutta la faccenda a mamma. E mi prendeva in giro, dandomi dello sprovveduto senza cervello. Lei ci rideva su, complice del mio ex migliore amico. Come se non bastasse, Checco mi metteva in bocca anche assurde falsità, come quella di essere un burattino di certi loschi personaggi che volevano far chiudere il Paradise per aprirci un night-club con spogliarelliste brasiliane e francesi, tutte assoldate da Vezio.

- Cosa ci fai qui?

Feci un salto e spalancai di colpo gli occhi, ripiombando nel mondo reale.

- Stavi dormendo? -, proseguì la voce. Alzai lo sguardo. Era lei, la ragazza alla finestra.

- Veramente mi stavo rilassando. Questo posto mi piace.

- Ah, allora scusa, non volevo disturbarti.

Sospirai. - Scusa tu, sono stato un po' scorbutico, prima. Ma non lo faccio apposta, è una questione di carattere.

- Allora hai un bel carattere, secondo me. Come ti chiami?

- Massa.

Le strinsi la piccola mano. Era morbida, delicata.

- Massa? Che bel nome -, disse lei sorridendo. - Non l'avevo mai sentito. Io invece mi chiamo Malù. - Sorrise, e mi sembrò di vedere il sole nei suoi occhi.

Che strano nome, pensai. Forse è straniera.

- Sono uscita per andare al pollaio di mio nonno a prendere delle uova per fare una torta. Sai, oggi è il mio compleanno e... stasera darò una festa.

- Davvero? Allora ti faccio tanti auguri! Quanti sono?

- Diciassette... L'anno prossimo però sono in quinta, ho fatto la primina.

- Davvero? Come Checco, allora.

- Chi è Checco? Un tuo amico?

- Sì, o almeno così credevo...

Finii per raccontarle del *Benellindson*, di papà, del bar e di mille altre cose che mi vennero in mente. Ascoltò il fiume delle mie parole senza battere ciglio, senza interrompermi nemmeno mezza volta, senza giudicare. Non fece commenti né tentò di trovare delle giustificazioni a quanto mi era capitato.

Eppure, proprio quel suo essere silenziosa e paziente mi trasmise una sensazione di calma, e per un momento mi sembrò di avere finalmente spezzato il circolo vizioso in cui ero caduto.

Malù aveva lineamenti delicati, con due occhi grandi così, dolci, che avevano il potere di tranquillizzarmi. Li fissavo imbambolato. Mi destò spiegandomi che doveva andare, altrimenti avrebbe fatto tardi.

- Però ti invito. Anzi, sei ufficialmente invitato al compleanno di Malù questa sera dalle otto e mezza al Coenobium.

Il mio umore era migliorato e le promisi che avrei fatto di tutto per passare a salutarla. Ma ero troppo curioso e di getto le chiesi cosa significasse il suo nome. Mi rispose che Ma stava per Maria e Lù per Luce... Era il soprannome che le aveva dato il nonno da piccola.

Mi piaceva, e pensai che mi avrebbe portato fortuna.

- E poi nonno dice che sono dolce proprio come una coppa Malù, quella con cioccolato e panna!

Con un leggero imbarazzo la salutai incamminandomi per rientrare in città.

Tornato a casa, in corridoio trovai mamma a spolverare la libreria: era così arrabbiata che nemmeno mi salutò.

Mi fiondai in camera e mi buttai sul letto. Ero talmente stanco che mi addormentai di colpo.

Come nel secondo tempo dei film, il mio sogno proseguì, e Checco era diventato il ragazzo di Magghy. Siccome non aveva il motorino per andarla a prendere, affinché gli prestassi il mio mi ricattò dicendomi che se mi fossi rifiutato avrebbe fatto pubblicare sul giornale locale che la mia prima volta avevo fatto cilecca.

Fortunatamente mi svegliai. Guardai l'ora, erano quasi le cinque del pomeriggio.

Sentii mamma programmare la lavatrice. Stava *sempre* a casa. A volte l'avevo spiata, e avevo notato che nei suoi momenti liberi le piaceva soprattutto affacciarsi sul terrazzo, e osservare quello spicchio di città. Non so cosa ci trovasse di bello nel panorama: da casa nostra si potevano ammirare ben due strade anonime con le saracinesche dei fondi in prima linea e i binari morti della ferrovia. In quell'angolo di visuale avevo atteso più volte che succedesse qualcosa di particolare, ma non era mai capitato. Eppure, quella era l'abitudine preferita di mamma, quasi fosse un rituale da ripetere ogni volta. Pensando a papà e alla crisi che aveva colpito il bar, però, mi chiedevo come mai non facesse niente per aiutarlo. In fondo era ancora giovane, e avrebbe potuto benissimo lavorare anche lei. Oppure no, se solo non avesse smesso di dipingere! Magari avrebbe potuto vendere ancora qualcuno dei suoi quadri.

Osservai la mia camera. Non la riconoscevo quasi più. Erano così tanti giorni che non ci badavo. Mi accorsi solo allora della montagna di magliette e di biancheria da lavare sparse sul pavimento. Ero sicuro che mamma le avesse lasciate lì di proposito, per mostrarmi quanto fossi irresponsabile.

Mi alzai, misi su un po' di musica e cercai di dare una sistemata.

Mi ero fatto una doccia scacciapensieri e me ne stavo lì davanti allo specchio a cercare di sistemarmi il ciuffo. Provai e riprovai almeno quattro volte, ma continuava a non piacermi. Forse ero io che non andavo. Anche i denti, che mi ero spazzolato per cinque minuti buoni, mi sembravano meno bianchi del solito.

Mi sentivo solo, ecco. La mia ragazza mi aveva lasciato, il mio migliore amico mi aveva deluso e la mia famiglia ce l'aveva con me. Poteva andare peggio di così?

Provai a buttare giù qualche schizzo del viso di Malù, ma non ero decisamente in vena. Aspettai in silenzio le otto e mezza e uscii per andare alla sua festa di compleanno. Chissà quanta gente ci sarà, pensavo. Ma chi se ne importa, la saluterò e poi via, a passeggiare per la città cercando di capire cosa mi sta succedendo, e magari anche a trovarci un senso...

Stranamente, il Coenobium era mezzo vuoto. Controllai l'ora. Le nove meno un quarto. Forse Malù mi aveva preso in giro. Ma tu guarda, mi mancava anche questa! Feci il giro della piazzetta e buttai un occhio all'interno del locale. In tutto, contai sette persone sparse su tre tavoli. Poi la porta del bagno si aprì e comparve Malù. La vidi sedersi a un tavolo vuoto. Ma dov'erano gli invitati? Incuriosito, entrai.

- Ciao, Malù, sei sola?

- Ciao. Be', come dire... In effetti sì, sono sola. Quella del compleanno era una bugia.

- Ah, sì? -. Ero sinceramente sorpreso. - Ma allora perché mi hai detto della festa e tutto il resto?

- Perché secondo me anche tu avevi bisogno di stare insieme a qualcuno, stasera.

Era vero, così vero che mi dimenticai di tutti i problemi e mi rifugiai in quei suoi grandi occhi smeraldo, bellissimi.

- Come ti hanno rubato il motorino? -, chiese lei a un tratto.

- Per la verità, *me lo sono* fatto rubare...

- Che vuoi dire? -, chiese sorpresa.

Mi sistemai accanto a lei e le raccontai per filo e per segno ciò che mi era successo. Parlammo, anzi, parlai per due ore filate, senza toccare cibo, bevendo birra. Il telefono ogni tanto squillava, ma non rispondevamo mai. Le raccontai di Magghy, della patente, ma anche dell'idea vaga di andare all'estero e del progetto della paninoteca.

- Insomma, tanta carne al fuoco ma ancora niente di preciso -, commentò alla fine del mio interminabile monologo.

- Già... Ma come faccio?

- Che vuol dire, come fai? Lo fai e basta! Decidi e ti metti sotto!

- Ti sembra facile...

- Scommetto che a scuola sei sempre sul filo della sufficienza. Non è così?

Ci mancava anche questa, adesso.

- In effetti... Ma che significa?

- Significa che sei così! Lo vedi? Ti arrabatti, sempre indeciso, e poi scarichi le responsabilità sugli altri, come sul tuo amico Checco per la paninoteca. Devi essere più determinato, smetterla di lamentarti e tirare fuori il coraggio di scegliere, capito?! Devi visualizzare il tuo obiettivo, devi allinearti con esso, allinearti! Devi credere nella tua luce! Credici! Altrimenti anche la tua vita resterà sul filo della sufficienza!

Sospirai e abbassai il capo. - Hai ragione -, ammisi. - Non avevo mai pensato alla mia vita da questo punto di vista; così dall'esterno, voglio dire.

Tra di noi scese un lungo silenzio.

Ero un po' imbarazzato, ma Malù mi tranquillizzò: - Scusa... non so cosa mi è preso, forse ho esagerato e ho perso la pazienza. Sarà per via di mio nonno... Con lui, non fai in tempo ad aprire bocca che ha già la soluzione per tutto. La verità -, continuò abbassando lo sguardo, - è che mi sei stato subito simpatico, e vederti così abbattuto, oggi pomeriggio, mi è proprio dispiaciuto.

- Passi molto tempo con tuo nonno?

- Be', nonno abita con noi. Papà lavora fuori città e torna solo il fine settimana, mamma fa i turni di notte, quindi... sì, passo molto tempo con lui.

- E tua cugina? Abita anche lei con voi?

- Oh no, solo quando gli zii sono fuori per lavoro. Le faccio da baby-sitter.

- E all'orto, ci vai spesso?

- Quasi ogni giorno, appena ho finito i compiti.

- Ti piace?

- Se mi piace? Io *adoro* la campagna. Da grande vorrei fare l'apicoltrice, e magari aprire un agriturismo, con piante di olivo secolare e tanti cavalli.

- Cavolo. Credo sia difficile.

- Sì, ma non mi importa, ce la metterò tutta per riuscirci.

Malù sembrava davvero determinata. Passò una cameriera e ordinai una seconda birra.

- Anche se...

- Anche se? -, domandai.

- Anche se ho un po' di paura.

Paura? Lei?

- Paura di cosa?

- Paura che un giorno, magari quando avrò finito la scuola, o peggio quando il nonno non ci sarà più, arrivi qualcosa a distruggere tutto il mio mondo...

Sul viso di Malù comparve un velo di tristezza.

Le accarezzai la mano, gliela strinsi forte. Volevo rassicurarla, volevo che continuasse a confidarsi, dirle che si sarebbe potuta aprire con me, ma allo stesso tempo non volevo forzarla.

Desidero che quella serata non finisse più. Sospirando appoggiai la testa sulla sua spalla. Malù era riuscita a farmi sentire a mio agio, e con lei tutto l'imbarazzo e la confusione degli ultimi giorni sembravano svaniti.

Alla fine della serata, ci baciammo. Un bacio appassionato, quasi a volerci liberare dalle nostre reciproche paure. Quasi violento, che non ci aspettavamo. Venne del tutto spontaneo, questa volta...

Nel preciso istante in cui le nostre labbra si staccarono, alzai lo sguardo e vidi Magghy.

Il cuore mi fece un salto fino in gola, poi si fermò. O almeno fu questa la sensazione che provai. Magghy? Come faceva a sapere che ero lì? Maledizione, forse era stato Checco a dirglielo, e chi sennò? Dopo che aveva spifferato a papà la storia del motorino, mi aspettavo di tutto da lui!

Magghy continuava a spostare lo sguardo da me a Malù, la bocca lucidissima, socchiusa. Vidi un lampo nei suoi occhi, e sulle guance le scesero due lacrime. A quel punto uscì di corsa dal locale. E io mi sentii uno stronzo totale.

Un fischio mi attraversò la testa, da un orecchio all'altro. Mi alzai e uscii a mia volta. Erano bastate quelle due lacrime a farmi capire che con Magghy non era finita.

- Perché tu -, continuava a ripetermi seduta su una panchina della piazzetta dove l'avevo raggiunta dopo una breve corsa, - è come se mi avessi tradita due volte! Capito? Due volteee! Io volevo costruire la nostra vita insieme, e invece ti trovo con un'altra?! E per di più te la stai baciando! -, si disperava Magghy. - Ma ti rendi conto di quanto male mi hai fatto? Sognavo di fare pace, e invece era solo un'illusione...

«Lontano, all'estero...», riecheggiò dentro di me.

Che disastro, non sapevo proprio cosa dirle né tanto meno cosa fare perché la situazione cambiasse. Ripensai alle parole di Malù, che avevo lasciato da sola al tavolo, senza una spiegazione. Mi sentivo terribilmente in colpa verso entrambe, e ancora una volta la mia unica reazione fu quella di chiudermi in me stesso, mentre la seconda birra entrata in circolo aveva spianato la strada a una grande confusione. Mi appartai in un angolo e sfogai tutta la mia frustrazione prendendo a calci e pugni un cassonetto dell'immondizia.

Magghy, sentendo quel rumore di colpi, cominciò a singhiozzare, poi a piangere rannicchiandosi su se stessa, come a voler scomparire. - Sei anche un violento, lo sapevo! Lo sapevo! Ma come ho fatto a innamorarmi di te?!

Intontito dall'alcool, sferrai un ultimo pugno con tutta la forza che avevo, e il cassonetto, già malridotto, si sfondò. Ritrassi la mano. Sanguinava. Avevo perso la sensibilità all'indice e al medio, ma quello era davvero l'ultimo dei miei problemi. Magghy cacciò un urlo e si prese la testa tra le mani, gemendo impaurita.

Non contento, cominciai a sferrare colpi con l'altro pugno. Mi sentivo come in preda a un istinto animale. Ripensai ancora alle parole di Malù. Ecco a cosa mi avevano portato tutte le mie indecisioni! A picchiare un cassonetto dell'immondizia puzzolente! Ero davvero caduto in basso.

Fu allora che due fari si avvicinarono, lentamente. Li osservai, poi vidi l'auto. Era una pattuglia dei carabinieri.

Si fermò e ne scese un omone alto e grosso in uniforme, con due folti baffi. - Lei, favorisca i documenti.

Oh, merda. Dalla padella alla brace. In un secondo mi passò la sbornia, mi passò l'arrabbiatura, mi passò tutto.

Cercai il portafoglio. Dove l'avevo messo? Alla fine lo trovai, nella tasca posteriore dei pantaloni.

Il carabiniere rientrò in auto lasciando la portiera aperta. Si sentì due o tre volte il rumore inconfondibile della radio di servizio.

- Venga, venga -, mi chiamò.

Magghy aveva smesso di piangere e guardava allibita la scena.

- Perché picchiava quel cassonetto? Le dava fastidio?

- No no, per carità.

- E allora? -, chiese il carabiniere che stava al volante. - Pensa di essere furbo?

Furbo? Ma che c'entra?, mi dissi. Ho un milione e mezzo di problemi e questo vuol sapere se penso di essere furbo. Magari, lo fossi.

- No, non lo penso. Scusi, sono solo un po' nervoso perché mi hanno rubato il motorino.

- L'ha sporta la denuncia? -, chiese quello alto e grosso toccandosi i baffi.

- Veramente no.

- Ma come? Le rubano il motorino e lei non sporge denuncia? -, continuò. - Perché? Forse ha qualcosa da nascondere?

Nascondere qualcosa? Oh santo cielo, ma no.

- Assolutamente no.

- E allora si sbrighi. Se i cittadini non denunciano i furti, è inutile poi lamentarsi che la merce rubata non si ritrova più. E la smetta di picchiare i cassonetti. Ha capito?

- Cos'ha fatto alla mano? -, chiese quello al volante.

- Ehm... Ho tirato un pugno al muro...

- Era duro, eh? -, sogghigno il più grosso.

- Decisamente...

Fortuna che non si accorsero che avevo danneggiato il cassonetto. Feci un profondo sospiro. Smaltita la paura, cercai di riprendere in mano la situazione. Com'era difficile, tutto così difficile. Pensai a Checco, cavolo, quanto mi mancava... Lui sì che avrebbe gestito quella situazione con lucidità!

Mi girai verso la panchina. Ma Magghy non c'era. Mi guardai intorno. Era sparita. Mi sentivo proprio uno stronzo.

Forse era tornata a casa. Era quasi mezzanotte. Mi avviai anch'io passando per le stradine del centro. La luna faceva capolino tra i vecchi palazzi. I piccioni dormivano nei sottotetti, le saracinesche dei negozi erano abbassate. Nonostante tutto, la città a quell'ora era immersa in un'atmosfera surreale. Pensai a Malù, a tutto quello che mi aveva fatto capire su me stesso. E io l'avevo abbandonata così, senza spiegazioni.

Svoltai all'altezza della biblioteca con l'intento di passare dalle scalette sotto le mura. E fu lì che trovai Magghy.

Era seduta di lato, alla fioca luce di un lampione. Era bellissima. Mi toccai la mano, mi faceva male.

Mi sedetti accanto a lei, e restammo in silenzio per un po'. Avevo voglia di abbracciarla, di chiederle perdono per quello che avevo fatto, di parlarle del nostro futuro insieme.

Feci tre lunghi respiri. Poi mi misi a parlare.

Mi uscirono le parole più belle che avessi mai pronunciato. Se mi fossi impegnato a dovere, sarei potuto diventare un disegnatore professionista, avrei portato a termine gli studi e mi sarei messo a guadagnare seriamente, mi sarei impegnato a far funzionare la nostra storia perché ci credevo e la amavo, e anche se all'inizio ci saremmo dovuti accontentare di una macchina usata, avremmo potuto cominciare a viaggiare, a partire da tutti i paesini della Toscana! Sì, potevamo riuscirci, sarebbe stato bellissimo, no? Il Benelli, ormai, faceva davvero parte del mio passato di adolescente...

Dopo quello che avevamo passato negli ultimi giorni, ero convinto che niente e nessuno ci avrebbero più diviso.

Magghy, provata da tutte quelle emozioni, si appoggiò teneramente alla mia spalla e mi strinse una mano. Rimanemmo lì, in silenzio, ancora per un po', poi ci baciammo, forte, fortissimo. Ne ero convinto più che mai: ci amavamo.

Mi accorsi di avere in tasca le chiavi del bar, e mi venne in mente un'idea dannatamente emozionante.

- Vieni, seguimi.

Era la prima volta che prendevo un'iniziativa del genere con lei. Ne ero orgoglioso. Avevo deciso che avremmo fatto l'amore al bar, su uno dei tavoli della saletta interna, come due veri amanti.

Arrivammo in via Sicilia. Lanciai un'occhiata alle finestre di casa di Checco. La luce della sua camera era ancora accesa. Che strano, pensai, lui che la mattina si alza sempre così presto è ancora sveglio a quest'ora...

La saracinesca del Paradise era leggermente alzata. La osservai meglio. Era proprio aperta. Possibile che papà si fosse dimenticato di chiuderla? Impossibile, pensai. Ma allora, cosa stava succedendo? Oh mio Dio, i ladri. Una scarica di adrenalina mi passò lungo la schiena. Pensai ai carabinieri, alla mia mano ferita, al Benelli.

A un tratto, mi accorsi di una moto parcheggiata sul lato opposto della strada, proprio di fronte all'ingresso dell'ormai ex campetto da calcio dell'Invicta. Le diedi un'occhiata più da vicino. Era una Yamaha Xt 500, bianca e rossa. La moto di Vezio. Allora era tornato. Mi chiesi cosa diamine ci facesse parcheggiata lì. E qual era, se c'era, un collegamento tra la moto e la saracinesca alzata. Mi abbassai per guardare dentro il bar. La luce era accesa, poi mi arrivarono delle voci. Riconobbi quella di Vezio. Vezio al bar...? Ma come aveva fatto a entrare? Stava forse rubando?

Tutto si chiarì dopo pochi istanti. All'improvviso, la saracinesca si alzò completamente e Vezio uscì, avvinghiato stretto a Monica.

Lo shock fu così inaspettato che svenni. Mi ritrovai seduto sul marciapiede, appoggiato con la schiena al muro del bar. Magghy mi dava dei colpetti sul viso, in silenzio. Quando realizzai quello che era successo, la prima reazione fu di scansarla con la mano. Monica stava dritta come un pesce lesso e si mordicchiava un'unghia. Tirò fuori la bomboletta per l'asma e aspirò. Vezio mi guardava stralunato, scuotendo la testa.

- Cosa stavate facendo? -, li aggredii.

Nessuno dei due rispose.

Quindi Vezio se la faceva con mia sorella! Allora significava che stavano insieme...

Con le forze che ancora mi rimanevano, mi scagliai contro di lui, sfogando tutto il mio risentimento. Lo colpii con una gomitata, e Vezio si piegò su di me cercando malamente di bloccarmi. Stavo per sferrargli una testata in pieno petto quando mi accorsi che aveva un vistoso cerotto sul braccio. Istintivamente, andai a battere proprio lì. Vezio cacciò un urlo e mi lasciò andare. Mi tirai indietro, ansimando. Perché non mi aveva mai detto niente? Io mi ero sempre confidato con lui. Si vantava delle ballerine brasiliane e delle francesi dalla voce sexy, e invece...

Ma per chi mi avevano preso, tutti e due, per uno stupido?

Guardai mia sorella, la camicetta nera le stringeva il seno sodo. Davanti a me faceva tanto la sostenuta, ma anche lei, in fondo... All'improvviso, la gelosia si impadronì di me. Il solo pensiero che

Vezio l'avesse toccata mi inorridiva, senza pensare a cos'altro poteva essere successo dentro al bar. La pressione mi schizzò alle stelle, le vene pulsavano nelle tempie. Quante frottole mi avevano raccontato!

Ero schifato. - Mi fate schifo! Capito? Schifo, tutti e due!

Con la testa incassata nelle spalle, deciso a non stare a sentire neanche una parola da loro, mi incamminai verso casa. La notte buia aveva completamente avvolto le strade di Grosseto.

Magghy mi seguiva come un'ombra, in silenzio.

Se tutto questo, come aveva farfugliato Vezio, aveva una spiegazione, be', al diavolo, non me ne fregava niente. Ora sì che capivo il motivo di tutti quei bei discorsi sull'esperienza all'estero. Così non mi avrebbe più avuto tra i piedi e si sarebbe potuto *dedicare* completamente a Monica. Che bugiardo! E se invece la stava illudendo per impadronirsi del Paradise e rilanciarlo alla faccia nostra? Non sapevo più cosa pensare! Ero stato trattato come un bambino delle elementari. Perché non mi aveva mai detto niente? Perché?!

Lo odiavo, odiavo quel dannato bar, odiavo tutto! Se solo non mi fossi fatto intortare da tutti quei suoi discorsi, io e Checco avremmo già potuto presentare la domanda per la paninoteca, e a quel punto gliel'avrei fatto vedere io, di cosa ero capace!

L'essermi rappacificato con Magghy era solo una magra consolazione a tutta la tristezza e la delusione che sentivo in quel momento. Era proprio un'estate maledetta!

«Devi smetterla di lamentarti e tirare fuori il coraggio di scegliere, capito?». La voce di Malù risuonò di nuovo dentro di me.

Quattordici

Era il venti di luglio. I cinque giorni appena trascorsi erano passati oscillando tra uno stato di apatia e uno di nostalgia non so neppure io di cosa, forse di un futuro che non avevo neanche fatto in tempo a programmare che già mi si era rivoltato contro. Papà mi trattava con sufficienza. Era il suo modo per farmi capire che l'avevo deluso. Aveva ripreso a tornare a casa per pranzo, dicendo che si era rotto di stare al bar aspettando che *non* arrivassero i clienti. Dopo mangiato si buttava sul divano e poi, verso le tre del pomeriggio, si rinfilava gli occhiali e tornava al lavoro sbuffando. Mamma mi obbligava a sbrigare le più noiose faccende di casa. Ma era il rapporto con Monica, che da quella sera non aveva più osato parlarmi, che in qualche modo si stava comunque trasformando. Lo avevo capito da come mi guardava. Stava cercando *un contatto*. Ma io avevo tirato fuori tutto il mio orgoglio, e a ogni suo tentativo facevo finta di niente.

Pian piano mi dimenticai anche del viso di Malù, solo le sue parole ogni tanto mi tornavano alla mente. In quei giorni, a volte avevo pensato di andare al Villaggio Curiel e chiederle scusa per come mi ero comportato. Alla fine, però, forse per vergogna, forse perché mi sarei sentito in colpa verso Magghy, lasciai perdere.

In camera, staccai tutti i poster, li arrotolati e li infilai nell'armadio. Non avevo più voglia di vederli sulle pareti, mi infastidivano. Lasciai solo la sciarpa della Lazio. Con una spugnetta pulii a fondo le Nike, che sistemai nella scarpiera del ripostiglio, e mi infilai le infradito. Erano più comode, e poi faceva caldo, caldissimo, alla tele avevano detto che quello era il luglio più caldo degli ultimi vent'anni.

Avevo preso l'abitudine di andare a casa di Magghy subito dopo pranzo. Ormai facevamo coppia fissa. L'unica stranezza dei nostri appuntamenti era che in tutti quei giorni non avevo mai incrociato né la madre né la sorellina. Non le avevo chiesto spiegazioni, in fondo non mi importava più di tanto, erano affari loro. Però, più passava il tempo, più sentivo che qualcosa non quadrava. Qualcosa mi andava stretto. Un pomeriggio, senza che le dicessi niente, Magghy se ne uscì con il discorso che la madre lavorava per una grande azienda farmaceutica e quindi spesso non tornava a casa.

Come spiegazione, però, non mi parve molto convincente. A parte gli ultimi giorni, anche papà non tornava quasi mai a casa, però lui doveva stare sempre al bar.

Non feci commenti, limitandomi ad annuire.

Facevamo l'amore e bevevamo Coca Light, poi, prima di cena, tornavo a casa. E il mese di luglio arrivò alla fine.

Quindici

Passando in corridoio, lanciai la solita occhiata al quadretto con la Madonna. Poi sul letto di mamma e papà notai l'album delle foto di famiglia. Senza farmi vedere, entrai a guardare. Chissà perché era stato tirato fuori. Lo aprii. La prima, era una foto in bianco e nero che riconobbi subito. Quella domenica sul Tombolo della Giannella. Io e Monica eravamo in primo piano, alle nostre spalle il mare calmo e scintillante. Dietro di me, papà sorrideva - aveva proprio il fisico da calciatore - e stringeva le spalle di mamma con le sue mani grandi. Lei era giovanissima, avrà avuto l'età di Monica. Gli occhi dello stesso colore del mare. Non mi ricordavo che fosse così bella. Io avevo sei o sette anni, capelli a pentolino e una bella finestra tra gli incisivi che mi dava un'aria simpatica. Sospirai, cercando di ricostruire quei ricordi così lontani nel tempo. Osservai quella stanza, in cui entravo di rado. Sul comodino di mamma, incastonata in una cornice d'argento, c'era la foto di un mazzo di incantevoli orchidee. Non l'avevo mai vista.

Con quella strana sensazione sotto pelle, dalla mia mente affiorò l'immagine del mio ex amico del cuore Checco. Erano due settimane che non mi facevo sentire. Sapevo che stavo sbagliando, ma in un modo o nell'altro avevo anche il *sentore* che, prima o poi, qualcosa sarebbe successo...

Una delle prime cose che mi aveva detto quando ci eravamo conosciuti era che secondo lui era stata una congiunzione astrale a farci incontrare. Qualche anno più tardi, quando cominciò ad appassionarsi alla Cabala, mi raccontò dei nostri angeli custodi: mi spiegò che gli angeli ci stanno sempre accanto e osservano le nostre azioni. Intercedono solo con coloro che sono puri di cuore, che amano senza giudicare e senza chiedere niente in cambio. Mi scrisse poi su un foglio il nome del mio angelo: *Nemamiah*. - Conservalo, Massa -, mi aveva detto, - e quando hai bisogno di lui, chiamalo!

Andai in camera e aprii il mio cassetto portaoggetti. Presi la scatolina di legno dove conservavo il chiodo arrugginito: dentro vi trovai anche quel biglietto. Dopo tanto tempo rilessi quel nome, *Nemamiah*, e mi venne un nodo in gola.

Dopo averlo annusato, misi in tasca il chiodo portafortuna e richiusi la scatolina.

Quella notte, non riuscii a prendere sonno. Avevo un gran caldo ed ero dibattuto all'idea che il passato non sarebbe più tornato, che con Checco non saremmo più riusciti a *ridiventare* amici come prima. La spensieratezza, la voglia di scoprire il mondo, un mondo che per noi iniziava appena oltrepassato il cartello di Grosseto, in un viaggio che finiva dritto dritto nel nostro letto, prima di addormentarci, stanchissimi ma contenti. La vita era uno scorrere di giorni, il nostro ritmo si incastrava perfettamente con quello delle stagioni. Era perfetto. Ma il tempo si muoveva solo in avanti, e io adesso ero maggiorenne. L'ultimo anno di scuola avrebbe segnato lo spartiacque ufficiale tra la vecchia vita e la nuova, e anche se la sentivo come scolpita dentro al cuore, forse avrei dovuto abbandonare per sempre *quell'idea del mondo* con cui ero cresciuto.

Presi il mio blocco e disegnai il mare. Disegnai anche due figure intente a contemplarlo. Eravamo noi, io e Checco. Sull'orizzonte, feci poi un puntino minuscolo. Una barca diretta lontano.

Guardai fuori dalla finestra. La notte ammantava la città di un fascino particolare. I lampioni accesi delle strade mi facevano compagnia. Sentii in lontananza due gatti che litigavano e un motorino sfrecciare chissà dove. Uscii dalla camera. Dormivano tutti. Dalla porta socchiusa, sentii papà russare. Dal salotto passai sul terrazzo a prendere un po' d'aria. Le mattonelle fresche mi diedero sollievo. Il Villaggio Azzurro dormiva.

Sedici

Finalmente, arrivò il giorno del tanto agognato esame pratico di guida. Avevo deciso di darlo dopo sole quattro lezioni. Diciottomila lire a botta non erano poche e poi, in fin dei conti, anche questa esperienza aveva perso il suo significato iniziale. Col passare dei giorni la patente era diventata come una sorta di tappa obbligata. È vero, mi sarebbe tornata utile, utilissima, ma cominciavo a rimpiangere il mio amato *Bennellindson*, che pur con tutti i suoi difetti mi aveva scorrazzato in sella per tanti anni facendomi scoprire gli angoli più suggestivi della Maremma.

Ripensai a Checco e ai contributi della Comunità Economica Europea. Chissà se il bando era già scaduto? Con questa domanda in testa mi incamminai verso la scuola guida.

Ero il primo. Salii in auto con l'istruttore. L'esaminatore era già sul sedile posteriore, come fosse stato un pezzo degli interni. Indossava la giacca e la cravatta ben stretta, e mi chiesi se non avesse caldo. Mi metteva in soggezione. L'istruttore mi disse di partire e di dirigermi verso la via Aurelia. Cavolo, pensai, la via più trafficata. Mi misi la cintura, controllai tutti gli specchietti e ingranai la prima. Mi scordai la freccia, e quando l'esaminatore me lo fece presente mi giustificai col fatto che non stava passando nessuno.

- Male -, osservò severo. - La freccia va messa *sempre*.

Deglutii, ma avevo la gola secca. Che palle questo, pensai tra me e me.

Procedevo con cautela, cercando di mantenere alta l'attenzione. L'istruttore mi disse di svoltare a sinistra, di conseguenza dovevo immettermi sulla seconda corsia. Stavolta misi la freccia. L'esaminatore non commentò. Svoltai.

- Ahi ahi -, fece subito dopo.

Cavolo, e adesso cos'era successo?

Guardai ovunque - cruscotto, plancia dei comandi... -, ma non capivo.

- Ahi ahi -, ripeté l'esaminatore. - Proprio non le vogliamo vedere, eh, queste strisce pedonali?

Non sapendo cosa rispondere, rimasi in silenzio.

- Quando vedi le strisce pedonali -, mi spiegò, - ti devi fermare.

- Ma se non c'è nessuno che deve attraversare?

- Non importa. Ti devi fermare *sempre*.

Uff, era proprio insopportabile.

Dopo il classico parcheggio in salita, che mi riuscì non so se per grazia ricevuta, l'esaminatore firmò con la faccia schifata la mia nuova patente di guida: un foglietto telato di quattro pagine di un rosa shocking.

La osservai per qualche istante, la misi nel portafoglio e mi diressi verso il bar. Avevo quasi voglia di ubriacarmi, desideroso com'ero di una nuova spensieratezza.

Osvaldo stava guardando la Tv. - Osvà, guarda -, gli dissi.

- Auuu! Ora sì che siamo a posto, Maremma maiala. Un altro dilinquente al volante! Che mondo è diventato questo! Che mondo!

Sorrisi. Mio padre ci guardava. Prese una bottiglia di spumante e cominciò a versarlo nei bicchieri. Riempì una ciotola di noccioline e se ne mise in bocca una bella manciata. Si unirono al brindisi anche gli altri unici due clienti.

- Speramo che metterai un po' de giudizio mo' -, disse papà masticando incessantemente. - Se solo l'usassi a dovere, quér cervello...

Entrò Monica. Osservò la scena e si ritirò in laboratorio. Se almeno mi prestasse la sua Uno Fire, pensai, potrei andarmene a fare un giro. Mi ero immaginato almeno un milione di volte alla guida di quella scatoletta azzurra.

Inaspettatamente, fu mio padre a prendere in mano la situazione. - Voijo vede se riesci a non combinà casini.

- Cioè?

- Mo'? -, chiamò mia sorella.

Monica aveva già capito le sue intenzioni.

- Che palle, papà, ma se succede qualcosa?

- Aò! E nun gufà, no?

Osvaldo rise e ripeté: - E nun gufà, aò!

Insomma, presi le chiavi della Uno e uscii. Misi in moto e ingranai la prima. Guardai di sfuggita le finestre di Checco, e mi parve di vederlo dietro a un vetro, come se stesse osservando i miei movimenti. Nell'abitacolo mi sentivo proprio un altro, più adulto, ma anche un po' a disagio. Non mi ricordai neanche una di tutte le raccomandazioni che mi aveva dato l'istruttore, la mia attenzione era concentrata esclusivamente sulla frizione.

Mi avviai verso il Villaggio Azzurro. A casa, fui accolto da un silenzio totale; mamma era distesa a letto. Mi avvicinai. Stava dormendo su un fianco, con Mila acciambellata accanto. Andai a buttarmi anch'io sul mio letto, e chiusi gli occhi.

Immancabilmente, sognai: stavolta, Checco era il proprietario di un famosissimo ristorante messicano, e una troupe televisiva era andata a intervistarlo. Per l'occasione si era messo in giacca e cravatta, e i capelli sparati lo facevano sembrare una versione giovanile di Einstein. Ero alla cassa: gli stavo dicendo che purtroppo mi mancavano tremila lire per saldare il conto e gli chiesi uno sconto.

Ma lui non ne voleva sapere. Diceva che il lavoro era lavoro e, se ne volevo approfittare, un'oretta di piatti sporchi da lavare mi avrebbe fatto bene. Io scoppiai in lacrime e in ginocchio gli confessai che proprio quella mattina avevo disgraziatamente tamponato con la mia macchina usata e poi mi ero accorto che avevo l'assicurazione scaduta. Checco scoppiò in una risata che rimbombò per tutto il locale e io allora cominciai a scavare una buca per sotterrarmi e sparire dalla faccia della Terra.

Mi svegliai di soprassalto, cercando di scacciare via quelle immagini. Mi infilai un paio di bermuda e una polo che non mettevo da tanto tempo. Mi aggiustai il ciuffo alla meno peggio, una spazzolata veloce ai denti ed ero di nuovo in strada.

Dal momento che le mie disponibilità erano assai limitate, pensai che avrei potuto portare Magghy dallo Zozzone a «festeggiare» la patente.

Quando ero con lei stavo bene, certo, eppure c'era qualcosa che mi rendeva irrequieto. Di colpo, mi accorsi che non volevo festeggiare proprio niente, non mi andava, mi sembrava stupido. Era una sensazione che mi colse inaspettata, perché dentro di me avevo sognato quel momento fino alla nausea.

La strada correva sotto le ruote della Uno. Per la prima volta misi la quarta. Arrivai a casa di Magghy e parcheggiai nel posto più largo disponibile: di fronte a un passo carrabile. Suonai. Come sempre, vidi uscire dal portone la sua amica Caty, che mi fece il suo consueto sorrisetto. Ma questa una casa non ce l'ha?, chiesi tra me e me.

Dal momento che la porta di casa di Magghy era aperta, entrai senza farmi tanti scrupoli. A ricevermi trovai una signora sui quarantacinque anni. Una vampata di calore mi attraversò da capo a piedi. Dal modo di vestire e da una certa somiglianza con Magghy, dedussi che si trattava proprio di sua madre.

Mi salutò. La voce era squillante, esattamente come al telefono. Mi aspettavo qualche domanda su di me o la mia famiglia, invece non mi chiese nulla di tutto ciò. Accennò solo a un viaggio che aveva in programma, poi chiamò la figlia.

Magghy arrivò su un paio di scarpe altissime. Indossava una camicetta con almeno tre bottoni aperti, il seno in evidenza. Mi vergognai un po' di trovarmi lì.

Magghy la rimproverò per non essere passata a cambiarle non ricordo quale vestito in non so quale negozio. I ruoli madre e figlia erano come invertiti. Monica, che pure sapeva essere antipatica, non si sarebbe mai permessa di parlare con quel tono a mamma.

Magghy mi disse solo: - Andiamo -. Io salutai la signora, che ricambiò senza nemmeno guardarmi, e uscimmo.

Sulla strada che portava dallo Zozzone non parlammo molto. In effetti, a ripensarci, non ci eravamo dati nemmeno un bacio.

Magghy si passò il lucidalabbra almeno tre volte. Mi chiesi il motivo. All'inizio lo trovavo un gesto sexy, ma ora capivo che era solo una sua tecnica per mettere in evidenza le labbra sottili. E poi, cominciava a darmi fastidio baciare sempre del lucidalabbra, sentirne in bocca il sapore. Insomma, pensai che forse avrei dovuto dirglielo. Arrivammo dallo Zozzone e lei ordinò le solite patatine fritte e Coca, «*Light*, mi raccomando». Ci sedemmo a uno dei tavoli esterni, stavolta sotto la tettoia di lamiera un tempo adibita a parcheggio. Intorno a noi, altri ragazzi parlavano e ridevano beati. La serata era umida, e le cosce nude mi si appiccicavano alla plastica della sedia.

Parlammo del più e del meno, come sempre tra noi, e a un certo punto Magghy se ne uscì fuori che sua madre aveva accettato un nuovo incarico di lavoro all'estero, in Svizzera.

Solo qualche giorno prima, alla parola «estero» dentro di me sarebbe esploso un carnevale. Adesso, invece, non mi faceva né caldo né freddo.

- In Svizzera? -, domandai. - Ma scusa, che lavoro è? E tu, piuttosto?

- Io... -, disse abbassando lo sguardo. - Mamma lavora per una grande multinazionale farmaceutica, o accetta, oppure addio alla carriera...

Addio alla carriera? Ma che cavolata era quella?

- Potresti venire anche tu -, propose. - Andremo ad abitare nel Canton Ticino e per la scuola non ci sarebbero problemi. Pensa che anche Caty vorrebbe trasferirsi. Quella, mi seguirebbe ovunque... Insomma, potresti frequentare l'Accademia di Belle Arti, dopo la maturità. Io mi iscriverò a Economia.

Io? In Svizzera?

- Non saprei... -, commentai.

- Non ti piacerebbe? Staremmo insieme tutti i giorni.

- Ma sì, mi piacerebbe, però non lo so... Ci devo pensare.

E la mia famiglia? E Checco? Come facevo a partire lasciandomi tutto alle spalle? Sospirai, pensando che, a quanto pareva, quello con Magghy era diventato un rapporto a tempo determinato.

- Ma tu allora hai già deciso -, ripresi il discorso.

- Io... Sì. E tu?

Rimasi in silenzio, grattandomi la testa. Mi vennero in mente almeno due miliardi di validi motivi per non partire. Accidenti, la sola idea di trasferirmi all'estero adesso mi faceva un po' paura. Appena un mese prima, sarebbe stato diverso... Come cambiavano le cose, come ero cambiato io!

«Devi smetterla di lamentarti e tirare fuori il coraggio di scegliere...». Ancora lei, ancora la voce di Malù risuonò nella mia mente...

- Ma come faccio a mollare tutto? Così, all'improvviso? -. La voce mi tremava per l'agitazione. - E poi c'è il bar...

- Che c'entra il bar? Mica ci lavori.

- Per ora. C'è in ballo un progetto di ristrutturazione con i fondi della CEE, io e Checco pensavamo di farlo diventare una paninoteca.

- Non me l'avevi detto -, esclamò Magghy incuriosita.

- Be'... ora lo sai.

Lei mi guardò sconcertata. - Perché adesso mi rispondi così? Che ti ho fatto, scusa?

- E come ti devo rispondere? -, le chiesi alzando le spalle. La verità è che mi sentivo demoralizzato.

- Ma allora sei proprio *stronzo*...

Uno stronzo? Perché mai sarei stato uno stronzo? *Non volevo* trasferirmi, punto e basta. In Svizzera poi, figuriamoci. Il formaggio coi buchi non mi piaceva per niente, e non c'era nemmeno il mare.

Secondo me lei l'aveva capito subito, e sotto sotto ne ero contento, perché la verità era che mi sentivo come liberato da un peso. A quel punto non me ne fregava proprio niente, poteva pensare ciò che le pareva. Io sarei rimasto a Grosseto.

Magghy per un po' non disse nulla, poi mi ordinò di accompagnarla a casa. Prima di alzarsi tirò fuori dalla borsetta quel dannato lucidalabbra e se lo passò nervosamente sulla bocca.

Quando mi ritrovai da solo, in macchina, mi sembrò che quel giorno fosse durato un mese.

Pensavo a Magghy, a tutti i baci che ci eravamo dati, a tutte le volte in cui avevamo fatto l'amore, alle promesse che ci eravamo scambiati e alle emozioni che avevamo vissuto insieme, ma più ci pensavo più la sentivo lontana, estranea. Evidentemente, non doveva essere lei la donna della mia vita. Cavolo, per settimane era stata un chiodo fisso nella mia mente e ora... C'ero caduto con tutte le scarpe dentro. Checco aveva davvero ragione.

Come faceva a non sbagliarsi mai? Non so perché, mi ricordai di Tesla e della sua teoria sulla luce. Me l'aveva spiegata proprio lui due o tre anni prima, sotto al Grande Cipresso. Mi era rimasta impressa perché si chiamava del «muro di luce». Non ci capivo granché di particelle elementari, ma secondo questa teoria modificando le onde elettromagnetiche si poteva alterare a piacimento un po' tutto: tempo, spazio, gli stessi oggetti. Dal «muro», mi disse

Checco, si può effettuare il teletrasporto e, cosa ancora più incredibile, *viaggiare nel tempo.*

Forse, chissà, lui ci riusciva...

Guidai senza meta. Mi ritrovai, guarda caso, proprio al Grande Cipresso: mi fermai e rimasi in silenzio a riflettere. Pregai che il bando non fosse già scaduto. Avrei fatto di tutto per partecipare. Mi sarei messo a studiare, studiare seriamente, ripagando Checco di tutti gli sforzi che aveva fatto. Era una promessa.

Una civetta cantava proprio sopra la mia testa. Alzai gli occhi al cielo, e mi accorsi del numero incalcolabile di stelle con cui era dipinto.

Diciassette

Quando entrai in casa, la luce della cucina era accesa. Seduti al tavolo, trovai Monica e papà. Posai le chiavi della Uno sul mobiletto verde e dissi a mia sorella di non preoccuparsi, non avevo combinato alcun danno.

A parte qualche frase di circostanza, dopo la zuffa con Vezio era la prima volta in cui cercavo di comunicare veramente con lei ma, come sempre, mi guardò senza rispondere. Solo che stavolta lo fece in modo diverso. Si voltò un attimo verso nostro padre, si alzò e uscì frettolosamente dalla stanza.

- Ma che le ho fatto? -, mi lamentai. - Possibile che sia sempre così scontrosa?

- Siedete 'n'attimo -, rispose papà arricciando il naso.

- Perché?

- Perché sì.

Mi sedetti accanto a lui sbuffando.

- Per un paio de ggiorni il bar starà chiuso... -, riprese.

Aggrottai la fronte. Che strano tono aveva usato.

- Ah, sì?

- Famo pe' sta' un po' insieme, sai com'è.

- Un po' insieme? Cioè?

Davvero, era la spiegazione più insolita che avessi mai sentito da lui.

- Pe' tu' madre.

- Che c'entra mamma?

Mi sentivo in colpa, ma non capivo per cosa. Papà che faccia il misterioso, Monica che se n'era andata non appena mi aveva visto. Insomma, cos'era successo?

- Papà! -, urlò mia sorella da camera sua. - E diglielo che mamma sta in ospedale!

Forse avevo capito male.

- In ospedale? -, ripetei. - Ma cosa state dicendo?

- Sì, ma è per dei controlli, niente de grave -, cercò di spiegare papà. - Aveva la pressione bassa, hai visto come so' 'sti dottori...

- La pressione bassa? Ma cosa dici? Sono maggiorenne e ancora mi nascondete le cose?! Basta! Bastaaa! -. Questa volta a gridare ero io.

Papà si alzò dalla sedia. - Ma te l'ho detto! Non è niente!

- Come niente?! Per la pressione bassa non si finisce in ospedale!

- Stai tranquillo. Deve fare degli esami e poi la rimandano a casa.

Uscii dalla cucina, e prima di entrare in camera mia guardai in quella dei miei, come per controllare. Mamma non c'era davvero.

Mi salì il sangue al cervello, martellandomi le tempie.

- Quando ce l'avete portata? -, gridai in preda al panico. - Quandooo?!

Sbucò papà. - Un paio d'ore fa. Ma stai tranquillo, è tutto sotto controllo.

- Tutto sotto controllo un cazzo! Ditemi che è successooo!

Ero così confuso. Non sapevo cosa pensare. Mi sentivo come un funambolo che, dopo aver camminato a lungo su una corda tesa, metteva un piede in fallo e si ritrova di colpo in caduta libera...

In terrazzo, Monica si confidò a lungo con me. Ero così preoccupato per mamma che tutta la rabbia covata per la sua storia con

Vezio si era dissolta in un attimo. Da alcune settimane, mamma si era accorta che qualcosa non andava. Era stanca, con sempre meno appetito, aveva persino perso qualche chilo. Un paio di giorni prima era andata dal medico per una visita di routine e lui si era subito insospettito, prescrivendo un sacco di analisi.

Era notte fonda ormai ma per me il tempo non contava più molto. Non riuscivo a smettere di pensare a quanto fossi stato cieco, *distante* da mamma. - Non mi sono accorto di niente -, continuavo a ripetere, - come uno scemo, di niente...

Monica stava lì, accanto a me. Le chiesi che malattia avesse, lei si limitò a dire che era qualcosa di brutto e che aveva a che fare con l'apparato riproduttivo.

- Vuoi dire che ha un cancro?

Monica abbassò la testa, stringendo gli occhi.

- È così? Dimmelo! È così?

- Dopodomani le faranno la biopsia -, disse sconvolta.

- La *biospia*? Che cos'è? Un'operazione?

- È un esame *invasivo*, significa che le devono prelevare un pezzetto molto piccolo di tessuto dall'utero ed esaminarlo.

- A cosa serve? Non capisco!

- Devono controllare se da quel tessuto si stanno sviluppando delle cellule... impazzite. Ma per il nostro medico le analisi parlano già piuttosto chiaro: c'è il rischio che debbano asportarle l'utero.

- Impazzite? Che vuol dire impazzite? Le cellule mica impazziscono! Mica hanno un cervello! -, risposi con ingenuità e rabbia.

Poi chiusi gli occhi e li strinsi forte.

- È terribile, tutto questo... -, disse Monica dopo una breve pausa, con una tristezza nella voce che non le avevo mai sentito.

- Ma poi? Sarà tutto a posto, vero? -, chiesi con un singulto.

Mia sorella mi guardò per un attimo. - *Tutto a posto...*

- Perché? Non sarà così?

Monica rimase in silenzio, poi tirò su con il naso. - Sì, spero di sì, ma comunque non sarà più come prima.

Compresi a cosa alludeva, e cercai di confortarla: - Mamma ha già noi, non penso che vorrà altri figli.

Monica mi guardò costernata, disse: - Sei proprio uno stupido se la pensi così. Noi donne siamo diverse da voi uomini. Siamo noi che portiamo dentro la vita. Ci avevi mai fatto caso?

No, non ci avevo mai fatto caso.

Venni assalito da una profonda inquietudine. Mi sentivo osservato da un occhio minaccioso e imprevedibile. Come sarebbero stati i giorni che ci attendevano? In che modo ce la saremmo cavata da soli, senza mamma, in casa?

Mi sentivo perso.

Monica interruppe le mie preoccupazioni dicendomi che andava a letto, e mi consigliò di fare altrettanto. Si avvicinò e mi accarezzò la testa. Sentii una specie di prurito all'altezza dello stomaco, non ricordavo l'avesse mai fatto prima di allora. Ma io, come uno stupido, non riuscii neanche a rivolgerle un mezzo sorriso.

Non avevo sonno e così rimasi lì, in terrazzo, a pensare e a osservare il malinconico splendore della città di notte. Uno spicchio di luna era dipinto nel cielo, nello spazio senz'aria dell'infinito. Riabbassando il capo, lo sguardo mi cadde sul piccolo vasetto dell'orchidea. Mi avvicinai. Era cresciuta. Tre belle fogliolette verde bottiglia puntavano verso il cielo. Ripensai a quando mamma aveva piantato i semi, assaporando ancora la carezza di Monica.

Dopo qualche minuto papà mise la testa fuori e anche lui insistette affinché andassi a dormire, ma gli dissi di non preoccuparsi per me.

Mi sistemai su una piccola sdraio che non usava mai nessuno, perché era la più scomoda. Dopo qualche minuto sentii di nuovo scostarsi la portafinestra. Mi girai ma non vidi nessuno. Solo in un secondo momento mi accorsi che si trattava di Mila. Iniziò a leccarsi il pelo stendendo le zampe e passandole sulle orecchie. Per lei, forse, niente era cambiato. O forse sapeva tutto; chissà quante volte mamma doveva essersi confidata con la micina... Ne sentiva anche lei la mancanza?

Mi misi a osservarla, riflettendo sulla piccola creatura che avevo di fronte. Solo allora mi resi conto che quella di Mila era stata da sempre una presenza discreta eppure, in ogni momento, in ogni giorno della sua esistenza, reale, *viva*, senza spiegazioni e senza rimpianti. Proprio come quella di mamma. I lunghi baffi della gatta accarezzavano l'aria e i suoi occhi fosforescenti rilucevano come pietre preziose nel chiarore lunare. Forse, in realtà, Mila era venuta lì per me, a darmi coraggio.

Poi, all'orizzonte, intravidi la breve scia di una stella cadente. Fu un attimo e non ebbi neanche il tempo di esprimere un desiderio, ma andava bene così, che senso avrebbe avuto una stella cadente che rimaneva lì a farsi osservare? Feci un profondo respiro e mi asciugai con la mano gli occhi gonfi di lacrime.

Cercai di mettere ordine tra le nozioni di anatomia che mi frullavano in testa, ma mi resi conto di avere solo vaghe idee. E io che mi consideravo *adulto*...

Rientrai dentro, fermandomi di fronte alla libreria in corridoio. Sfilai il volume dell'enciclopedia sull'anatomia umana e lo sfogliai fino ad arrivare al capitolo dedicato all'apparato riproduttivo femminile. Sapevo che le ovaie sono due ghiandole, e che è al loro interno che si sviluppano le cellule uovo. Ma che l'utero fosse «l'organo destinato ad accogliere l'uovo fecondato e a sostenere lo sviluppo del germe» era già una nozione di cui non avevo molta cognizione... Lessi: «germe». Come il seme di un frutto, pensai. E ancora, le tube di Falloppio, il collo dell'utero, la tasca di Douglas, ma anche il clitoride, la vagina... Mi tornavano alla mente certe battute fatte in classe durante le lezioni di biologia, ma era la prima volta nella mia vita che quelle parole venivano associate a un avvenimento importante, cariche di un significato a cui non avevo mai pensato. Osservai tutte le immagini con un'attenzione davvero speciale. Poi richiusi il volume e lo rimisi al suo posto.

Tornai di nuovo in terrazzo, con il pensiero fisso a mamma e alla malattia che covava in lei. Chiusi gli occhi. Nel profondo del mio cuore, pregai per la prima volta il mio angelo *Nemamiah* che tutto potesse risolversi per il meglio in breve tempo.

Quando li riaprii, la luna era scomparsa. Nella penombra, delle nuvole basse sembravano fumo sospeso. Poi, a un tratto, tutti i rumori cessarono e minuscole gocce di pioggia iniziarono a bagnare le mattonelle del terrazzo. Le osservai emozionato. Quanto tempo era passato dall'ultima volta! Ne ero sicuro, quella pioggia era venuta per me. Mi avvicinai alla balaustra, chiusi gli occhi alzando il viso al cielo e aspettai che l'acqua mi bagnasse completamente.

Diciotto

Dopo una notte praticamente insonne, un paio di minuti prima delle sette decisi di alzarmi. In cucina, in piedi, Monica stava bevendo il caffè. Un vago odore di cipolla aleggiava nell'aria.

- Papà?

- È già uscito. Siediti, fai colazione.

La tavola era apparecchiata. La mia tazza al solito posto, tre fette biscottate già spalmate con la mia marmellata preferita su un piattino. Monica posò la tazzina e andò al fornello. Tornò con il latte e me lo versò nella tazza. La osservai. Aveva preparato tutto.

- Esco a fare delle commissioni -, disse poi riempiendo d'acqua il pentolino, che lasciò nel lavello.

- Okay.

Non sapevo il programma della giornata, ma fu lei a mettermene al corrente: - Oggi mangeremo presto, poi andremo da mamma. Se ci riesci, metti a posto almeno camera tua.

Perché non ci sarei dovuto riuscire?

Monica, da nostra madre aveva preso la stessa gestualità, lo stesso modo di parlare. Li avevo avuti sotto gli occhi tutti i giorni, ma ci feci caso solo in quel momento.

- Posso fare anche qualcos'altro.

- Lascia stare -. Quindi se ne andò.

Ma io non volevo sentirmi inutile.

Pensai a Checco, e quel pensiero, come una fitta improvvisa, si impadronì di me. Provai a cercarlo al telefono, ma sua nonna mi disse che non era in casa. Non lo sentivo da un sacco di tempo. Non mi sembrava possibile. Avevo proprio sbagliato tutto, e forse avevo rovinato per sempre la nostra amicizia.

Sospirai. Coraggio, Massa, mi dissi. Solo in casa, cercai di capire da dove iniziare. Prima di tutto, presi i miei panni sporchi e li sistemai sulla lavatrice, dividendo la biancheria colorata dal resto. Non sapevo se andava bene, ma lo feci lo stesso.

Decisi poi di mettere a posto in cucina. Sparecchiai, lavai le tazze e le stoviglie e le sistemai nella credenza. Per capire dove andassero, però, persi un po' di tempo. Mi arrabbiai con me stesso per essere arrivato a diciotto anni senza sapere dove stavano i cucchiaini.

Tornai in camera. Rifeci il letto. Il lenzuolo continuava a pendere da una parte, ma lo lasciai così. Volevo controllare il resto della casa. La porta di camera dei miei era aperta. Papà aveva lasciato le ante dell'armadio accostate. Le chiusi. Osservai il lato del letto dove dormiva mamma. Feci un profondo respiro e uscii. Percorsi il corridoio. Poi cambiai idea e tornai indietro. Entrai di nuovo in camera mia e alzai completamente l'avvolgibile della finestra: la stanza aveva bisogno di essere arieggiata. In corridoio, mi accorsi che lo specchio sopra al mobiletto dell'ingresso era leggermente storto. Lo raddrizzai. Mi guardai intorno. La porta della stanza di Monica era socchiusa. Entrai. Le lenzuola del letto ben tirate, il poster di Madonna accanto alla scrivania. Su una mensola, alcuni orsacchiotti in fila mi guardavano. Mi sedetti sul suo letto. Non ero abituato a trovarmi lì. Non avevo mai provato interesse a entrare in camera sua, a curiosare tra le sue cose. Quella volta, però, avevo sentito come una sorta di *bisogno*: volevo conoscerla meglio, entrare nel suo mondo, sentirla più vicina...

Quando uscii, mi venne in mente di controllare la carta igienica in bagno. Il rotolo era stato appena cambiato. Sistemai accuratamente gli asciugamani e ordinai come meglio potei i prodotti per la rasatura di papà.

Pensai che c'erano sicuramente altre cose da sistemare ma, cavolo, non sapevo *quali*. Avevo sempre dato per scontato che non ci volesse poi molto a gestire una casa, ma adesso capivo di aver sempre sottovalutato la questione.

Dalla finestra della cucina osservai le nuvole grigie lasciare di nuovo spazio al sole dell'estate.

Era quasi mezzogiorno quando Monica rientrò e mi trovò in salotto sul divano con la Tv accesa, a rimuginare, il pensiero fisso a mamma. Posò le chiavi sul mobiletto dell'ingresso e la vidi andare in cucina senza dire nulla. Lasciò la porta aperta. Aprì uno scomparto della credenza, e poi intravidi gli scacchi blu e bianchi della tovaglia svolazzare. Mi alzai e la raggiunsi; stava stendendo la tovaglia sul tavolo, e pensai di darle una mano. Dal cassetto presi tre forchette e tre coltelli, e li sistemai sul tavolo. Mi spostai a sinistra e allungai la mano sul ripiano del lavello, ripetendo la stessa operazione con i bicchieri. Quindi olio, sale, pepe. Cos'altro poteva servire?

- I tovaglioli? -, mi ricordò Monica, quasi leggendomi nel pensiero.

Li prese e li sistemò da sola.

- E l'acqua? Il vino per papà? -, mi incalzò.

Mi affrettai a prenderli.

Nel frattempo, Monica aveva tirato fuori dal frigo una grande insalatiera. Dall'odore di cipolla capii subito che al mattino aveva preparato la panzanella.

Quando nostro padre rientrò, mia sorella ci passò sopra un filo di olio e completò sminuzzandoci del basilico. La portò in tavola e ci servì. Per me, tolse tutti i cetrioli e al loro posto aggiunse una dose doppia di pomodori. Papà prese la mia parte di cetrioli, e chiese più cipolla. Prima di sedersi, Monica tirò fuori dal frigo ancora un piattone colmo di formaggi e affettati toscani. Aveva pensato proprio a tutto.

Consumammo il pranzo in silenzio, lentamente, come se il tempo ci avesse concesso una tregua. Per la prima volta non c'era mamma a capotavola.

Mi sentivo il cuore in gola, mi sembrava di vivere in un film. Chissà lei cosa stava facendo? Stava pensando a noi? Era preoccupata?

Monica si alzò, sparecchiò e disse che era ora di uscire.

Andai in camera a prepararmi. Avrei fatto vedere a mamma la patente, e magari le avrei raccontato di Magghy. Chissà cosa avrebbe commentato.

L'ospedale, lungo il viale che portava a Siena, era un enorme e grigio parallelepipedo a sei piani. Dava l'impressione di trovarsi lì per sbaglio, come un monolite piombato all'improvviso nel tranquillo paesaggio grossetano. Arrivammo all'ingresso principale e svoltammo verso i parcheggi, dalla parte opposta della strada. Monica portava un sacchetto con alcune posate, dei bicchieri di plastica e altre stoviglie; papà la borsa da viaggio con gli indumenti e la biancheria di ricambio; io due bottiglie d'acqua e due succhi di frutta.

All'edificio si accedeva tramite una salita tortuosa, intervallata da una fila di alti pini, che brulicava di gente. Il complesso era davvero imponente, con decine di finestre anonime, squallide. Ero sorpreso. Non me lo ricordavo così imponente, così austero, quasi fastidioso. Ci dirigemmo al gabbiotto dei visitatori. Era l'ora del passo, nell'aria un brusio di voci, il calpestio incessante di chi andava e veniva. L'addetto alla portineria, un uomo basso e ben vestito, ci indicò il piano e il numero della stanza di mamma. Superammo il bar. In vetrina, la mia attenzione fu attirata da una scatola di cioccolatini con la foto di un'orchidea bianca. A lei sarebbe piaciuta.

- Papà, voglio prendere una cosa per mamma qui al bar dell'ospedale. Andate su, vi raggiungo.

Entrai. Un grande calendario elettronico mi ricordò che era venerdì cinque agosto 1994.

Mi svuotai le tasche. Contai undicimilaottocento lire. Poi controllai il prezzo sulla scatola. Dodicimilacinquecento. Cavolo. L'unica era farmi fare un piccolo sconto. Andai alla cassa ed esposi sinceramente il problema. Inaspettatamente, la signora del bar non mostrò la benché minima riserva, anzi, fu così gentile che arrotondò a undicimila. Si vede che ero stato convincente. Ne fui così contento che le strinsi la mano, mi misi la scatola sottobraccio e uscii.

Davanti agli ascensori c'erano diverse persone in attesa, così decisi di salire a piedi. Superai una porta seguendo le indicazioni per le scale.

Non c'era nessuno. Mi piombò addosso un'ondata di nostalgia. Pensai a mamma. Cominciai a salire, lentamente, col fiato quasi sospeso. Le scale, vecchie e sporche, erano state tinteggiate di celeste, con i gradini in pietra consumati in certi punti. I muri, di un colore smorto - come me in quel momento -, salivano e sembravano non finire mai. Mi sentivo tutto irrigidito. A testa bassa, osservavo i miei piedi in marcia. Il petto mi andava su e giù, e cominciavo a sentirmi in preda all'ansia. Mi fermai tra un piano e l'altro, e respirai profondamente. Dovevo resistere, non farmi assalire dalle emozioni *forti* e dalla paura ancor più *forte* che a mamma potesse accadere qualcosa di tremendo. A poco a poco, l'angoscia di rimanere solo si impadronì del mio cuore, ma in un batter d'occhio il panico aveva preso il suo posto e io credetti di morire. Come avrei fatto senza di lei? Fu allora che alcune immagini si affastellarono nella mia mente.

Ero neonato, e mamma mi teneva in braccio e mi accarezzava, e mi baciava, e mi nutriva, con tenerezza. Poi mi ritrovai bambino. Era il primo giorno di scuola: mamma mi aveva accompagnato e ora mi stava dicendo che sarebbe andata via, che mi avrebbe lasciato da *solo*. Mi lanciava baci con la mano per salutarmi. Io mi sentivo abbandonato, perché avevo paura che nessuno mi sarebbe più venuto a prendere.

Un rumore di passi mi fece trasalire. Erano di un signore che scendeva le scale. Scossi il capo e continuai a salire. Così com'erano venute, quelle immagini perse nella memoria tornarono a chiudersi nei cassetti misteriosi della mia mente. L'unica mia certezza era che stava accadendo qualcosa di importante, che mi sarei portato dentro per sempre...

Al piano, pur essendo l'ora di pranzo, c'era una penombra particolare. Sembrava che tutte le cose fossero spente. Un uomo in camice bianco sbucò da una curva del corridoio. Il cuore pompò veloce, ma il medico mi oltrepassò a testa bassa, mentre un lembo del camice aperto si gonfiava allo spostamento d'aria.

Arrivai in una saletta d'aspetto, che al contrario del corridoio era immersa nella luce naturale del giorno. Un ficus alto due metri stazionava in un angolo, vicino a un tavolino basso di vetro su cui erano poggiate alcune riviste. Dalle enormi finestre, Grosseto appariva diversa, mi sembrava finta, distante.

Imboccai il corridoio del reparto di ginecologia. In fondo, vidi papà. Guardava fuori da un grande finestrone con gli infissi di alluminio. Lì vicino Monica, appoggiata con la schiena allo stipite di una porta. Forse mamma si trovava al di là, in quella camera.

L'adrenalina accelerò nelle vene, e io mi sentii di nuovo rigido, affannato, con gli occhi gonfi di pianto. Avrei voluto essere solo, in quel momento, per non sentire la vergogna nel liberare tutta l'emozione che avevo dentro, come una seconda pelle che mi stringeva l'anima.

Nostro padre si avvicinò alla porta nell'atto di bussare, ma proprio in quel momento quella si aprì, e ne uscì un medico. Si misero a parlare. Monica li osservò, tirò fuori il suo inalatore e aspirò due volte, poi, dopo aver infilato la testa dentro, entrò in camera. Mi affrettai a seguirla.

Mamma! E Checco. Checco?

Il letto era inclinato e mamma stava parlando con lui, che era seduto su uno sgabellino accanto alla finestra. Fu l'immagine più emozionante che avrei potuto vedere.

Allora non ero solo...

Checco mi salutò alzando un sopracciglio, a mamma si illuminarono gli occhi e si mise a piangere silenziosamente.

Ancora oggi, ripensando a quella scena, sento lo stomaco salirmi in gola.

- Chicco -, disse con un filo di voce.

Mi sfilai da sotto il braccio la scatola di cioccolatini e gliela offrii: - Ecco, è per te.

- Oh... è per me!

Tirai fuori anche la patente: - E questa.

Mamma la osservò: - Bravo... Mi raccomando, adesso... Non correre...

- Ti abbiamo portato tutto quello che può servirti -, disse Monica, sforzandosi di sorridere mentre svuotava la busta. - Ho preso un paio di riviste e qua ci sono posate e bicchieri di carta. I ricambi ce li ha papà di là con tutto il resto. Se vuoi vedere la televisione in camera, stasera ti porto la mia.

Mamma si strinse le mani al petto. - Grazie, tesoro, ma non ti preoccupare, va bene così. Non ce n'è bisogno.

Il suo viso, i suoi occhi azzurri, le sue mani affusolate. Le guardavo, e in cuor mio speravo che prima o poi tornassero a dipingere.

Parlammo ancora qualche minuto. Mamma scherzò sulla biopsia che le avevano fatto, su quel termine dal suono così ridicolo, poi aggiunse che desiderava riposare un po'. Uscimmo.

Checco si mise seduto nella saletta d'aspetto.

Monica mi prese sottobraccio: - Vieni.

Non so perché, ma solo in quel momento mi accorsi di quanto fosse cambiata, di quanto fosse «grande».

- Non voglio che tu te la prenda con Vezio.

Non mi aspettavo parlasse di lui.

- Vezio si è davvero affezionato a me, e io, sì insomma, anch'io a lui. Ma c'è una cosa che devi sapere.

- Cioè?

- Cioè che lui non è quello che pensi.

- Cioè...?

- Non è vero che fa il barman nei locali alla moda in giro per l'Italia.

Che significava «non è vero»? Dove voleva arrivare?

- Ma cosa stai dicendo?

- E non è vero nemmeno delle ballerine, delle sue mille conquiste...

Ero senza parole.

- Per carità -, proseguì, - magari usa un po' troppo l'immaginazione, ma secondo me tutte quelle cose le ha viste in qualche film...

- Ma... Vezio?

- Sì, Vezio. In realtà è un avventizio.

- Un che?

- Un avventizio. Lavora nei campi. Fa le stagioni. Quando c'è lavoro lo chiamano e lui parte. Ha le sue conoscenze.

Continuavo a credere che Monica volesse solo difenderlo. Ma certo la sua era una difesa piuttosto insolita.

- È un bravo ragazzo, in fondo. E comunque un lavoro, anche se precario, ce l'ha -, aggiunse con una punta di amarezza.

Vezio un *avventizio*? Mi sembrava uno scherzo.

- Ma perché allora se ne va in giro a raccontare certe cose? Ma papà? Lo sa?

- Nessuno lo sa. Solo io. Con me si è confidato. Quanti sogni, quante speranze. L'ultima volta ha anche pianto, poveretto...

Vezio... piangere? Mi sembrava impossibile. - E perché ha pianto?

- Perché... -, ripeté Monica sospirando. - Era giù di corda. Dietro a quel suo modo di fare in fondo è molto fragile, e poi è stanco, stanco della campagna, stanco delle pesche, dei pomodori, della fatica, degli orari massacranti... Insomma, mettiti nei suoi panni. Senza contare che ha cominciato a bere un po' troppo, per i miei gusti. Gliel'ho detto un milione di volte, ma credo che si sia messo a frequentare altri bar...

Mi sembrava assurdo. Vezio a raccogliere frutta e pomodori nei campi? A bere e piangere perché era depresso?

- Ma perché è depresso?

- E perché, secondo te?

- Che ne so? Non mi ha mai detto niente.

- Perché non è contento della vita che fa. Non ha mai avuto il coraggio e la costanza di impegnarsi a fondo, di imparare davvero un mestiere, di cercarsi *davvero* un lavoro. Avrebbe voluto viaggiare, ma alla fine gli unici viaggi che può permettersi sono per andare a fare la stagione da qualche parte...

Mi chiesi se quelle parole, in fondo, non fossero rivolte a me. E lei? Ci stava insieme? Non riuscii a trattenermi dal chiederglielo.

- Macché insieme... -, fece spallucce. - Non cambierà mai, e io voglio un uomo accanto, non un immaturo.

- Allora, l'altra volta non avevate appena...?

- Ma che ti salta in mente? Tu sei pazzo. Non ti sei nemmeno accorto che era ubriaco e aveva ancora gli occhi gonfi di lacrime...

- Perché eravate al bar, allora?

- Mi aveva chiamato dicendo che aveva *bisogno* di bere ma non aveva un soldo in tasca. Era disperato. Singhiozzava come un bambino. Cosa dovevo fare? Non me la sono sentita di abbandonarlo e così gli ho dato appuntamento al bar. Sono stata una scema, perché pensavo di cavarmela con un paio di Bellini, e invece alla fine s'è scolato una bottiglia intera di spumante.

- Ah... E come ha fatto a tornare a casa, a Gavorrano?

Monica mi guardò. - Anche a te ha detto che stava in campagna, in un podere vicino Gavorrano, eh? In realtà vive in un buco. Qui a Grosseto, nella zona industriale. Ma ora basta parlare di lui, adesso ci sono cose più importanti... Pensiamo a mamma, e smettila con le tue paranoie da fratello geloso.

Arrossii. Mamma. Monica. Vezio. Quante cose non avevo capito... Adesso - perché il tempo mette ordine in tutto - interpretavo gli eventi in maniera completamente diversa. Perché bisogna sbagliare per rendersi conto di avere sbagliato? Com'era tutto complicato!

Poi papà chiamò Monica. Checco leggeva un libro. L'avevo accusato di non essersi fatto gli affari suoi spifferando a mio padre del Benelli. L'aveva fatto per aiutarmi, lo so, e aveva pure cercato di prendersi parte della colpa. Con lui ero stato proprio uno stronzo, un *vero* stronzo, altro che con Magghy... Sarei voluto tornare indietro, stringergli la mano e dirgli: «Grazie, amico mio», ma ormai era troppo tardi.

I suoi occhialetti da intellettuale, le sue smorfie, i suoi commenti: ecco cosa mi mancava di più. Io, da solo, giravo a vuoto, ero sprecato. Insieme, invece, ci rafforzavamo a vicenda. Eravamo come il principio del Tao: non esiste nero senza bianco, positivo senza negativo...

Lo raggiunsi.

- Se la montagna non va da Maometto... -, sospese le parole.

- ... Maometto va al mare -, completai convinto.

Mi guardò, si tirò su gli occhiali e scosse la testa.

- Sei sempre il solito -, sospirò. - Vieni, siediti.

Mi accomodai.

- Grazie, Checco. Lo so che avrei dovuto dirtelo prima, ma l'ho capito solo ora.

- Per cosa?

- Primo, perché sei qui; secondo, per il Benelli. Lo so che l'hai detto a papà per aiutarmi.

Checco annuì. - Sai, da quando la mia non c'è più, Luisa la sento un po' come una seconda mamma; perciò tu sei mio fratello, e tra fratelli non ci si preoccupa di certe cose.

Ero così contento di avere un amico come lui. Sapevo che non avrei trovato le parole giuste per dirglielo, così rimasi zitto.

- Sai cosa mi ha detto Monica? -, esclamai a un tratto. - Che Vezio non fa il barman.

Checco sorrise. - Lo so.

- Lo sai?

- Lo so. Vezio fa l'avventizio.

- Di' la verità. Te lo ha detto prima Monica. Giusto?

- Monica? Acqua, caro mio. L'ho proprio visto, una volta.

- E quando?

- L'anno scorso.

- Ma dove?

- Vicino a Saturnia. Avevo accompagnato nonna alle terme e stavo tornando a casa in pullman. A un certo punto l'autista rallenta e comincia ad andare a passo d'uomo. Per almeno dieci minuti. Poi accelera improvvisamente per fare un sorpasso. Indovina? Di un trattore. E chi c'era alla guida? Proprio lui. Vezio. A torso nudo, con i calzoni tutti sporchi di terra, gli occhiali a specchio e il ciuffo che gli svolazzava al vento.

- Non ci posso credere. Perché non me l'hai mai detto?

Checco sorrise. - E che te lo dicevo a fare? Lui era felice di raccontarti le sue fantasie, e tu felice di ascoltarle...

Eh già, era proprio finita un'epoca, constatai.

- Ma lo sai, adesso che ci penso, che qualche volta me lo sono chiesto?

- Cosa?

- Come mai Vezio avesse sempre qualche benda o cerotto sulle braccia. Non era, come diceva lui, per via dei bicchieri che si rompevano troppo spesso.

- Ma del lavoro in campagna...

- Certo. E poi, era sempre così abbronzato. E quelle mani rovinate... altro che brillantante! Ora sì che capisco!

- Altroché, era tutta colpa del solleone dei campi...

Mi passai una mano tra i capelli. Dovevano essere in disordine, ma non aveva importanza.

- Il bando è già scaduto, scommetto... -, cambiai discorso.

Checco si girò di scatto. - Veramente hanno concesso una proroga.

- Sul serio? Allora possiamo sempre provare! -. E sul suo viso si allargò un sorriso luminoso.

- Inforco lo Zip e volo a casa a riordinare le carte. Ci sentiamo dopo!

Noi tornammo alla macchina. Fuori, il caldo era opprimente. Nel tragitto verso casa nessuno aprì bocca. Guardavo scorrere la città, le case, i negozi, le persone. Chissà quante storie si portavano dentro, quanti destini. Non ci avevo mai pensato prima.

Poi papà disse: - Ai laboratori dell'ospedale so' riuscito a farmi dare subito i risultati della biopsia.

Monica si girò di scatto. - Cosa dicono?

- Quello che sospettavamo...

Monica si mise a piangere. Dal sedile posteriore, mi allungai verso di lei e le diedi un buffetto affettuoso sulla testa. Ero preoccupato, certo, ma fiducioso.

- Ma nun ve dovete preoccupà! È così piccolo che a malapena se vede!

- Quando ci sarà l'operazione? -, chiese Monica. Si soffiò il naso.

- Domani. Del resto, già 'o sapevamo che pe' sicurezza è meijo asportà tutto, no? Andrà tutto bene. State tranquilli. E poi, me raccomando, quanno tornerà a casa nun se dovrà stancà.

Monica si girò dalla mia parte: - Capito?

- Sì, *badrona*.

Ero sicuro che alla fine ogni cosa si sarebbe risolta, ma avevo paura.

Dopo cena, andai da Checco a lavorare al progetto.

Erano quasi due mesi che non mettevo piede nel suo appartamento, e comunque non ci andavo mai molto spesso. Il mio amico, quando era a casa, studiava o aiutava sua nonna in qualche faccenda. Mi accolse proprio la vecchietta, in vestaglia. Mi diede un bacio in fronte. Checco le fece prendere le pasticche per la circolazione e la accompagnò nella sua stanza. - Nonna, mi raccomando! Se ti scappa la pipì premi il bottone che ti penzola sul letto. Capito?

Andammo nella camera-studio. La casa di Checco era davvero grande, e la sua stanza più del doppio della mia. Le altissime librerie erano come sempre stipate di libri, di musicassette e di mille altri oggetti: conchiglie, piantine di cactus, bizzarre fotografie in bianco e nero. In un angolo, sul trespolo, il pappagallo di legno che aveva comprato a Venezia durante una gita. Il suo piccolo telescopio di fronte alla finestra, il mega planisfero alla parete e il globo luminoso sul comodino. Altri aggeggi, di cui ignoravo da sempre la funzione, erano sparsi qua e là nel solito disordine. Per terra, sopra i tappeti dai fantasiosi disegni, diverse paia di Adidas. Checco chiuse la porta e dietro vidi che aveva attaccato il poster di Jimmy Courier mentre alzava la coppa del Roland Garros. In mezzo a tutti quegli oggetti inconsueti stonava vedere quel tipo con la racchetta.

Accese la luce. Era blu, «blu relax», come diceva lui.

- Cos'è questa storia del bottone? -, chiesi.

- Non te l'avevo detto? Ho costruito un piccolo sistema di allarme per ogni evenienza. Nonna preme il bottone e mi parte lo stereo. Quando preme una volta si sintonizza su Radio Grosseto, quando schiaccia due volte su Rete Toscana Classica. Così so subito di cosa ha bisogno.

Pensa tu cosa si era inventato!

- Ma passiamo a noi -, disse. - Il progetto deve essere corredato da planimetria del locale, disegno a colori dei nuovi arredi, dettaglio degli impianti firmati dal geometra e controfirmati dai tecnici, pianificazione commerciale, utilità per la collettività e linee di massima sulla programmazione artistica con relative lettere d'intenti da parte di enti o associazioni legati al territorio e interessati a inserirci nel loro circuito di promozione culturale... Ah, e la banca deve metterci a disposizione il credito finanziabile. Poi...

- Poi? -, chiesi sbigottito. - Non è ancora finita? Ma come facciamo a procurarci tutte queste carte?

- Ragazzo di poca fede. Ma per chi mi hai preso, per un mangiapane a tradimento? Stai tranquillo. Ho parlato con un vecchio collega di mamma, che conosce il proprietario del terreno dell'ex scuola calcio. Potrebbe esserci la possibilità di affittarne una porzione per la stagione estiva. Ci pensi? Una paninoteca all'aperto! Ah, e poi c'è un'altra cosa interessante a livello fiscale: «Impresa familiare». Coinvolgendo Antonio e Monica le tasse si abbatterebbero di molti punti percentuale... Ma tu, piuttosto, hai finito il disegno dell'insegna?

- Eh? Be'... Ancora no, non ho avuto tempo.

- See, figuriamoci. L'*impegnuomo*, ti voglio chiamare.

- Ma no, dai, ce l'ho tutto in testa però.

Checco mi fornì carta e matita e mi mise al lavoro. Mi sfilai le scarpe e mi sdraiai sul tappeto.

- Forza, allora, esprimiti -, mi incitò. - Allineiamo i nostri intenti. Tira fuori quel poco di buono che è in te!

Gli lanciai una scarpa e lui la evitò per un pelo. Erano quasi le dieci. Pensai a mamma. Chissà se stava dormendo. Mamma, non avere paura.

Ma adesso ero lì, davanti al foglio bianco, per creare l'insegna del mio primo locale. L'avrei dedicata a lei.

Scrissi più volte il suo nome: *Luisa*, Luisa, LUISA. Poi mi venne un'idea. - E se lo chiamassimo «Mammaluisa»?

- See... Mammaliturchi! -, esclamò Checco.

A me invece piaceva. Va be', prima o poi lo avrei convinto...

Mi misi a fare schizzi prendendo spunto da un arabesco all'angolo del tappeto. Checco tirò fuori non so quali libri e si mise a sfogliarli prendendo appunti.

- È da un po' che non mi parli di Magghy -, disse a un tratto.

Feci spallucce. - È finita... Ma ora non mi va di parlarne.

- Oookaaay -, cantilenò.

Ci rimettemmo al lavoro.

Non ricordo che ora fosse quando crollai letteralmente al tappeto.

Mi svegliò Checco, infilandomi un cubetto di ghiaccio dentro la maglietta.

- Waaah!

- Vai a casa, Massa. Prenditi lo Zip. Ci vediamo domani.

Seguii il suo consiglio.

Avevo quasi dimenticato quanto potesse farti sentire libero correre in motorino col vento in faccia e l'odore di erba bagnata che ti riempiva le narici.

L'aria fresca della notte mi ritemprò. La mia insegna sarebbe stata la più bella e originale mai apparsa in città. Mamma ne sarebbe andata orgogliosa.

Appena toccai il letto, sprofondai nel sonno.

Potevo fare a meno dell'immancabile sogno?

Ero solo al Paradise e stavo bevendo una mega tazza di latte fumante. Non so perché, ero contento. A un tratto appare Checco, con una cresta verde tipo punk. Io lo guardo meravigliato e rido. Lui mi chiede che cosa ho da ridere, poi ordina un bicchiere bello pieno di amaro Averna. Glielo riempio fino all'orlo. Dopodiché mi dice che sarebbe partito. Partito? E per dove? «America. Sanford, Seminole County, Florida. Vado da Jimmy». Gli chiedo perché si sia fatto quella strana cresta verde e lui mi risponde: «Perché l'America è la patria della libertà». Tracanna l'Averna e mi dice addio.

Mi svegliai di soprassalto. Guardai l'ora. Erano le cinque e mezza del mattino. Che sogno strano, proprio Checco che se ne andava... Impossibile.

Dai meandri della mia mente affiorò l'immagine della madre di Magghy. La Svizzera... Chissà se ci metterò mai piede, mi domandai.

Poi pensai a mamma. Forse stava ancora dormendo. Mi venne un brivido all'idea che poche ore dopo sarebbe andata sotto i ferri del chirurgo.

Diciannove

In silenzio, mi alzai e andai in cucina. Era sempre buio, ma qualcosa di impercettibile, nel cielo a est, stava cambiando. Mi appoggiai al davanzale della finestra a osservarlo. Nell'aria, i primi cinguettii degli uccelli: la città si stava risvegliando.

Dopo mezz'ora l'orizzonte si era tinto di azzurro e violetto. Com'era magnifica, la natura. Sfumature sempre nuove accompagnavano il lento sorgere del sole. Un miracolo che si ripeteva da miliardi di anni. Quando spuntò, da dietro le colline basse, era come un fuoco arancione.

Rimasi incantato.

Dopo qualche minuto papà entrò in cucina. Si preparò il caffè in silenzio.

Pensai fosse un buon momento per accennargli l'idea del progetto della paninoteca. In fondo, avremmo potuto lavorarci tutti insieme: Checco aveva detto che la gestione familiare sarebbe stata conveniente per le tasse. In quel momento ci raggiunse anche Monica. Rimuginai ancora un po', ma alla fine non riuscii a dire niente.

Ogni cinque minuti controllavamo l'orologio. L'operazione di mamma era prevista per le undici.

Poco prima dell'ora x, squillò il telefono. Rispose papà.

- Sì?... Sono io.

Ascoltò in silenzio. Un silenzio carico di attesa.

Io e Monica ci guardammo. Poi papà riattaccò e rimase un attimo a fissare il vuoto.

- Papà? -, chiese mia sorella. - Chi era? Per mamma?

- No, no... Mo' però devo annà, devo annà... Voi, venite più tardi. Capito?

Lo raggiungemmo subito.

Monica durante il tragitto non aprì bocca nemmeno una volta.

Quando arrivammo al reparto lei cominciò ad agitarsi. Io ero in confusione totale.

Vedemmo papà, e Monica gli corse incontro. Lui le disse qualcosa e poi successe il finimondo. Mia sorella si mise a gridare. Urlò qualcosa che lì per lì non compresi, poi cadde a terra, svenuta.

Ero come paralizzato. Cosa stava succedendo?

Poi lo scoprii. Mamma era in rianimazione.

Me lo feci ripetere un'altra volta, stringendo i pugni.

Avevo capito bene. L'operazione, che era stata anticipata alle otto, era riuscita, ma l'antibiotico che le avevano somministrato subito dopo conteneva un eccipiente al quale era allergica.

In quel preciso istante mi crollò il mondo addosso.

Un'allergia.

- Ma com'è possibile?! -, continuava a ripetere papà.

I medici, visibilmente imbarazzati, replicarono che purtroppo una volta su mille... Papà disse che in un ospedale non potevano succedere quelle cose, che avrebbe denunciato tutti, chiamato i giornali. A un tratto, dal momento che uno dei medici seguitava a pregarlo di stare calmo, lui non ci vide più e lo colpì con un pugno. Quello cadde a terra dritto, come il tronco di un albero. In un secondo si radunò lì attorno un manipolo di infermieri e altro personale, e tutti gridavano: - Si calmi! Si calmi!

Monica era stata portata su un lettino in ambulatorio e non dovette assistere a quella scena drammatica. Furono minuti terribili.

Papà rifiutò di prendere un calmante e si mise a camminare avanti e indietro nella saletta d'aspetto.

Cosa sarebbe successo a mamma? Non potevo saperlo.

Mi chiusi in un bagno e cominciai a piangere.

Perché proprio a lei? Perché il destino le si era accanito contro? Perché non la lasciava in pace? E io, cosa *avrei dovuto* fare per aiutarla?

Erano tutte domande inutili.

Nel tardo pomeriggio tornammo a casa. I medici avevano detto che le prossime quarantotto ore sarebbero state delicatissime. In macchina, Monica non la smetteva di lamentarsi, e alzava la voce agitata.

Dal pianerottolo, sentimmo che il nostro telefono stava squillando. Mi affrettai ad aprire la porta di casa ma non feci in tempo a rispondere.

- Sarà stato l'ospedale? -, chiesi.

Le grandi dita di papà composero nervosamente il numero del reparto. No, non erano stati loro a telefonare.

Mila miagolò venendoci incontro, ma la casa era diversa. Qualcosa era definitivamente cambiato. Tutti i miei progetti, il mio futuro, in un solo colpo erano stati spazzati via da un cazzo di sciroppo. Niente che potessimo fare sembrava avere un senso. Mi sentivo terribilmente in colpa per tutto.

Ripassai dentro di me la litigata con mamma prima di andare al campeggio. Che stupido! Che immaturo!

Monica si chiuse in camera sua. Negli ultimi giorni era stata lei a prendere in mano le redini della casa. Aveva preparato da mangiare, fatto il bucato e stirato, tenuto in ordine le stanze e pensato anche a Mila, la gatta di mamma. Sentendo i suoi gemiti, mi sembrò veramente tutto finito...

Cosa ne sarebbe stato di noi? Papà andò sul terrazzo e si accese una sigaretta. Erano almeno dieci anni che non fumava, e vederlo con la sigaretta stretta tra le labbra mi rese ancora più inquieto.

Dopo un po' squillò di nuovo il telefono, e un brivido freddo mi percorse la schiena. Risposi io.

Era Checco. Oh, Checco... Gli raccontai cosa era successo. Mentre gli parlavo, tutto mi sembrava così assurdo. Lui rimase in silenzio, poi disse solo: - È arrivato.

Gli domandai cosa intendesse.

- Il momento della verità.

Attesi un suo ulteriore commento, ma aggiunse solo di chiudermi in camera, abbassare la tapparella e rimanere al buio.

Chiesi spiegazioni, ma lui rispose: - Non fare domande.

Nel silenzio nero della mia stanza, provai a seguire le sue istruzioni. Nella mia mente, però, si accavallavano immagini senza sosta. Vidi mamma sdraiata su un letto bianco, gli occhi chiusi, macchinari che le pompavano aria nei polmoni. Vidi papà nel laboratorio del bar che si tagliava con un coltello affilato e poi ancora Monica, mentre dava uno schiaffo a Vezio e gli sputava in faccia.

Quelle sequenze si ripeterono non so quante volte, quando a un certo punto, tra di esse, si inserì l'immagine del mare.

Era calmo. Ascoltavo le piccole onde frangersi delicatamente sulla riva, in un flusso e riflusso continuo. Al largo, poi, vidi un peschereccio. Gabbiani volavano sopra poppa stridendo. Il loro richiamo si trasformò nel suono del respiratore che avvertiva i medici di un imminente problema. Cercai di ricacciare indietro quel pensiero, ma non ci riuscii. Nella sequenza successiva, una bara veniva trasportata giù, lungo delle scale.

Feci un respiro profondo. Non avevo controllo sui miei pensieri.

Alzai l'avvolgibile e presi il walkman. Mi infilai le cuffie, schiacciai «play» e Michael cominciò a cantare con la sua voce d'angelo *Man in the mirror*.

Checco suonò prima di cena.

Entrò in camera e mi abbracciò. Era la prima volta da quando eravamo amici che ci scambiavamo quel gesto d'affetto.

Mi consegnò un libro e, senza dire altro, se ne andò. Lessi il titolo:

Gli angeli custodi
Preghiere

Pensai a *Nemamiah.* Mi aveva lasciato solo?

Aprii il libro:

La vita che stai vivendo è solo un breve tratto del percorso che la tua anima compie nello spazio-tempo. Il collegamento con questo Tutto è l'Angelo custode che hai accanto. Sembra incredibile, ma è proprio così: in questo preciso momento, il tuo Angelo ti sta osservando, e lo farà per sempre, perché tale è la Legge dell'Universo...

Che legge poteva mai essere quella che aveva lasciato che mamma si ammalasse? Non capivo. Avevo sempre creduto, è vero, che tutto fosse perfettamente regolato da qualcosa, o da qualcuno. Ma come facevo, adesso, a fidarmi di quest'idea? L'autore del libro era certamente uno di quei tipi che nella vita avevano avuto tutto. Facile, così. Sfogliai velocemente le pagine, osservai di nuovo la copertina e poggiai il libro sul comodino. Non volevo illudermi un'altra volta. Grazie, Checco, ma non so se questa volta funzionerà...

Quella notte, i miei sogni furono tormentati da creature mostruose. Davanti al letto vidi passare esseri metà uomini metà insetti, o anfibi, che emettevano suoni che non avevo mai sentito. Volevo gridare ma dalla gola non mi usciva niente. L'ultimo, una specie di animale verde scuro con quattro braccia ma senza mani, e un muso dalle sembianze femminili talmente gonfio che sembrava sul punto di scoppiare, sbucò da sotto il materasso facendomi sobbalzare e svegliandomi di colpo.

Mi sedetti sul bordo del letto. Ero in un bagno di sudore, i nervi a fior di pelle. Non mi era mai capitato di sognare dei mostri. Se avessi incontrato in un incubo un personaggio come Freddy Krueger ero certo che non mi sarei mai e poi mai messo a urlare come una femminuccia. Ora, però, capivo che la realtà è un'altra cosa. Mi sembrò di essere appena ritornato dall'inferno. Oh, cavolo...

Venti

Quando il sette di agosto arrivò, mi sentivo letteralmente a pezzi.

Rimuginavo su quelle ultime settimane, cercavo di riordinare gli avvenimenti, di fissarmeli bene in mente. Volevo capire perché stava succedendo tutto questo proprio a me. Alla mia famiglia.

Per tutta la giornata aspettammo che mamma reagisse in qualche modo, ma non ci furono novità. Con papà i medici si riservarono un bollettino aggiornato per la mattina successiva.

Scese di nuovo la notte, una notte la cui oscurità mi faceva paura. Rimasi fino a tardi a fissare le luci dei lampioni giù in strada, senza pensieri, o meglio, senza speranze.

Intorno alle due squillò il telefono. Lo stomaco mi arrivò in gola, poi risprofondò nelle viscere.

Monica si precipitò a rispondere. Dopo qualche secondo cominciò a gridare.

Mio dio... No, nooo!

La testa mi prese a girare all'impazzata.

- Cos'è successo?! -, urlò papà piombando in corridoio. - Parla! Parla, santo cielo! Parlaaa!

- Oh no, oh no -, singhiozzò Monica. - Hanno detto che è meglio se andiamo.

Ci precipitammo.

L'ospedale sembrava disabitato. In rianimazione, un medico chiese a papà chi cercasse. - Ah, venga, venga.

Tornò da noi dopo un minuto.

- Purtroppo nun ce stanno belle notizie. La situazione s'è aggravata. Er core è sotto sforzo, ma la cosa peggiore è che vostra madre non reagisce agli stimoli, e nun sanno perché... -. Papà abbassò lo sguardo, sconsolato. - Dovemo pregà, dovemo solo da pregà... -, mormorò abbassando lo sguardo.

Monica gli chiese di essere più preciso, ma lui scosse la testa. - Nun lo so, nun so più gnente, più gnente... -. Non aveva più nemmeno la forza di parlare. Tirò fuori di tasca un fazzoletto e si soffiò il naso.

Eravamo in balìa degli eventi, senza differenze tra noi, tutti uguali, impotenti di fronte a quella situazione insensata.

Quella notte, seduto nella poltroncina di plastica della rianimazione, presi la mano a mia sorella e la strinsi forte. Monica, ti voglio bene, avrei voluto dirle...

Un'infermiera uscì dal gabbiottino e ci invitò a prendere un caffè. Non ricevette risposta. Poi, quando non ce lo aspettavamo più, arrivò il medico e ci disse che i parametri erano rientrati nella norma. Il cuore di mamma era stato trattato farmacologicamente e si era ripreso. Ci consigliò di tornarcene a casa.

«Nella norma»: non dimenticherò mai quelle due parole. Le ripetevo di continuo dentro di me. Nella norma per chi? Sicuramente non per noi: quella non era certo la nostra «normalità». La nostra vita familiare era sconvolta, il nostro equilibrio precario appeso a un filo.

Rimanemmo un'altra ora. Sul viso di Monica continuavano a scendere lacrime silenziose. L'intensità del suo legame con mamma era straordinaria. Mi ci erano voluti diciotto anni per capirlo.

Le dicevo di stare tranquilla, e intanto le accarezzavo i capelli. Cos'altro avrei potuto fare, se non ricambiare le sue manifestazioni di affetto?

Alla fine ce ne andammo, lasciando mamma sola.

Era quasi l'alba. Papà e Monica si trascinarono stancamente a letto, a me invece il sonno era passato. Mi scaldai un po' di latte e mi soffermai a guardare il fuoco sul fornello. Nel silenzio della casa, mi concentrai sul crepitio della fiamma. L'avevo sentito non si sa quante volte, l'avrei riconosciuto tra mille tanto era abituale. Fu allora che, come un lampo improvviso, mi ricordai che qualche tempo prima avevo visto alla Tv una trasmissione su delle persone che, ascoltando suoni a loro familiari, erano riuscite a superare stati di assoluta apatia, uscendo addirittura dal coma. Perché non avrebbe potuto funzionare anche con mamma?

Ma sì, certo. Il walkman aveva la funzione per registrare. Non persi tempo. Lo presi, ci infilai una cassetta vergine, controllai che le pile fossero cariche e schiacciai il pulsante «Rec».

Registrai il rumore della fiamma del gas per circa due minuti poi, mentre bevevo il latte, aprii e chiusi tutti i cassetti della cucina, lo sportello del frigorifero, del freezer. Scostai tutte le sedie e le rimisi a posto. Mi spostai in bagno. Aprii il rubinetto della doccia e tirai lo sciacquone.

Erano suoni che mamma sentiva da una vita, *doveva* riconoscerli. Mi sembrò davvero di fare qualcosa di giusto, di utile, e nel mio cuore riaffiorò una briciola di speranza.

Avevo speso tutti quegli anni cercando di acchiappare i sogni, vivendo solo per me stesso e credendo così di vivere in armonia con la natura. Ora, invece, mi sentivo come *risvegliato* e con il bisogno di *fare*, fare qualcosa di concreto, di *reale*. Mi tornarono in mente le parole di Malù: «Devi essere più determinato... credere nella tua luce». E non era certo pregando gli angeli che ci sarei riuscito.

- Ciao, mamma -, dissi al minuscolo microfono del walkman. Come poteva non riconoscere la *mia* voce?

Registrai ancora per un po', alternando rumori di casa a parole o brevi frasi a effetto.

- Volevo dirti che con Magghy ci siamo lasciati.

Pausa.

- Sul serio, non sto scherzando. Avevi ragione tu... M'aveva dato de vorta er cervello...

In corridoio, incrociai Mila. Drizzò la coda e venne a strofinarsi sulle mie gambe, facendo le fusa. Orientai il microfono del walkman sul suo musetto.

- Mamma, questa è Mila. Anche lei ti aspetta!

Schiacciai «stop», ricacciai indietro il groppo alla gola e respirai profondamente. Riaccesi di nuovo: - Forza, mamma, non mollare.

Più tardi, Checco mi chiamò per sapere se c'erano novità. No, non c'erano novità. Mi chiese se stavo leggendo il libro che mi aveva prestato, gli risposi che lo avevo iniziato.

- Non demordere, Massa, ci vuole pazienza, ma poi i risultati arrivano! *Concepire*, devi *concepire*! Ricordi?

Non aggiunsi altro, lo salutai e andai in ospedale. In tasca, walkman e cuffie.

Comunicai al caposala le mie intenzioni. Mi disse che succedeva spesso. Gli chiesi cos'era che succedeva spesso: - Che si risveglino i pazienti?

- No, che facciano loro ascoltare musica.

- Non è musica. Sono i rumori di casa.

Mi fissò un po' stupito. - Mah, fa lo stesso.

Non faceva lo stesso. I rumori di casa sono ben diversi dalla musica. E poi c'era la mia voce. Cosa poteva saperne, lui?

Gli consegnai il walkman supplicandolo di fare sentire subito la cassetta a mia madre. Disse che l'avrebbe fatto il prima possibile, e se ne andò.

Mamma, svegliati: tornando a casa, quel pensiero continuava a martellarmi dentro.

Venni richiamato alla realtà dai rumori dalla cucina. Monica doveva essere rientrata e stava preparando la cena.

La raggiunsi e, senza farle domande, cominciai ad apparecchiare la tavola. Mi avvicinai al lavandino per prendere i bicchieri, e lei mi sorrise.

Quando papà arrivò, ci sedemmo e cominciammo a mangiare.

Prima delle nove chiamò Checco e mi disse di andare da lui.

- Devo parlarti urgentemente. Ti aspetto tra venti minuti al massimo.

Cosa stava succedendo?

Quando mi aprì, indossava una strana vestaglia.

- Ma cosa ti sei messo?

- Non fare domande, vieni, vieni, andiamo nella camera-studio.

Al centro della stanza, illuminata come al solito di «blu relax», aveva allestito una sorta di altarino con strane statuette e due grandi cuscini verdi, uno dei quali aveva delle righe dorate.

- Accomodati.

Mi sedetti su quello a righe.

- Non lì.

- Perché no?

- Perché è quello del maestro.

- Ah. E chi è?

- Come chi è? Sono io -, disse mentre si spalmava una specie di olio sul viso.

- Ma che stai facendo?

- È olio essenziale di lavanda. Aiuta.

- A cosa?

- A cosa? Un po' a tutto.

Mi stavo innervosendo. Non avevo voglia di stare lì a perder tempo con certe stupidaggini. Almeno, non in quel momento.

- Che ore sono? -, chiese.

- Le nove e dieci.

- Benissimo. Tra dieci minuti iniziamo.

- Iniziamo cosa? -, domandai esasperato.

Checco avvitò il tappo del vasetto dell'olio e lo ripose su una piccola mensola. Si pulì le mani con una salvietta e poi prese un piccolo volume dal ripiano più alto della libreria. Lo aprì, mentre quel forte odore mi penetrava il cervello e mi spalancava i polmoni. Ero un po' infastidito.

- Ecco, adesso faremo un viaggio.

- Un viaggio? Cosa stai dicendo?

- Quello che ho detto. Mentre i nostri corpi rimarranno qui, seduti sui cuscini, noi cercheremo di andare da Luisa.

- Da mamma? E come? Col pensiero?

- Abbi pazienza e vedrai.

Checco chiuse la finestra e accese delle candele. Lo osservavo con attenzione. Era tutto troppo insolito e lui troppo serio per essere solo un gioco.

Alle nove e venti in punto spense la luce e si accomodò sul cuscino.

Salmodiò una specie di poesia, una poesia bellissima, che parlava di fiori celesti e cieli paralleli. Non avevo mai sentito niente del genere. Non so come spiegarlo, ma era commovente. Quindi accese lo stereo.

- Chiudi gli occhi -, disse calmo, - e segui la voce. Concentrati sul tuo respiro. Inspira, espira. Fai come me. Inspira, espira...

Chiusi gli occhi seguendo il respiro di Checco.

- Ecco, così. Bravo. Adesso ci sei solo tu, solo tu...

Volevo fidarmi di lui. Sapevo che *potevo* farlo. Per qualche secondo sentii salire l'ansia, ma dovevo controllarla, lasciarla fluire via.

Improvvisamente, avvertii ancora più forte l'odore di lavanda, all'altezza degli occhi, poi una specie di soffio caldo mi colpì proprio al centro della testa, sulla fontanella. Un calore intenso, come fuoco, mi scese lentamente al centro degli occhi, pian piano arrivò alla gola e alla fine raggiunse il cuore, dove esplose all'improvviso investendomi di una luce bianca, calma e avvolgente. Non sentivo più il mio corpo né quello di Checco accanto, o meglio, c'era, ma era solo *presenza*... Ebbi la sensazione di sollevarmi verso l'alto e di uscire da me stesso dal centro della testa, come fossi fatto di vapore. C'era *qualcosa* a spingermi verso quello che percepivo come infinito. E mi sentivo invaso da un senso di pace. Di comprensione per tutto, per tutti. Vedevo la luce passare dal bianco totale all'oro, all'indaco. C'era un silenzio assoluto, e improvvisamente apparve il fusto del nostro Cipresso. Eravamo lì, tutti e due, seduti e pieni di luce, come in un bozzolo. Era questa, ora, la mia sensazione. Mi sentivo protetto. Non avevo più paura. Fu allora che una voce flebile mi ordinò di andare da lei...

Non so spiegare come, ma quella sera riuscii davvero a vedere mamma, anche se per un solo istante. Aveva le cuffie, gli occhi chiusi. Ed era bella, oh quant'era bella...

Se devo essere sincero, nemmeno adesso so cosa fosse di preciso quel viaggio che Checco chiamò «astrale». Durò così poco, ma per me fu *vivido*, indimenticabile.

Era notte fonda e non riuscivo a dormire. Sentivo i battiti del cuore nel collo, nelle orecchie. Mi giravo e rigiravo nel letto senza trovare pace. Cosa mi stava succedendo? La visione del Grande Cipresso e quella di mamma erano state così nitide che non riuscivo ad accettare l'idea che si trattasse solo di immaginazione. *Doveva* esserci qualcos'altro, qualcosa che nemmeno la scienza era in grado di spiegare.

Accesi la lampadina sul comodino e presi in mano il libro sugli angeli.

Nemamiah, se davvero esisti, da qualche parte nell'universo, dammi un segnale della tua presenza...

Ventuno

Uscii prima delle sette, il libro in tasca. Ero diretto in centro.

Le strade erano ancora deserte. L'edicolante, due spazzini, il bar sulla piazzetta del museo che stava aprendo. Alcuni piccioni tubavano sotto le grondaie sbattendo le ali, come se volessero sgranchirle.

Entrai nel convento di San Francesco e mi sedetti nella prima fila. Ero solo, e c'era una pace indescrivibile. Il crocifisso sospeso mi osservava. Meraviglioso. Quando ci ero entrato, alcune settimane prima, era stato diverso. Adesso mi sentivo come a casa, come se fossi all'interno di un corpo più grande, più sicuro. Avevo ritrovato la speranza.

Mi spostai nella cappella affrescata. Era illuminata da un'unica lampadina. Si respirava un'atmosfera di raccoglimento. Di fronte alla piccola statua di Gesù erano disposte poche sedie. Poi mi accorsi che su una di esse c'era qualcuno, un uomo. Probabilmente stava pregando. Ero sorpreso, non mi aspettavo qualcuno lì.

Mi accomodai anch'io e cercai di respirare profondamente. Non sapevo di preciso a cosa servisse, ma dentro di me speravo di poter *rivedere* mamma, e trasmetterle un messaggio.

Chiusi gli occhi e cercai di concentrarmi. Inspirare, espirare... Niente.

Quando li riaprii, quell'uomo era accanto a me. Il cuore mi salì in gola. Lo guardai meglio, era un frate. Infilò la mano in una tasca della tonaca e tirò fuori un piccolo oggetto.

- Questo è per te, ragazzo. Conservalo e fanne buon uso.

Era un rosario.

- Ma secondo lei -, gli chiesi senza pensarci due volte, - gli angeli esistono davvero?

Il frate mi guardò dritto negli occhi.

- Esistono perché *noi* esistiamo.

- Allora sono veri. Ma riuscirò mai a parlare con loro?

Il frate sorrise. Aveva un sorriso bellissimo, che trasmetteva pace. - Certo. Con la voce interiore.

- E come?

- Lo vuoi sapere davvero?

- Sì.

- Be', allora, tanto per cominciare, devi imparare ad *ascoltare*, e non a chiedere.

- Non a chiedere?

- Certo. Non devi *mai* chiedere.

- Ma come faccio a ottenere qualcosa se non posso chiederla?

Il frate mi venne più vicino. - Lo scoprirai da solo, figliolo -, disse sfiorandomi la testa con la mano. - Abbi pazienza, e vedrai.

- Pazienza... Anche il mio amico mi dice sempre di avere pazienza.

- Vedrai -, ripeté il frate alzandosi, - che alla fine la tua determinazione sarà premiata.

Uscì dalla cappella senza fare rumore. Passando, lasciò una scia profumata, familiare. L'annusai.

Decisi di portare il rosario a mamma. Dovevo *ascoltare*, ascoltare e avere pazienza, e si sarebbe svegliata.

- Per favore, vorrei consegnare a mia madre un portafortuna -, dissi al caposala.

L'infermiere mi guardò con la solita espressione assente e mi rispose che non appena fosse stato possibile glielo avrebbe portato lui stesso in camera.

- No, devo farlo io.

L'infermiere storse il naso. - Non è consentito entrare in rianimazione senza autorizzazione.

- Io *sono* autorizzato.

- E da chi?

- Da me stesso in quanto figlio.

Lui mi guardò a metà tra l'incredulo e l'offeso.

- Mi dispiace. Non è proprio possibile.

- Prova a fermarmi -, e intanto stavo già superando il gabbiottino.

- Ehi, su, ragazzo, non ti agitare. Vieni qua.

Ma ero già a metà corridoio.

- E va bene, ma solo cinque minuti, capito? Cinque minuti!

Su un carrellino per i medicinali vidi una penna, la presi al volo ed entrai nella stanza di mamma senza prestargli ascolto.

Mamma. Erano due giorni che stava così. Un paio di tubicini nel naso, il lenzuolo tirato sul petto, gli occhi chiusi. Accanto al letto, due macchinari con dei grafici incomprensibili che viaggiavano sullo schermo.

Oh, mamma!

Il mio walkman era sul comodino, le cuffie avvolte intorno. Presi il rosario e glielo misi in mano. - Mamma, tieni, è per te, da parte mia -, le sussurrai in un orecchio. - Quanto sei bella... Te l'ho mai detto? E ti voglio bene, un mondo di bene.

Le baciai la mano, poi mi misi seduto. - Rimango qui, mamma, non ti lascio sola.

Ancora poco più di un mese, e sarebbe ricominciata la scuola. L'ultimo anno e poi la maturità. Promisi a me stesso che mi sarei impegnato di più. Dovevo dimostrarle che ero cambiato, che ormai ero un uomo. Inoltre, c'era ancora in ballo il progetto della paninoteca. Se avessimo vinto il bando e ottenuto il finanziamento, avremmo rinnovato completamente il Paradise, e sarebbe diventato l'attività di *tutta* la famiglia.

Sfilai il libro dalla tasca e lo aprii. L'introduzione era preceduta da una pagina bianca. Avrei disegnato l'angelo di mia madre, *Aladiah*. Presi la penna e mi misi all'opera. Mamma, grazie di avermi trasmesso il tuo dono.

Era un'emozione unica, disegnare un angelo. La penna scivolava sul foglio, la mia mano era sicura e i miei occhi studiavano l'immagine che pian piano prendeva forma. La sua testa elegante rivolta al cielo, le braccia accoglienti, le grandi ali spiegate come in volo. Anche la più piccola sfumatura era importante.

Ricordai il mio primo disegno, quel pomeriggio ad Albinia quando vidi mamma dormire sul divano, un raggio di sole sottile sul viso. Avevo otto anni. Rubai uno dei suoi fogli e uno dei suoi carboncini e in silenzio la immortalai, in tutta la sua bellezza. Agii d'istinto, mosso da una sensazione di trasporto, quasi magica. Al suo risveglio, trovò il disegno accanto a lei e, spiandola nascosto dietro la porta, la vidi asciugarsi le lacrime sorridendo.

Guardai l'angelo *Aladiah*, dopo tanto tempo ero di nuovo contento. Guardai mamma, ed ebbi la sensazione che da un momento all'altro avrebbe aperto gli occhi per ammirare il suo angelo custode. Staccai delicatamente la pagina e la misi nel cassetto del comodino.

Dopo circa mezz'ora si affacciò un infermiere. Mi disse che non potevo più rimanere lì, ma gli risposi che per me era invece del tutto possibile, perché ci sarei rimasto lo stesso.

Mi chiese di ripetere, non aveva capito. Così gli chiarii il concetto: - Oh sì, ha capito benissimo. Io rimango qui. Non esco.

Lui entrò. Ribadì che quelle erano le regole. Senza regole, un ospedale, come del resto qualsiasi altra struttura, non poteva funzionare.

Replicai che quelle erano le mie, di regole. In fondo, non davo fastidio a nessuno. Anzi.

- Io mia madre da sola non ce la lascio più. Lei ha bisogno di me. Capito?

Se ne andò senza dire altro.

Ero riuscito a farmi valere. Ero orgoglioso di me stesso. E anche mamma lo era, ne ero convinto. Le accarezzai dolcemente la mano.

All'ora di pranzo arrivarono papà e Monica. Mi chiesero da quanto tempo fossi lì. Mia sorella mi mise un braccio intorno alle spalle e vi si appoggiò con la testa.

Circondammo mamma della nostra presenza, sperando che qualcuno, da qualche parte, potesse accorgersene.

Dopo circa mezz'ora entrarono due medici e dissero che dovevamo lasciare la stanza. Io invece volevo rimanere ancora. Papà e Monica mi invitarono a seguirli fuori, ma fui irremovibile. - Verrò a casa a piedi, ormai sono abituato.

I medici non erano assolutamente dello stesso parere, e come al solito ne seguì un battibecco. Papà cercò di farci arrivare a un compromesso, e alla fine riuscii a spuntarla. Mi dissero che, in via del tutto eccezionale, per quella sera potevo rimanere.

Avevo mangiato un panino che mi aveva portato Monica dal bar dell'ospedale. Ormai fuori era buio. Mi sentivo un po' stanco, e chiusi gli occhi ripensando al frate e alla scia profumata che aveva lasciato dietro di sé.

- Preghiamo insieme -, disse piano una voce alle mie spalle.

Mi girai. Era Checco. Entrò in punta di piedi. Era tutto vestito di nero, compresa la visiera da tennis. - Tieni -, e mi consegnò un foglio piegato in quattro.

- Come sei entrato? -, gli domandai a bassa voce.

- Come un ladro, direi.

Aprii il cassetto del comodino e gli mostrai il mio disegno dell'angelo di mamma. - Guarda.

Lo osservò qualche secondo. - Caspita... A volte quel poco di buono che c'è in te funziona davvero.

Sentimmo dei passi in corridoio. Checco sgattaiolò sotto il letto di mamma. Si affacciò un'infermiera, diede un'occhiata in giro, mi salutò con un cenno del capo e uscì.

- Pericolo scampato.

- Okay -, fece Checco dal basso. - Comunque penso che rimarrò qui sotto, se non ti dispiace. Si sta bene, e poi sento meglio Luisa.

Mi chinai. Checco si era sdraiato e aveva chiuso gli occhi.

Nella penombra della camera, presi la mano di mamma e me la portai al cuore.

Il mio amico recitò sottovoce: - La creazione di tutte le cose, nel cerchio zodiacale che si ripete all'infinito. Guidaci nell'universo come fanno le api con il polline dei fiori.

Quindi mi disse di aprire il foglio e leggere.

Ero emozionatissimo. Mi schiarii la voce.

Invocazione: cancella da me le conseguenze dei miei errori passati / e ti prometto di non vacillare mai più / sulle pietre sopra le quali inciampai. / So che la terra dipende dal Cielo / che il corpo dipende dallo Spirito / e che la riuscita dipende dalla nostra Volontà / e dalla tua Grazia. / È questa Grazia, che ti chiedo / Angelo Aladiah. / Il tuo Divino e onnipotente appoggio...

Feci tre respiri profondi, *ascoltando* il mio corpo, come mi aveva insegnato Checco. Sentii un piacevole formicolio. Mi alzai e baciai mamma sulla fronte. Poi guardai sotto al letto, e sentii un tuffo al cuore. Checco stringeva forte gli occhi, cercando di trattenere le lacrime. Si era commosso...

Quasi bisbigliando, parlammo di tante cose. Gli raccontai di come era andata a finire con Magghy, della sua mania del lucidalabbra, della Svizzera, di quanto fossi stato ingenuo a pensare che fosse lei, la ragazza giusta. Gli raccontai anche di Malù, dei suoi occhi verde smeraldo e delle sue parole di incoraggiamento. Lui seguì il mio discorso in silenzio, e alla fine disse solo che era «giusto così».

Ci chiedemmo come sarebbe stato l'ultimo anno di scuola, e come avremmo poi affrontato il futuro. Checco mi confessò, e la cosa mi colpì non poco, di non avere intenzione di iscriversi all'università: - Vorrei continuare a studiare per conto mio nella camera-studio, e poi non posso lasciare sola nonna, lei ha bisogno di me... -. Fu così che finimmo col parlare del senso della vita, e di quello della *cosiddetta* morte...

- Checco? Ma allora, durante le nostre meditazioni, se non esistono barriere temporali, deve essere possibile anche catapultarsi in un'altra dimensione, oltre il «muro di luce» che aveva ipotizzato Tesla. Potremmo vedere la nostra vita come in un film, e magari tornare ancora più indietro, per capire *chi* siamo davvero ora, e magari riuscire a sistemare alcune cose del passato, sbloccare certe emozioni...

Alla fine, ci addormentammo tutti e due: io sulla sedia; Checco, con due rotoli di carta igienica a mo' di cuscino, sotto il letto di mamma. Le ultime parole che mi aveva detto erano state che la carne, le ossa, erano solo un involucro, «perché il tempo dell'anima non finirà mai. È questa la vera legge, Massa...».

Ventidue

Erano passate da poco le cinque quando mi stropicciai gli occhi, ancora mezzo intontito. - Checco, è mattina... -, dissi a bassa voce. - Tra poco passano gli infermieri. Forse è meglio se vai.

Mi abbassai a guardare sotto il letto. Se n'era già andato.

Osservai con calma il viso di mamma. Ogni angolo poteva rivelare il più piccolo movimento.

Passò qualche minuto. - Forse è meglio se vado anch'io, adesso. Ci vediamo più tardi, mamma... -. La baciai.

Prima di rientrare a casa mi feci una passeggiata. Sul retro del foglio che mi aveva dato Checco mi fermai a disegnare uno scorcio di città su cui non mi ero mai soffermato: era un piccolo incrocio nei pressi della stazione degli autobus. C'erano una palazzina Art déco, salmone e azzurra, tutta decorata, e sul piano stradale una modesta bottega di cornici. Al di là del vetro, il corniciaio picchiava con un martello sulle assi di una grande cornice dorata. Mi sbrigai a fissare sulla carta anche quel momento. Così, lo avrei portato per sempre con me.

Papà era seduto al tavolo di cucina e sfogliava una rivista. Bevve un sorso di caffè e fece un lungo sospiro.

- Viè qua -, mi disse. - Guarda che robba.

Girò la rivista dalla mia parte. Osservai bene. - Cos'è, un camper?

- Meijo. È 'na cabbina.

- Una cabina? Di cosa?

- Ma come de cosa, aò? È uno Scania. 'Na bbestia, eh?

- Un camion?

- Eh.

Sembrava una camera d'albergo.

- Bello, davvero... Ma che ci devi fare?

- Eh... fijo mio, che ce devo fa'... -, sospirò distrattamente.

Aprii il frigo, presi il cartone del latte e misi il pentolino sul fuoco. Che c'entrava, ora, la cabina del camion? Lo sbirciai con la coda dell'occhio. Sfogliava la rivista con grande interesse. Anche quello, in fondo, era un modo per distrarsi. Povero papà.

Feci colazione. Quando gli chiesi dove fosse Monica, mi rispose che era al bar. Papà aveva deciso di riaprirlo. Mi vestii e andai a darle una mano.

Per la strada, pensai che era arrivato il momento di parlarle del progetto di ristrutturazione. Chissà cosa avrebbe pensato. Gestione familiare: era questo il punto di forza. Mamma ne sarebbe andata orgogliosa, e gli affari sarebbero migliorati a vista d'occhio...

Arrivai in via Sicilia e mi fermai al portone di Checco. Suonai. Progetto, progetto, progetto.

- Checco, raggiungimi al bar, dobbiamo lavorare al progetto. Sbrigati!

- Checco è uscito -, rispose la vocina fioca di sua nonna.

Chissà dov'era andato. Va be', pensai, prima o poi sarebbe rientrato.

Monica, seduta su uno sgabello dietro al bancone, osservava pensierosa il bar vuoto.

- Osvaldo? -, chiesi.

- È in montagna. Torna dopodomani. Fa caldo, vero?

- Siamo ad agosto.

- Già...

- È passato Checco, per caso?

Monica ci pensò un attimo. - In effetti, un'oretta fa l'ho visto sfrecciare con il motorino.

Ma chissà dov'era andato?

- Secondo te mamma si risveglierà mai? -, domandò all'improvviso mia sorella.

Mi avvicinai al bancone. - *Deve* risvegliarsi. Dobbiamo starle vicino con il pensiero.

Abbassò il capo: - Sì...

- Io e Checco presenteremo domanda per un bando della CEE.

- Che bando?

- Per ristrutturare il Paradise.

- Ristrutturare il bar?

- Sì. Potremmo farci una paninoteca, a gestione familiare, per abbattere le spese. E poi abbiamo un'idea fantastica. Checco ha fatto i conti e secondo lui è fattibile: da giugno a settembre potremmo affittare il campetto e allestire una sala all'aperto, magari con un palchetto per tenere piccoli concerti o, che so, proiettare qualche film. Come fanno sul lungomare.

Monica mi guardò senza dire niente.

- La CEE offre finanziamenti agevolatissimi -, continuai, - e ti dà il 30% a fondo perduto. Sai che significa?

- Sì, lo so.

- E allora? -, la incalzai. - Non ti sembra un'ottima idea?

Monica si alzò dallo sgabello, prese uno straccetto e cominciò a strofinare il lavello. - Secondo me non funzionerà...

- Ma come no? Funzionerà, ne sono sicuro. E poi c'è Checco. Lui non si può sbagliare.

- Non lo so... È rischioso. Troppo rischioso.

- Ma perché? -. Passai anch'io di là dal banco. - Dimmi perché. Cos'è che non ti convince?

- Sono i *soldi*. Che noi non abbiamo...

Maledetti soldi... - Ma Checco mi ha detto che l'importo finanziabile è del 100%! Capito? Il 100%! Non dovremo sganciare nemmeno una lira!

- Sì, ma se le cose non vanno come previsto? Il finanziamento va ripagato lo stesso, lo sapevi? E poi, bisogna vedere se il progetto viene approvato. Ci vogliono il geometra, i tecnici, un sacco di altre cose...

- Ma possiamo farlo. Basta impegnarsi! Guardati intorno. In questa zona non ci sono paninoteche. Pensa al Coenobium. In quel quartiere non c'era nemmeno un ritrovo. E ora ci va mezza città.

Monica si grattò la testa.

- Pensaci.

Sospirò. - E tu credi che potrebbe funzionare...

- Ma certo! E poi un minimo di rischio dobbiamo pur metterlo in conto, è così che funziona. Anche a scuola ce lo ripetono sempre. Cavolo, sì che può funzionare! Però ci *dobbiamo* credere, dobbiamo *allinearci*, come dice Checco... -. La guardai negli occhi. - Dai!

- Va bene -, cedette guardandosi le mani, - qualunque cosa voglia dire Checco, *allineiamoci*... Facciamolo per mamma.

Ero elettrizzato. Le dissi che sarei rimasto lì con lei tutta la mattina e le chiesi come potevo aiutarla, ma alzò le spalle, non c'era proprio niente da fare.

Ancora esausto per via della nottata in bianco, alla fine decisi dunque di tornare a casa, buttarmi sotto la doccia e riposare un po'.

Trovai papà che dormiva sul divano, la testa piegata all'indietro. Andai in bagno. Davanti allo specchio, mi osservai il petto, le braccia, le vene del collo, il ciuffo che scendeva. Mi sentivo così diverso, come se fossi un altro nel corpo di sempre.

Poi notai un piccolo neo sul collo. Non l'avevo mai visto prima. Checco diceva che, quando nella nostra vita succede qualcosa che ci segna nel profondo, anche il corpo ne viene segnato, come fosse la cartina geografica della nostra esistenza: - Siamo collegati, Massa, con tutto...

Ancora una volta, aveva avuto ragione.

- Ho deciso -, dissi. Ero a casa di Checco, seduto di fronte allo specchio del bagno. Lui mi guardava la testa. Il suo cespuglio biondo sembrava un girasole scoppiato.

- Sicuro sicuro? -, domandò.

- Sicuro.

Checco si grattò la fronte. - Che tu sia benedetto, caro Massa.

Impugnò le lunghe forbici e... *Zac*! Il ciuffo cadde a terra silenzioso.

Lo guardai. Il *mio* ciuffo... Be', adesso non lo era più.

- E adesso? -, chiese il mio amico.

- E adesso continua. Vai, taglia tutto.

- Ma tutto tutto?

- Tutto.

Fu così che mi ritrovai completamente rasato. Certo, con qualche scalino per via del taglio con le forbici, ma Checco aveva fatto davvero un buon lavoro.

Quanto tempo avevo passato con il tubetto di gel in mano cercando la pettinatura perfetta!

Feci un sospiro e mi alzai dalla sedia.

- Questo è il momento del non ritorno -, disse Checco.

- Già...

- Però manca ancora qualcosa.

Mi guardai di nuovo allo specchio. - Cosa? -. Non mi veniva in mente niente.

Poi Checco si mise seduto al mio posto. - Eccomi.

- Cioè?

- Ora tocca a me...

Rimasi a bocca aperta. - Vuoi tagliarti il cespuglio?

- È necessario. Per completare l'opera. Le cose, o si fanno per bene, o non si fanno per niente.

- Checco, ma dici sul serio?

- Forza, forza! -, smaniò. - Qui ce n'è da tagliare, non perdere tempo!

Dopo tanti anni abituato a vederlo così, col cespuglio, tagliare quei riccioli mi sembrò davvero strano. Lavorai in silenzio, e quando anche l'ultima ciocca cadde a terra, non potei far a meno di esclamare: - Oooh...

Il mio amico aggrottò la fronte, anche per lui era surreale vedersi così. Poi, sul suo viso apparve un timido sorriso. - Sono diverso, eh?

- Decisamente...

Sembrava proprio un altro.

- Ma sono sempre io! -. Guardò per terra. - Caspita! Quanti capelli! Si potrebbero vendere. Vediamo un po'... Calcolando una media di circa centosessantatré capelli per centimetro quadrato, dalla mia testa ne dovrebbero essere caduti circa centocinquantottomila. Pensando al valore...

- Eh no, dai, non ricominciare con tutti questi numeri! Ti prego!

- Infatti scherzavo. Non potrei mai vendere i miei capelli. Ci sono tutti i miei ricordi, dentro.

Sì, era sempre, inconfondibilmente lui...

Poi Checco mi munì di carta e matita, e schizzai velocemente un nostro ritratto allo specchio.

Era divertente disegnare tutti gli scalini che avevamo in testa, ma lo spasso maggiore fu sicuramente immortalare l'espressione che aveva deciso di assumere Checco: bocca leggermente aperta a culo di gallina, occhi sbarrati e capo inclinato di quarantacinque gradi. Mi ricordò le smorfie che facevo a mamma quando ero piccolo.

Ci spostammo nella camera-studio, e passammo in rassegna l'album fotografico delle gite scolastiche, ridendo e ricordando le piccole grandi avventure trascorse. Il volume dei capelli di Checco era aumentato di anno in anno, mentre il mio ciuffo a forza di usare il gel era diventato così rigido che alla fine, nella foto scattata in piazza Unità d'Italia a Trieste, nemmeno la bora era riuscito a scalfirlo. Erano passati solo pochi mesi, ma mi sembravano anni.

A un certo punto Checco disse che voleva farmi un regalo. Frugò in uno scaffale della libreria e mi consegnò un libriccino. Lo guardai: era *L'amico ritrovato*, di Fred Uhlman.

- Parla di una ricongiunzione spirituale. I protagonisti potremmo essere noi. Io Konradin, e tu Hans. Che ne pensi?

- Non so chi siano -, ammisi, - ma se lo dici tu...

- Certo che lo dico io. La loro amicizia supera gli ostacoli del tempo, come farà la nostra. Nel libro, a distanza di molti anni, Hans scopre che l'amico Konradin non solo non lo ha dimenticato, ma ha fatto la scelta più coraggiosa che un uomo possa fare... -. La sua voce si incrinò.

Sentii l'emozione stringermi lo stomaco, gli occhi gonfiarsi di lacrime.

Lui se ne accorse e si fece più vicino. Appoggiò la sua testa alla mia. Sentivo la sua pelle, le ossa del suo cranio contro il mio. Fu come entrare nei suoi pensieri. Eravamo vivi. - Adesso siamo ancora più forti di prima: ricordatelo, Massa.

Ventitré

Erano cinque giorni che mamma stava in ospedale.

Papà camminava avanti e indietro nel corridoio di fronte all'ingresso della rianimazione. Quando io e Monica lo raggiungemmo, prima guardò la mia testa, poi guardò mia sorella. - Se Dio vuole s'è taijato quei capelli da pischello.

Senza troppi giri di parole, ci raccontò che la mattina, prima di smontare, l'infermiere che aveva fatto il turno di notte in rianimazione gli confidò di aver assistito a un episodio insolito.

Era da poco passata la mezzanotte, quando gli era parso di vedere entrare qualcuno nella camera di nostra madre. Insospettito, e allarmato, era corso subito a controllare. Aveva aperto la porta, infilato la testa dentro e spostato lo sguardo da una parte all'altra. La stanza era vuota. - Ma c'era un odore, impercettibile, come di fiori, come una brezza... non so... lavanda forse, sì ecco, come di lavanda! Ma le ripeto, dentro non c'era nessuno, sor Antò, nessuno!

Entrammo in camera. Era tutto come al solito. Il walkman sul comodino, il rosario intorno a un polso di mamma, i macchinari con i monitor in funzione. E quell'odore di lavanda di cui aveva parlato l'infermiere... Lo dissi a Monica e papà, ma loro non sentivano nulla. Mi venne in mente il frate del San Francesco, che non avevo più incontrato, e un brivido mi passò lungo la schiena.

- L'infermiere ha detto di avere visto qualcuno entrare in camera? -, chiese Monica. - Be', ecco, magari è stata un'allucinazione. Non è che aveva bevuto?

Dentro di me, speravo invece che fosse tutto vero, che *qualcuno*, magari *Aladiah*, l'angelo di mamma, avesse per così dire compiuto un piccolo miracolo e lasciato dietro di sé una scia profumata.

Papà era nervoso. Girellò per la camera un minuto o due, poi uscì. Possibile che né lui né Monica sentissero quest'odore, seppur leggerissimo?

- Secondo me invece non è tutto come al solito -, dissi a Monica. - Guarda bene mamma.

Lei si avvicinò subito al letto.

- Cos'ha?

- Non è mai stata così bella...

Con il cuore gonfio di emozioni, anche quella mattina uscimmo dall'ospedale senza di lei.

Secondo i medici, più tempo passava più era difficile che si risvegliasse.

Non lo dicevo a nessuno, nemmeno a Checco, ma ogni giorno mi recavo nella piccola cappella affrescata del San Francesco. Non per pregare, o almeno non solo per quello. Ci andavo per ascoltare il silenzio.

Nel libro sugli angeli c'era scritto che la nostra vita si svolge su tre livelli distinti, e io ci credevo, perché ogni volta che mi accomodavo sulla sediolina e chiudevo gli occhi lo provavo sulla *mia pelle*. Vedevo mamma e potevo toccarla, sentirne il calore. E poi, qualche giorno prima, le avevo parlato. Sì, proprio così. Era il mio piccolo segreto. Ci eravamo scambiati solo due parole, ma per me significavano tutto.

Quella mattina, decisi però di sedermi su una panca di fronte all'altare. Aprii il libro che mi aveva regalato Checco e cominciai a leggere. Ero emozionato, e mi immersi in quelle pagine completamente rapito. Non avrei mai creduto che una storia potesse sprigionare tanta forza. Che potessi riconoscermi in quelle parole messe insieme a una a una da qualcuno che aveva vissuto una vita così diversa dalla mia. Ora capivo perfettamente cosa intendeva Checco quando me ne aveva parlato.

Circa a metà libro, alzai gli occhi sul crocifisso di Duccio. Lo osservai, e quel viso dipinto mi parve sorridere.

D'un fiato arrivai alla fine.

Non mi ero accorto delle lacrime che mi rigavano le guance. Quel sentimento che chiamiamo amicizia è davvero in grado di compiere qualsiasi cosa ...

Durante la cena, io, papà e Monica avevamo parlato a lungo. O meglio, avevo parlato io, buttando fuori tutte le sensazioni che mi avevano accompagnato fino a quel momento. Mi sentivo come ispirato, protetto dall'*alto*. Era difficile spiegare a parole *cosa* sentivo, ma proprio questa difficoltà ne aumentava il valore.

Prima, a ogni incomprensione, mi chiudevo in me stesso, e il mio istinto di ribellione prendeva il sopravvento. Era impossibile controllarlo, anzi, neanche lo volevo: per me, nel mondo regnava la stupidità. Tutti gli altri sbagliavano. Poi, mi ero reso conto che quello stupido ero io. Perché ero io che non andavo oltre le apparenze. Una volta sistemato il mio orticello, credevo di avere la coscienza a posto e di essere in *armonia con la natura* semplicemente girando qua e là per le strade di campagna. Per tutto il resto, be', che ci potevo fare, io?

Almeno una volta nella vita tutti abbiamo avuto questo tipo di pensieri.

Ma quanti di noi se ne sono *veramente* liberati?

Mentre parlavo, papà mi osservava con attenzione, l'espressione sorpresa. Mia sorella invece faceva finta di niente, ma il suo volto tradiva interesse. Mi sentivo al centro dell'attenzione, anzi, *ero* al centro dell'attenzione. E avvertivo la responsabilità delle mie parole.

Monica sparecchiò. Papà non disse niente, ma quando si alzò dalla sedia mi passò un braccio sulle spalle. Un brivido mi attraversò il collo, e si conficcò nel cuore. Poi andò verso i fornelli e dalla busta che aveva lasciato sul ripiano accanto al lavello tirò fuori una mela, una pesca, una pera, due albicocche, un kiwi e una manciata di prugne. Li lavò e si rimise seduto. Attaccò dalla pera. Tra le sue mani, sembrava una miniatura.

Io e Monica lo guardavamo incuriositi.

- Dove hai preso quella frutta, papà? È tutto chiuso, oggi è San Lorenzo -, osservò mia sorella.

- A 'na bbancarella sulla vecchia Aurelia, pe' annà a Braccagni.

- E che ci facevi, laggiù? -, domandai.

- Nun te preoccupà.

Papà mangiò tutta la frutta, con gusto.

- Lo sapevate che la frutta de staggione è tre volte più nutriente della frutta de serra?

Che discorso era quello? Ero un po' preoccupato. Papà era così strano, ultimamente.

Monica gli disse che sì, lei lo sapeva.

- E tu? -, mi chiese.

- Penso di sì, insomma, è normale -, risposi. Ma continuavo a non capire.

- Bene -, aggiunse. - E sentiamo un po', secondo voi pesa di più una mela o una pesca?

- In che senso? -, chiese Monica.

- Voglio dire, pesa di più un metro cubo di pesche o uno di mele?

- Non saprei, papà...

- Voglio fare una prova -, continuò.

- Che prova, pa'? Ma perché ci stai dicendo queste cose?

- Statte zitto. Prendi un foijo e scrivice 'na serie de lettere, a caso. Sotto scrivice 'n'antra serie più piccola, e sotto ancora 'n'antra ancora più piccola. Hai capito?

Ero un po' disorientato, ma presi carta e penna e scrissi le lettere. Gli mostrai il foglio. - Va bene?

- E però nun me lo devi fa' vede!

- Perché?

- Perché sennò a che serve? Va' là! Mettite ar muro. Devo indovinà le lettere, no?

Questa poi, sì che era una novità. Indovinare le lettere. Chiesi spiegazioni, ma non riuscii a cavargli una parola di bocca. Alla fine, disse solo che avremmo saputo tutto al momento giusto.

Camminavo così volentieri ormai, che quando Monica mi aveva detto che se volevo potevo prendere la Uno, mi ero sentito quasi in imbarazzo a rifiutare. Le strade erano tranquille e quell'ora della sera, poi, era la mia preferita. Verso la costa, tra un palazzo e l'altro, i colori del tramonto pitturavano il cielo a grandi campiture arancio e violetto.

Percorsi via Sauro al fresco dei platani. Superai la trattoria sulla curva e scesi le scalette del sottopasso ferroviario. Checco mi aveva detto di portare con me l'orchidea di mamma, e che quella sarebbe stata una notte indimenticabile.

Arrivato in via Sicilia mi fermai di fronte al portone, senza suonare il citofono. Erano le nove in punto, e il portone si aprì come sincronizzato. - Perfetto! -, esclamai. Ma poi mi accorsi che non era Checco. Uscì una signora, indossava un lungo vestito scuro con un cappello a falde larghe orlato di rosso e una borsa di pelle piuttosto grande. Mi guardò.

- Mi scusi, sto aspettando un mio amico, credevo fosse lui.

Il portone intanto si era richiuso, ma la signora era sempre lì, nella penombra, e mi guardava.

- Mi scusi ancora, signora. Ero proprio convinto che fosse il mio amico, è sempre puntualissimo.

La signora non disse niente, ma a un certo punto, dopo aver fatto un lungo sospiro, aprì la borsa e ci frugò dentro. Estrasse una penna e un piccolo quaderno. Lo aprì e ci scrisse sopra qualcosa. Me lo mostrò.

Era quasi buio, ma si poteva ancora leggere: «Sei sempre il solito. Sono io! Ti piace il vestito?».

Guardai meglio. Tirò su la testa. Cavolo, era proprio Checco.

- Ma come ti sei combinato?

- Dobbiamo fare una cosa, per Luisa.

- Ma dove andiamo?

- Come dove? Da Luisa.

- Ma sono le nove, non ci faranno passare. Non possiamo approfittare ancora della disponibilità dei medici. Non mi sembra giusto.

- Secondo te perché allora mi sarei vestito così, da prete?

- Da prete? -, chiesi. - Mi sembra più un vestito da donna.

- Ma che dici? E il saturno, allora?

- Il che?

- Il saturno, il cappello! Va be', c'ha il bordo rosso, ma capirai chi se ne accorge.

Mi chiedevo cosa diavolo avesse in mente. Lo guardai meglio. In effetti, era proprio un vestito da prete. - E questa borsa? -, gli chiesi.

- C'è lo stereo a pile.

Lo stereo a pile? Oh, santo cielo.

- E poi, guarda -. Tirò fuori una vistosa collana con una croce e se la mise al collo. - Forza, forza. Procediamo! -. Si tolse il saturno, s'infilò il casco e inforcò lo Zip. - Monta su. Ah, e ricordati questo nome: Saturno.

Parcheggiammo sulla via Senese. Checco suggerì di passare dal retro. - Tu -, disse, - mi raccomando, seguimi, stammi appiccicato. E ricordati, sono un prete, io. Nessuno ci farà domande, al massimo ci saluteranno. Penseranno che stiamo andando da qualche vecchietto moribondo. Ma... ah ah aaah! -, Checco fece una risata beffarda. - Sappiamo entrambi che così non è!

Scrollai il capo. Corremmo giù per una lunga discesa debolmente illuminata. Non c'era nessuno. Un'ambulanza era parcheggiata da una parte. Entrammo da una porta di servizio e ci ritrovammo in una specie di sotterraneo. Una fitta rete di tubi gialli correva lungo il soffitto. Nell'aria uno strepitio continuo, simile a quello delle caldaie. Mi guardai velocemente in giro, era un labirinto di corridoi, ma Checco sapeva dove andare. Lo seguii, stringendo il sacchetto di carta con l'orchidea. Il mio amico camminava veloce, col vestito nero e il cappello ben calzato sulla fronte. Oltrepassò una piccola porticina. Ecco le scale.

Cominciammo a salire. Ai piedi, Checco calzava un paio di Adidas nere, le tre strisce rosso fuoco si intonavano al bordo del saturno dello stesso colore. Nella mano destra, la borsa.

Arrivammo al piano della rianimazione senza incontrare anima viva. Ormai fuori era buio pesto. Da un finestrone, le luci di Grosseto brillavano. Checco si fermò di schianto e si girò verso di me. - Devi andare al gabbiottino del reparto, scusarti con l'infermiere per l'orario, e poi dirgli che mi stai accompagnando perché devo *assolutamente* pregare. Se ti chiede il motivo, aggiungi che tra poche ore è l'undici di agosto, ed è prevista una solenne invocazione -, Checco guardò l'orologio, - dall'una e venti all'una e quaranta del mattino, che per l'appunto è domani undici agosto 1994. Domande?

- E tu, che farai mentre io sarò impegnato con lui?

- Che farò? Farò così -, e simulò una specie di sorriso benevolo. - Il classico sorriso da prete.

L'infermiera che era di turno si stupì soprattutto per l'orario, secondo lei francamente inopportuno.

- Purtroppo l'unico momento possibile è proprio questo -, cercai di convincerla. - È una preghiera rituale, che si tramanda da tremila anni -. Guardai Checco. - Vero, padre?

Lui sorrise, gli occhi coperti dal saturno, e annuì inclinando il capo di lato.

L'infermiera non era per niente convinta, ma di fronte a un prete cosa poteva fare? Disse solo che non le era mai successo niente del genere.

- C'è sempre una prima volta -, la confortai.

Salutò Checco con un «Arrivederci, padre», al che lui aprì la borsa e tirò fuori una specie di santino, su cui era disegnato un monaco, o qualcosa del genere, circondato da svariati animali. In primo piano, un maiale. La scritta in basso recitava: «*Sanctus Antonius Abbas*, il santo eremita, patrono degli animali. Prega per noi». Checco baciò il santino e lo consegnò all'infermiera.

Entrammo in camera di mamma quasi in punta di piedi e chiudemmo la porta. La lucina gialla di emergenza illuminava fiaccamente il pavimento.

Mi avvicinai a mamma e le presi la mano, la portai al viso e la strinsi forte. - Mamma, mamma, so che riesci a sentirmi. Stanotte rimarremo qui con te, io e Checco!

Presi l'orchidea e la posai sul comodino, poi ci sedemmo ai lati del letto. Checco si tolse il saturno e lo poggiò in fondo al letto.

- Per prima cosa -, disse, - dobbiamo *allinearci* per prendere in mano la nostra vita, tutta la nostra vita.

Qualche giorno prima Checco mi aveva regalato un altro libro, e finalmente avevo capito cosa intendeva con tutta quella storia dell'*allineamento*. Era un saggio di Leonard Orr e Konrad Halbig sul «rebirthing»: insegnava a *respirare*. Proprio così. A respirare, l'atto spontaneo per eccellenza, che a quanto pareva non molti sanno fare come si deve. Per questo le persone vivono una vita in cui non si riconoscono, perché non sanno respirare. Eppure, a volte basterebbe guardare un neonato nella culla mentre dorme e osservare il movimento del suo ventre. Il segreto della respirazione è in quel movimento, il massaggio naturale per la rigenerazione interna. Tutto qui.

Con gli occhi chiusi, seguivo il ritmo del suo respiro profondo. Era come pregare nel silenzio di noi stessi.

Mi bastarono pochi minuti per sentirmi completamente avvolto da un calore indescrivibile. Poi ebbi come la sensazione di tuffarmi nel vuoto.

Checco mi chiese cosa vedessi.

- Sono in cucina, ad Albinia.

- E quanti anni hai?

- Mmh... Sei. Anzi, sette.

Dopo qualche minuto, riuscii a mettere bene a fuoco e mi accorsi che vicino a me c'era mamma. Indossava un grembiule colorato, e dal profumo nell'aria capii che stava preparando la panzanella. Lo dissi a Checco.

Lui mi guidò per la stanza, e mi chiese di descriverla dettagliatamente. I mobili erano semplici, proprio come li ricordavo. Il piccolo televisore in bianco e nero, con due lunghe antenne sulla sommità, stazionava sul ripiano più basso della credenza. Sul cavalletto, vicino alla finestra, una tela di un incantevole paesaggio d'estate. Poi, all'improvviso, vidi Checco. Era lì, seduto sul tavolo.

- Ci sei anche tu...

- Ti ho raggiunto... Ma aspettiamo che Luisa finisca di preparare la panzanella -, disse sottovoce dall'altro lato del letto. - Poi potremo mangiare.

Nella mia mente, i fotogrammi continuarono a viaggiare. Mamma finì di condire il pranzo e portò i piatti in tavola. Io la guardavo, e avevo gli occhi pieni di lei.

Checco mi spronò a continuare. - Che sensazioni provi?

- È strano... Ma... è come se non riuscissi a parlare, sento come un nodo in gola.

- Cos'è che ti blocca?

- Non lo so... mi sento rallentato, come in uno spazio fuori dal tempo.

- Rilassati, respira a fondo e visualizza questo nodo alla gola, *ascoltalo*, *osservalo*, ma senza giudicare. Il nodo è un *maestro*, è lì per parlarti, per aiutarti...

- Sì -, risposi espirando profondamente. - Vorrei dire a mamma che le voglio bene. Ma non ci riesco.

- Diglielo! Coraggio! Nessuno è qui per giudicarti, nessuno. Siete solo tu e lei. Lasciati andare, lascia andare il respiro e sciogli questo nodo... Ora!

Il cuore accelerò i battiti. Presi un ultimo, profondissimo respiro e, buttando fuori l'aria con forza, liberai le parole rimaste inchiodate lì per tutti quegli anni: - Mamma, ti voglio bene!

Poi mamma mi abbracciò, e quell'abbraccio fu l'emozione più grande che avessi mai provato. Le sue braccia mi stringevano, la mia testa era accoccolata sul suo petto. Come quando ero bambino. E mi sembrava così reale che pensai davvero di rivivere un momento passato. Come aria che riempie i polmoni, il suo amore inondava il mio piccolo cuore. Era stato così semplice dire quelle parole. Semplice e liberatorio.

Checco scese dal tavolo e mi venne vicino toccandomi una spalla: - Bravo, amico mio. Bravo.

Avvolto nel torpore di quell'emozione, mangiammo tutti insieme la panzanella, in silenzio.

- Ora -, disse Checco dall'altro lato del letto dopo pochi minuti, - lasciati andare, fluttua sopra quella scena e ritorna qua. Possiamo aprire gli occhi... Bene. Stasera, ventuno agosto, giorno di reggenza del Serafino *Mahasiah*, siamo qui per risvegliare Luisa dal suo sonno primordiale. Per questo ho chiesto un consiglio al mio angelo *Mebahel*. E lui me l'ha dato: lo stereo a pile. Stasera ci sarà un concerto.

Checco estrasse dalla borsa il piccolo stereo portatile, tutto rattoppato dal nastro adesivo e dalle figurine dei suoi tennisti preferiti. Al posto della manopola del volume, una forchettina da frutta che seppi serviva anche da antenna di emergenza. Aprì lo scomparto e soffiò sulle testine. Quindi prese le cassette, ne scelse una e la infilò dentro. Mi guardò. - Per sicurezza, terremo il volume molto basso, non vorrei *risvegliare* tutto l'ospedale! -, rise.

- Si comincia. Johann Sebastian Bach, *Suite n. 5 per violoncello solo.*

La musica inondò delicatamente l'aria, come fosse un profumo trasportato da un alito di vento.

Non avevo mai ascoltato niente del genere, ma mi bastarono poche note per capire che quella musica non apparteneva solo a *questo* mondo, ma al cosmo intero. Era incredibile come da un singolo strumento potesse sprigionare una tale intensità di emozioni. La sentivo dappertutto, in ogni parte di me.

Checco si alzò, lentamente, andò al centro della stanza e cominciò a muoversi con movimenti sinuosi, felpati.

Con il vestito nero e la catena al collo, era tremendamente buffo e al tempo stesso così serio, come se per lui quello non fosse un travestimento. Sembrava un derviscio sufi, uno di quegli asceti mistici del Medio Oriente alle prese con una lenta danza roteante.

Stringevo la mano a mamma e con un dito, in aria, seguivo la musica ondeggiando come un direttore d'orchestra. Poi le accarezzai il viso, le baciai la mano.

Quando il suono del violoncello si interruppe, mi chiesi se il silenzio che seguiva non facesse parte del brano, tanta era l'intensità delle emozioni che mi sentivo dentro: pace, fiducia, ma anche determinazione.

Checco disse che il concerto proseguiva con Rachmaninov, *Concerto per pianoforte e orchestra n.* 2, terzo movimento. Si sfilò le Adidas.

- Massa, se non ti dispiace tornerei sotto come l'altra volta. Vorrei stare vicino a Luisa -. Dopodiché si sdraiò sotto il letto di mamma e schiacciò «play».

- E ora -, disse, - immergiamoci nello spazio siderale...

Appoggiai la testa sulla spalla di mamma, sentivo il suo cuore battere. Nella semioscurità della stanza, quella musica mi riempì di una pace infinita.

Era l'una e venti quando Checco tirò fuori il suo libro di preghiere e, da sotto il letto di mamma, cominciò a invocare a bassa voce:

Mahasiah! Angelo Luminoso della Santa Medicina, panacea universale, che guarisce tutti i mali, quelli dell'anima, del cuore, del corpo; ti chiedo di stendere il tuo balsamo provvidenziale su tutte le mie ferite, le mie inquietudini e i miei tormenti. Sì, ero cieco, ma ora ci vedo. Ero sordo, ma ora ci sento, e il mio desiderio ardente è di venire al Vero, alla Verità, alla Luce che rende liberi...!

Strinsi le labbra, come a cercare la massima concentrazione. Poi, mi ricordai del mio disegno dell'angelo. Lo presi dal cassetto del comodino e lo appoggiai sul petto di mamma, all'altezza del cuore.

Alle cinque e mezzo, Checco uscì da sotto il letto e mi disse di aiutarlo. - Dobbiamo spostare Luisa verso la finestra. Tra poco spunterà l'alba.

Con molta attenzione, sfrenammo le ruote del letto e lo avvicinammo al finestrone. Fuori, il primo chiarore del giorno si stava lentamente affacciando all'orizzonte, dietro ai contorni morbidi delle colline.

- Che spettacolo... -, ammirò Checco. Prese lo stereo e cambiò cassetta. - Beethoven, *Sinfonia n.* 6, detta «Pastorale». Esprime i nostri sentimenti più sinceri, perché è vero che secondo la Sapienza Antica ci sono sette Mondi, che nell'universo ci sono miliardi di galassie, ma noi siamo *qui*, governati da Madre Natura che ci appartiene e alla quale apparteniamo, e ci siamo *ora*, e per me il nostro è il pianeta più bello di tutti, non lo cambierei per niente al mondo... Massa, Luisa, questa musica è per voi...

Osservai il sorgere del sole col fiato sospeso. Il mio cuore batteva all'unisono con quello di mamma.

- Abbracciala, Massa, abbracciala! -, mi esortò Checco.

Mi alzai di scatto e la strinsi forte. - Mamma! Adesso puoi svegliarti. Perché io ti amo, ti amo! -, le sussurrai piano.

Checco schiacciò «stop», mentre un timido raggio di sole illuminava il volto di mamma.

Il mio amico riprese il suo saturno, rimise lo stereo nella borsa e mi disse di andare: - Dobbiamo passare dal Grande Cipresso. Per rendergli omaggio.

Poi baciò mamma sulla fronte. Io ero immobile davanti al letto, e trattenevo il respiro. Checco mi scosse e mi disse di sbrigarmi.

Uscimmo dalla stanza. L'infermiere di turno lo guardò confuso, salutandoci senza sapere cos'altro fare. Checco lo benedisse velocemente. Era esilarante.

Al Grande Cipresso, l'aria del mattino era frizzante. Scendemmo dallo Zip e Checco si sfilò la veste. Avevo una voglia matta di abbracciare quell'albero, così mi avvicinai, allargai le braccia più che potei e strinsi forte il tronco, fino quasi a farmi male. Era una sensazione straordinaria, impagabile. Sentivo che qualcosa mi stava proteggendo... forse era Dio, non lo sapevo bene.

Ventiquattro

Erano passati due giorni dalla preghiera e dal «concerto» nella camera di mamma. Li avevo trascorsi a casa, quasi ad attendere una svolta, un segnale dall'alto. O semplicemente che qualcuno chiamasse dall'ospedale e ci dicesse che lei aveva aperto gli occhi, che stava bene.

Due lunghissimi giorni, a fare zapping alla Tv in cerca di un documentario sugli animali o sperando che trasmettessero una puntata speciale di *Quark*, con Piero Angela a spiegare teorie sul risveglio delle persone in stato d'incoscienza o cose del genere. Ma nulla. Giusto i soliti cartoni, il *Gioco delle coppie*, Ambra e le ragazze di *Non è la Rai* che facevano finta di cantare dimenandosi.

Era stato Checco a stabilire che avrei dovuto passare quel tempo da solo con me stesso, a riflettere. Ma su cosa c'era ancora da riflettere? Era un po' nervoso, anzi molto. Avevo troppi pensieri in testa, mi sentivo come appena uscito da un frullatore...

Seduto sul divano del salotto, le immagini della mia prima volta con Magghy andavano e venivano, *Serenata rap* ancora in sottofondo. Poi papà tirava un pugno al dottore, Monica urlava e sveniva, i fili del *Benellindson*, la badante albanese del podere. Ora, Checco era un prete e la musica classica si mischiava a Jovanotti. La Comunità Economica Europea, il bando, le norme, la testata a Vezio, poi Vezio che guidava il trattore...

Mi veniva da vomitare, mi girava la testa, tremavo, sudavo e mi sentivo mancare... Iniziai a respirare lentamente. «Il segreto è nel respiro, Massa...», risentivo la voce di Checco. Poi arrivò Malù, con gli occhi smeraldo come il mare, il suo profumo di libertà e le sue parole decise e chiare: «Devi smetterla di lamentarti e tirare fuori il coraggio!». Il disegno che feci a mamma da piccolo e lei sul divano che si commuoveva, io mentre la spiavo, il nostro abbraccio nel nostro ultimo viaggio da soli fino a ritrovarci nella cucina di Albinia. E ancora, i tubicini freddi di plastica nelle narici di mamma, i suoi occhi chiusi, spenti, il mio orecchio sul suo petto, il cuore che batteva quasi impercettibilmente, la bara in lontananza che scendeva dalle scale e sfilava via...

Dovevo respirare, profondamente, come fanno i bambini nella culla...

Cambiai posizione sul divano e *decisi* di respirare. Uno, due, tre respiri lunghi e profondi, le mie mani poggiate sul ventre; ancora un altro respiro profondo, lento, ancora più lungo...

Avvolto da una luce forte, luminosissima, intravedo il Grande Cipresso. Inizio a sentirne il richiamo e *decido* di fluttuare verso di lui. L'aria ora è leggera, e io sono sereno, calmo: è una dolce brezza sopra il capo, all'altezza della fontanella. Intravedo una figura scura sotto al Cipresso; mi avvicino, vengo investito dall'odore intenso di lavanda appena colta e poi scorgo una mano che stringe un rosario, e infine un sorriso. È lui, lo riconosco, il frate del convento di San Francesco. Lo guardo, e tutti i miei sensi vengono catturati da quell'aura di pace interiore che emana. Mi abbraccia, e io mi sento leggero, inondato di profumo. La testa inizia a girare di nuovo, mi manca il respiro, voglio prendere fiato ma non ci riesco, mi sento inchiodato al divano, a pancia in su, le mani che non si muovono.

So che devo farmi il segno della croce, ci riesco con difficoltà, prendo un respiro profondo, violento, come quando si riemerge dall'acqua dopo una lunga apnea. Ho le lacrime agli occhi.

Decido di uscire, a piedi, forse sono le sei o le sette di sera, ho bisogno di camminare. Mi avvio verso la strada che porta a Principina, lentamente, non ho fretta. Devo raggiungere il Grande Cipresso, sento che qualcosa sta attendendo il mio arrivo.

Sobbalzai, svegliandomi di colpo, col cuore in gola, le mani tremanti e un suono acuto, penetrante, nelle orecchie.

Mi alzai di scatto, non capivo dove mi trovavo. Mi passai le mani sul viso a stropicciarmi gli occhi, scossi la testa a destra e sinistra, un grosso sospiro e mi misi in piedi. Mi precipitai al telefono. Stava squillando. Ecco cos'era quel suono acuto... Ma avevo un po' paura. Paura di ricevere una brutta notizia. Paura della realtà. Avrei voluto tornare al Grande Cipresso. Lì mi sentivo sereno. Gli squilli si facevano sempre più insistenti.

Rispondi, Massa, rispondi!

Alzai la cornetta bruscamente, ma non ebbi il coraggio di chiedere chi fosse.

Poi una voce calda come un raggio di sole arrivò a squarciare il mio cupo cielo interiore.

- Chicco, Chicco...

- Maaa...-, e non riuscii a continuare.

- Chicco!

- Mammaaaaa!

Iniziai a gridare, a chiamarla. Era così facile respirare in quel momento.

- Mamma, mamma!

- Chicco, amore di mamma! Sono io... Sono mamma, sì! Vieni, amore, siamo tutti qui... Io sto bene... È passato, è tutto passato.

Iniziai a singhiozzare. Forte.

Libero di fare. Libero di essere me stesso.

Libero di correre da lei. Libero.

Venticinque

Passarono giorni intensi, nuove energie stavano risvegliando il mio desiderio di fare, fare qualcosa per me stesso, per la mia *nuova* famiglia. Per noi.

Più convinto che mai, decisi allora di riprendere e rendere pubblico il progetto di ristrutturazione.

Verso le sette di sera, io e Checco ci facemmo coraggio e andammo al bar a parlare con papà, sicuri che l'idea di rilanciare il Paradise fosse ottima, sicuri che lui si sarebbe entusiasmato quanto noi e che la sua approvazione avrebbe segnato il punto di inizio della nostra svolta. Soprattutto della mia. Sarei diventato il più giovane imprenditore della provincia, e non solo. Appena maggiorenne e già titolare di un'attività. Sognavo troppo? Forse sì, ma in quel momento per me era l'unico obiettivo che riuscivo a visualizzare. Checco era stranamente silenzioso, e non capivo il motivo.

Facevo molto affidamento sulle sue conoscenze tecniche e sulle norme che aveva studiato per il bando della Comunità Economica Europea. Sarebbe stato lui a esporre tutti i passaggi pratici. Io ero il fantasista, il finalizzatore, proprio come «Giorgione» Chinaglia; lui mi avrebbe lanciato a rete. Eppure, proprio mentre ci stavamo sedendo tutti e tre a uno dei tavolinetti tondi in acciaio leggermente ossidato, un'ulteriore conferma del degrado di quel bar ormai semideserto, il mio amico fece una smorfia strana, come di chi parla il linguaggio dei segni. Capii subito, da quella bocca chiusa storta da una parte come se qualcuno gliel'avesse cucita con del filo, che Checco, il mio migliore amico nonché spalla di un attacco che avrebbe scardinato le difese più resistenti, quel giorno non voleva partecipare all'azione finale...

E fu così. Non spiccicò una parola, una che fosse una. Seguiva i miei discorsi e i miei vani tentativi di illustrare il *nostro* progetto: mi impappinai mentre snocciolavo norme di cui non ricordavo minimamente numero né diciture varie; mi si arrotolava la lingua nel tentativo di spiegare le stesse trasformazioni del bar. Ogni tanto Checco mi faceva una smorfia di sostegno come a voler sottolineare certe parti del mio discorso, oppure alzava lo sguardo al cielo come se volesse imprecare contro qualcuno.

Tutto sommato, il suo ghigno finale fu di approvazione: bocca piegata leggermente all'ingiù, sopracciglia leggermente contratte all'insù e oscillazione del capo nell'atto di chi annuisce. Per me, era come aver superato il mio primo vero esame della vita... Soddisfatto e incoraggiato da quella *promozione*, iniziai a osservare papà, che in tutto quel mio chiacchierare affannato ma energico non aveva fatto alcuna smorfia né detto mezza parola: era rimasto tutto il tempo con il naso arricciato all'insù e gli occhiali appoggiati sulla punta, a fissarmi senza battere ciglio. Io e Checco, dopo la mia domanda di rito: - Be', allora che ne pensi, lo facciamo, papà? -, rimanemmo appesi per secondi interminabili a quella sua strana espressione, che tutto sommato sembrava tradire un certo interesse.

Nulla.

Checco guardò me, io guardai papà che a sua volta fissò Checco, poi si alzò, andò nel retrobanco e tirò fuori dei fogli, che passò a al mio amico ordinandogli di mettersi in fondo alla parete, tenendoli ben in vista. Ancora una volta tutte quelle letterine minuscole. Fu allora che collegai ogni cosa. Era un test della vista per l'esame di guida. Ma sì, il camion!

Che c'entrava, ora? Papà chiuse gli occhi e mi disse di controllare se indovinava le lettere. Iniziò a spararne a raffica: prima riga, seconda riga a scendere, terza riga anch'essa perfetta, quarta riga uguale, tutto rigorosamente a occhi chiusi, e poi l'ultima, quella dai caratteri minuscoli, e via anche lì, tutte indovinate, tutte a memoria.

Checco mi guardò divertito. Poi gridò: - Grande, Antonio!

Papà si tirò su gli occhiali soddisfatto, tolse il grembiule, sfilò gli zoccoli che portava per stare in piedi tutto il giorno dietro al bancone e si infilò al volo le sue *AsiSc*. Si diresse al contatore elettrico e iniziò ad abbassare tutte le levette. A una a una, le luci del Paradise si spensero come quelle di un albero di Natale il sette gennaio. Lasciò accesa solo la lampada del retrobanco. Il bar ora sembrava il set di un film. Poi tirò fuori un enorme cartello arancio fluorescente e con un pennarellone blu scrisse a caratteri cubitali «VENDUTO» e, più sotto e più piccolo, «Chiuso per sempre». Ero incredulo. Rimasi tutto il tempo a fissarlo, senza guardare nemmeno una volta il mio migliore amico.

Poi papà venne verso di me, mi cinse le spalle con le sue manone e mi guardò dritto negli occhi. - 'Sta vita nun fa' pe' te, fijo mio, damme retta, nun fa' pe' te! Ho venduto er bar, finalmente se semo levati tutti li buffi da dosso e mo' rinasco, fijo mio, rinasco! Ho preso 'a patente der camion e da domani comincio a lavorà pe' 'a BT, 'a Braccagni Trasporti, «frutta e verdura pe' tutte 'e staggioni», e pijo pure du mioni ar mese puliti puliti! Tu devi da studià, sognà, devi da seguì l'istinto tuo. Devi da *vive*, nun poi fa' 'sta vita de sacrifici e de rinunce! Devi vive, vive, fijo mio!

Sentii un nodo stringermi la gola. Guardai Checco, e lui mi fece cenno di abbracciare mio padre. Non attesi nemmeno mezzo secondo. Proprio come con mamma, in quel viaggio a ritroso nel tempo, mi sentii nuovamente leggero, forte, protetto tra le sue braccia. Non ricordavo quando era stata l'ultima volta che avevo abbracciato mio padre, ma era stata molto, tanto, troppo tempo prima.

L'idea del progetto della paninoteca svanì in quell'abbraccio. Dopotutto ne ero contento, o forse solo sollevato.

Appena mi sciolsi dall'abbraccio, Checco mi guardò e con le mani mi mimò il suo okay. Sentii le sue parole nella mia mente, come un messaggio telepatico: «Ben fatto, mio caro Massa, ora sei pronto». Anch'io gli risposi allo stesso modo: «Ti voglio bene, mio grande amico».

Ormai era calata la notte, e io e Checco eravamo seduti sul muretto dell'ex scuola calcio Invicta, sul lato opposto del Paradise, in silenzio.

Le porte a vetri del bar erano spalancate. Nella luce soffusa che proveniva dal retrobanco, osservavamo papà che parlava tra sé e sé, e le scartoffie che gli volavano di mano. Ogni tanto andava al telefono accanto al soffietto del laboratorio, componeva un numero e ritornava dietro il bancone, prendeva la sua manciata di noccioline e con il solito ghigno la ingoiava senza pensarci un attimo. Sembrava un matto, un matto che da più di un'ora compiva sempre le stesse azioni, come a seguire un cerchio, o meglio un circuito prestabilito da qualcun altro. Un burattino di legno, con quelle sue mani enormi, pilotato da un marionettista che si divertiva a sua insaputa. Finché un'ultima manciata di noccioline non gli cadde completamente di mano.

Fu in quel momento che mi girai verso Checco, e lo vidi che teneva gli occhi chiusi, come fosse addormentato. Non mi fece neanche aprire bocca che disse: - Guarda che non sto dormendo, sto solo calcolando dentro di me il tempo siderale dell'istante esatto in cui Antonio ha fatto cadere le noccioline.

- Che vuoi dire? -, risposi sorpreso.

- Voglio dire che, secondo i miei calcoli, d'ora in poi Antonio inizierà a essere libero, inizierà una nuova fase della sua vita.

- E come lo sai?

- Stasera Saturno, *il saggio*, uscirà dal suo sole, e tutte le cose ormai cadute saranno ricostruite su nuove fondamenta, più *sincere*.

- Ah... -, sospirai, pensando al famoso cappello di Checco che avrei dovuto tenere a mente.

Checco mi guardò e sorrise impercettibilmente.

- Sai, Massa, devo confessarti che *quel giorno* io ti aspettavo, sapevo che saresti entrato nella mia vita da quel raggio di sole, e che la nostra sarebbe stata un'amicizia indistruttibile, dal tempo, dalle durezze della vita.

- Ma dai, Checco... Come facevi a saperlo, il nostro incontro è stata una semplice casualità!

- *Casualità*! -, rispose lui facendomi il verso.

Allora iniziò a spiegarmi che dopo circa tre mesi dall'inizio della nostra amicizia, quando ancora mamma ogni tanto lavorava al bar, lui aveva avuto modo di passare diverso tempo con lei.

Si confidavano sulla vita e sui reciproci desideri inespressi. Checco le spiegava le sue teorie, su come avesse fatto Michelangelo a dipingere la Cappella Sistina in quel modo, con quali gradi di inclinazione avesse tenuto il pennello, quali colori avesse usato e come fossero riusciti a conservare quei toni caldi lungo i secoli... e altre teorie secondo le quali forse qualcuno sceso dal cielo aveva trasmesso a quegli artisti capacità energetiche particolari, grazie alle quali avevano creato quelle opere, usando solo le onde *theta* del pensiero. Mamma ribatteva che poteva essere possibile, ma sosteneva convinta che invece era frutto solo di un dono interiore che andava coltivato, con passione e dedizione continua. Questi confronti diventarono un appuntamento quasi fisso tra loro, per il caffè del dopo pranzo. Non che fossero sempre d'accordo, spesso discutevano animatamente, ma poi ogni volta finivano con grandi risate...

- Luisa per certi versi mi ricorda mia madre; in lei rivedo la sua stessa gentilezza d'animo -, proseguì Checco.

Rimasi in silenzio ancora per un po'. Non sapevo se essere geloso o semplicemente orgoglioso di quelle parole.

- Una sera, dopo che Luisa mi aveva rivelato quando eri nato, corsi subito a casa e feci dei calcoli astrali con le nostre date e ore di nascita. Ero troppo curioso di vedere se le mie intuizioni avevano delle fondamenta.

Continuavo a rimanere in silenzio a guardarlo; mi sentivo come in una bolla, come se quel marionettista che pensavo muovesse papà ora stesse muovendo i miei, di fili...

Checco mi spiegò che noi siamo come l'uomo vitruviano racchiuso in un cerchio, che la nostra testa è posta a Nord e i nostri arti seguono i restanti punti cardinali. - Noi siamo al centro dell'universo -, mi ripeteva Checco, - e siamo collegati col tutto. Noi siamo il Sole, e tutti gli altri pianeti del sistema solare ruotano attorno al nostro cerchio; come la Luna influenza le maree, la semina, favorisce le nascite, così tutti gli altri pianeti influenzano la nostra vita, il nostro percorso. Resta a noi saperli ascoltare. E sai cosa ho scoperto, caro Massa?

- Cosa? -, risposi imbambolato.

Continuò dicendomi che aveva sovrapposto i nostri cerchi astrali, e aveva scoperto ben quattro congiunzioni, fortissime: cioè, se avessimo disegnato le nostre carte astrali con i dovuti calcoli siderali, pianeti del calibro di Urano, Plutone, Nettuno, e la stessa Luna, sarebbero risultati congiunti alla perfezione.

- Che significa, Checco?!

- Significa! Significa!

- Che siamo uguali?

- Che siamo legati da un karma *simile*, perché siamo anime *simili*, che devono compiere *quasi* lo stesso percorso nella vita. E per questo *devono* sostenersi...

Checco chiuse gli occhi, volgendoli alle stelle. Io feci altrettanto.

Stavolta fu lui a porgermi la *nostra* domanda: - Massa? Ma secondo te, la vita è così com'è, è già fatta... Mi spiego meglio. Voglio dire, la vita, in generale, è così e basta, è già stata scritta da qualcuno, o ce la scriviamo da soli e non lo sappiamo?

Ci fu un attimo di silenzio. Io sorrisi al cielo, pieno di noi e di quel momento, e con decisione risposi: - E se invece lo sapessimo, mio caro vecchio Checco?

Ventisei

Presi la macchina di Monica e mi diressi verso casa di Checco. Stranamente, la vecchia Uno Fire era tirata a lucido, come se mi dovesse condurre a un matrimonio. Era solo un caso, o mia sorella lo aveva fatto per me? Non lo sapevo. Comunque, il profumo al mango dell'Arbre Magique mi dava un po' alla testa e mi rendeva ancora più allegro ed euforico, quasi mi fossi fatto di chissà quale sostanza, il sorriso stampato in bocca.

Checco scese e col suo solito modo di fare un po' goffo salì in macchina, diede una veloce annusata, mi guardò dritto in faccia e mi disse: - Lo sai che il mango eccelle per il suo ricco contenuto in oligominerali, dal potassio al magnesio allo zolfo, oltre che a numerose fibre e glucidi?

Lo guardai ancora una volta stupefatto; stavo per scoppiare a ridere, ma mi trattenni e lo lasciai proseguire.

- E per questo, mio caro vecchio Massa, è considerato un frutto molto energetico che può infondere un forte senso di euforia e freschezza! E ha anche un effetto alquanto lassativo!

A quel punto scoppiai a ridergli in faccia, e un copioso schizzo di saliva partì dalla mia bocca come un missile terra-aria per andare a schiantarsi proprio sulle sue labbra socchiuse, che forse attendevano un mio commento. La sua faccia rimase così, inchiodata, di ghiaccio e incredula. Per alcuni secondi rimase a fissarmi nelle pupille poi, con un gesto a metà tra lo stupito e lo schifato, si passò la mano sulla bocca ribaltando gli occhi a simulare uno shock anafilattico. Finse di morire agonizzando sul sedile della Uno. Esalato l'ultimo respiro, cominciò a ridere, contagiando presto anche me. Per dieci, lunghissimi minuti, con i crampi allo stomaco, ridemmo fin quasi allo svenimento, poi ebbi un lampo. Inchiodai, misi in folle e tirai il freno a mano.

- Guida tu!

Non ci pensò su un attimo. Ci scambiammo di posto simulando una specie di lotta greco-romana, braccia e gambe si incrociarono più volte come bastoncini di sciangai in una partita all'ultimo sangue, e alla fine riuscimmo a invertirci i ruoli.

Volevo proprio vedere cosa sarebbe riuscito a combinare.

Spinse la frizione, fissò il cambio e, dopo pochi secondi, inserì bruscamente la prima. Pieno di gioia, con gli occhiali storti e la fronte imperlata di sudore, mi chiese: - Dove la porto, signore?

- In via Sicilia, prego.

- Ma come, siamo già in via Sicilia!

Per fare il giro del palazzo e ritornare davanti all'ormai ex bar Paradise passarono all'incirca trenta sudatissimi e faticosissimi minuti, ma furono sicuramente i più spensierati di tutta quella lunghissima estate... Checco fece grattare il cambio per un'ultima volta passando dalla seconda alla prima; la vecchia Uno Fire singhiozzò come ubriaca, e si fermò nuovamente davanti al portone. Mise in folle e con quel suo sguardo da scienziato pazzo si voltò verso di me. Ci guardammo dritti negli occhi come se non ci fossimo mai conosciuti prima; sulle nostre teste mal rasate stavano ricrescendo i capelli, e notai un nuovo neo su un angolo della sua fronte. Sorrisi ripensando al mio. Poi mi voltai verso lo specchietto retrovisore e lo girai con la mano fino a inquadrare i miei occhi. Mi fissai per alcuni secondi, dritto nelle pupille, e allora rividi il giallo intenso di quell'immenso campo di girasoli, e il *Benellindson* rosso Ferrari sul cavalletto.

Ora Checco mi stava osservando riflesso dallo specchietto del mio vecchio scooter, mi fece un largo sorriso e, grattandosi la testa, disse: - L'estate è già finita, mio vecchio Massa...

Mi venne da abbracciarlo forte e, respirando profondamente, vidi ancora noi seduti ai piedi del Grande Cipresso.

Afferrai il suo cranio rasato e me lo portai alla fronte, pelle contro pelle, ossa contro ossa, poi, tirandomi indietro, risposi sospirando: - Sì... L'estate è già finita. È ora di tornare a casa...

Per la prima volta, ero stato io a insegnare qualcosa a quel cervellone del mio miglior amico del cuore. Sì, *il mio miglior amico del cuore*.

Perché è così che ci si chiama da piccoli, ed è bello ripeterselo e sentire come risuona dentro.

La divinità dell'uomo

Un'antica leggenda indù racconta che vi fu un tempo in cui *tutti* gli uomini erano Dèi. Essi però abusarono talmente della loro divinità, che Brahma, Signore degli Dèi, decise di privarli del potere divino e di nasconderlo in un posto dove fosse impossibile trovarlo.

Il problema principale fu dunque quello di trovare un nascondiglio.

Quando gli Dèi minori furono riuniti a consiglio per risolvere questo dilemma, Essi proposero la cosa seguente: - Seppelliamo la divinità dell'uomo nella Terra.

Brahma tuttavia rispose: - No, non basta, perché l'uomo scaverà e la ritroverà.

Gli Dèi allora replicarono: - In tal caso gettiamo la divinità nel più profondo degli oceani.

E di nuovo Brahma, Signore degli Dèi, rispose: - No, perché prima o poi l'uomo esplorerà le profondità di tutti gli oceani e sicuramente un giorno la ritroverà e la riporterà in superficie.

Gli Dèi minori allora conclusero: - Non sappiamo dove nasconderla, perché non sembra esistere, sulla Terra o in mare, luogo alcuno che l'uomo non possa una volta raggiungere.

E fu così che Brahma disse: - Ecco ciò che faremo della divinità dell'uomo: la nasconderemo nel suo *Io* più profondo e segreto, perché è il solo posto dove non gli verrà mai in mente di cercarla.

A partire da quel tempo, conclude la leggenda, l'uomo ha compiuto il periplo della Terra, ha esplorato, scalato montagne, scavato la terra e si è immerso nei mari alla ricerca di *qualcosa* che si trova *dentro di lui*...

Gli autori

Francesco Serino

Nasce a Grosseto nel 1978. Laureato in Storia contemporanea, a diciassette anni vince la sezione giovani del premio internazionale di ceramica di Vietri sul Mare; ha interpretato la parte di Orsino in un lungometraggio ispirato alle commedie shakespeariane e disegnato la copertina di un EP per un gruppo rock. Ha fatto l'aiuto cuoco e oggi lavora in una libreria e collabora con una piccola casa editrice.

È un grande fan del compositore austriaco Gustav Mahler e dello scrittore giapponese Haruki Murakami. La profonda amicizia che lo lega a Massimiliano Varrese è iniziata nel 1989.

Massimiliano Varrese

Nasce il 5 gennaio 1976 a Roma, ma vive la sua infanzia e l'adolescenza nella Maremma toscana per poi fare ritorno nel 1995 nella capitale, dove viene scoperto da Raffaella Carrà che lo lancia in *Carràmba! Che fortuna*.

Alterna il lavoro a teatro con la grande passione per la danza, che lo porta a solcare il palcoscenico nello show TV *Stasera pago io* di Fiorello, i palchi di tutta Italia con Paola&Chiara e quelli di tutto il mondo al seguito della ex Spice Girl Geri Halliwell, per la quale appare nel video *It's raining men*. Protagonista di fortunate serie TV tra cui *Il bello delle donne*, *Grandi domani*, *Carabinieri* e *La sacra famiglia*. Al cinema ha lavorato con Omar Sharif in *Fuoco su di me*, premiato alla Mostra del Cinema di Venezia. Sempre a teatro, ha interpretato Step nel musical *Tre metri sopra il cielo*, ottenendo il Premio Vittorio Gassman come miglior giovane talento. Premiato poi dalla Norman Academy per le qualità morali, civili ed etiche, ha ricevuto la Medaglia Beato Angelico nella Chiesa di S. Maria Maggiore in Roma, premio universale per tutte le arti e gli artisti.

Da sempre appassionato di scrittura e composizione di canzoni, collabora e firma brani con noti autori e musicisti italiani, tra cui A. Sparagna, L. Angelosanti e F. Morettini. Attualmente collabora in teatro con il pianista M. Mastrini, noto per le opere classiche suonate al contrario.

Studioso di arti marziali e discipline olistiche, attualmente si sta diplomando come operatore in Discipline naturali.

Ideazione e coordinamento
Antonio Monaco

Foto di copertina
Laura Cusano
www.lauracusano.com

Progetto degli interni e copertina
Sonia Lacerenza

Redazione
Paola Costanzo
Maria Teresa Sirna

Impaginazione
Portalupi Editore s.r.l.

Stampa
A4, Chivasso (To)

I lettori che desiderano essere informati
sulle novità pubblicate dalla nostra casa editrice
o esprimere le proprie considerazioni su questo libro
possono scrivere, o comunque rivolgersi a:

EDIZIONI SONDA
corso Indipendenza 63
15033 Casale Monferrato (Al)
Tel. 0142 461516 – Fax 0142 461523
E-mail: sonda@sonda.it

KEVIN BROOKS
UNA CANZONE PER CANDY

TAMAR
VERETE-ZEHAVI
La vita
Graffiata

YVES GREVET
MÉTO
LA CASA
SONDA

KOPANO MATLWA
COCONUT
Nera fuori
Bianca
dentro